ENDORSEMENTS

Matthew 24–25, often called the "mini apocalypse," is a minefield of biblical interpretation, primarily related to the timing of its fulfillment. I can't think of a better guide to carefully walk with through these chapters than Thomas Ice. He is a careful, contextual scholar who leaves no stone unturned. I highly recommend this book to all who want to understand this key prophetic passage.

—Mark Hitchcock, Ph.D.
Senior Pastor, Faith Bible Church, Edmond, OK
Associate Professor of Bible Exposition,
Dallas Theological Seminary

As one who teaches eschatology, I often say that no one has a better grasp of Jesus's Olivet Discourse than Thomas Ice. Not only is Ice's understanding of the Discourse thoroughly biblical, his views on Matthew 24–25 have been formed and vetted through many chapters, books, and debates over several decades. His futurist presentation of the Olivet Discourse is the best I have seen and soundly refutes other views. Now, to our benefit, all of this knowledge and insight comes together in this book, *Understanding the Olivet Discourse*. I highly recommend it and will be promoting it to my students and all who are interested in Jesus's words in Matthew 24–25.

—Michael J. Vlach, Ph.D.
Professor of Theology
Shepherds Theological Seminary

Matthew 24–25, otherwise known as the Olivet Discourse, represents pivotal chapters in anyone's eschatological system. Unfortunately, dispensationalists have been historically somewhat murky on the subject by offering conflicting interpretations. Some see Church Age teaching incorporated into these chapters. Such an approach opens the door to much eschatological confusion regarding date setting revolving around the Parable of the Fig Tree (Matt. 24:32–34). Moreover, others seek to find the rapture in Matthew 24:36–41. Such a schizophrenic interpretive approach unwittingly opens the door to non-pretribulation rapture perspectives, such as post-tribulationalism, pre-wrath rapturism, and even partial rapturism. In such a confusing environment, the eschatological and exegetical approach to these chapters offered by Dr. Thomas Ice, Executive Director of the Pre-Trib Research Center, is desperately needed. Here, Ice not only demonstrates that Matthew 24:4 and following are exclusively future as relating to the future 70th week of Daniel and not the events of A.D. 70, but he demonstrates also that this material (Matt. 24ff.) exclusively concerns the nation of Israel in the tribulation period wholly subsequent to the rapture of the church. In other words, this material has nothing to do with the Church Age. In order to get unconfused on a pertinent subject, I heartily recommend this work.

—Andy Woods, J.D., Ph.D.
Pastor-Teacher, Sugar Land Bible Church
President, Chafer Theological Seminary

UNDERSTANDING THE OLIVET DISCOURSE

A Futurist Interpretation of Matthew 24–25

THOMAS ICE

STONE TOWER PRESS

Understanding the Olivet Discourse
A Futurist Interpretation of Matthew 24–25

Stone Tower Press
7 Ellen Rd.
Middletown, RI 02842
stonetowerpress.com

Now revised, the 39 chapters this book appeared originally over several years written by the author in *Pre-Trib Perspectives,* the bi-monthly publication of the Pre-Trib Research Center.

Unless otherwise stated, all Bible citations are from the *Holy Bible: New American Standard Bible.* 1995, 2020. La Habra, CA: The Lockman Foundation.

Paperback ISBN: 978-1-7368651-8-7

Formatting and cover design by Amy Cole, JPL Design Solutions

Cover image: *Jesus on Mount of Olives* (1892) by Enrique Simonet 1892, Museo Nacional del Prado, Madrid, Spain, Public Domain

Printed in the United States of America

TABLE OF CONTENTS

Introduction vii

1. Context and History Matters 1
2. The First Question of Matthew 24:3 9
3. The Temple's Destruction 17
4. The Timing of Matthew 24:4–14 25
5. False Christs of Matthew 24:4–5 31
6. False Messiahs, Wars, and Fear in Matthew 24:5 39
7. Empires at War in Matthew 24:6–24:27a 47
8. Famines and Earthquakes 55
9. A Time of Persecution 63
10. Hatred and False Prophets 71
11. Increased Lawlessness 79
12. The Kingdom Gospel 87
13. The Abomination of Desolation 95
14. Fleeing to Safety 103
15. The Greatest Time of Tribulation 111
16. Tribulation and Context 119
17. Days Cut Short 127
18. Beware of False Christs and False Prophets 135
19. A Public Appearing 143
20. A Proverb of Warning 151
21. Tribulation and Transition 159
22. Understanding Figures of Speech 167
23. Dark Skies 175
24. Astronomical Abberations 181

25. Shaking of the Heavens 189
26. A Sign in the Sky 197
27. Mourning Tribes 205
28. Global Gatehring 213
29. Identifying the Elect 221
30. Parable of the Fig Tree 229
31. Interpreting "This Generation" 235
32. The Temporal and the Eternal 243
33. "Like the Days of Noah" 251
34. Two, Then One 259
35. Prepared and Alert 265
36. Faithfulness in Service 271
37. Parable of the Ten Virgins 277
38. Parable of the Five Talents 285
39. Judgment of the Sheep and Goats 295

Conclusion 303
Bibliography 307
About the Author 317

INTRODUCTION

The Olivet Discourse is one of the preeminent passages of Bible prophecy recorded in the New Testament. It is also the longest prophetic teaching of Jesus recorded in the Synoptic Gospels (Gospel of Matthew, Gospel of Mark, Gospel of Luke). In the pages that follow there is a methodical analysis and study of Jesus's prophetic sermon from a futurist perspective.

Much of this presentation appeared in an earlier format as part of the monthly newsletter *Pre-Trib Perspectives* beginning in October 2002. The following pages are a revision of those earlier articles with some additional material.

Any person seeking to understand the breadth, fullness, and details of Bible prophecy will, at some point in his or her study, spend time with the words of Jesus in Matthew 24, 25, and parallel passages. Bible prophecy cannot be understood fully apart from the words of Jesus in those passages. It is those words and a study of them that readers are encouraged to pursue in the following pages. As you do so, may you be richly rewarded.

1

CONTEXT AND HISTORY MATTERS

"The Olivet Discourse, delivered shortly before Jesus' crucifixion, is the most important single passage of prophecy in all the Bible. It is significant because it came from Jesus Himself immediately after He was rejected by His own people and because it provides the master outline of end-time events."

Dr. Tim LaHaye[1]

The Olivet Discourse, so named because Jesus gave it while on the Mount of Olives overlooking Jerusalem and the Temple, is an important passage for the development of anyone's view of Bible prophecy. It is comprised of our Lord's teaching on Bible prophecy that is found in Matthew 24–25, Mark 13, and Luke 21. Because one's interpretation of the Olivet Discourse greatly affects whether one is a premillennialist or anti-millennialist, futurist or preterist, or pretribulationist or posttribulationist, this study offers an extensive interpretation of Matthew 24–25 from a futurist (premillennial pretribulational) perspective.

THE CONTEXTUAL SETTING FOR JESUS'S DISCOURSE

The setting for the Olivet Discourse, at least for Matthew's account, is found in preceding events leading up to Matthew 24. Christ had presented

Himself to the nation Israel as their Messiah, but they rejected Him. Not only did the people reject Him, but their rulers did so as well. Thus, Jesus rebukes and exposes their hypocrisy and unbelief in Matthew 22 and 23. Jesus notes that this present generation of Jewish leaders is like those from previous generations who killed the prophets (23:29–36). He then tells the Jewish leaders, "Truly I say to you, all these things shall come upon this generation" (23:36). What things? It will be the curse of judgment, that will come upon the Jewish people through the Roman army in A.D. 70. "All hope for a turning of Israel to God in repentance has gone," notes Dr. Stanley Toussaint. "The King therefore has no alternative but to reject that nation for the time being with regard to its kingdom program. The clear announcement of this decision is seen in these verses of Matthew's Gospel."[2]

In spite of the fact that the Jewish people deserved the approaching judgment, like a caring parent about to administer a just punishment, Christ cries out, "O Jerusalem, Jerusalem, who kills the prophets and stones those who are sent to her! How often I wanted to gather your children together, the way a hen gathers her chicks under her wings, and you were unwilling" (23:37). Jesus wants to gather His people (as He will in 24:31), instead, He will scatter them via the A.D. 70 judgment (Luke 21:24).

Jesus then declares in 23:38, "Behold, your house is being left to you desolate!" To what does the house refer? In the context of this passage it must be a reference to the Jewish Temple. Matthew 24:1–2 presents a discussion by Jesus with His disciples about the Temple. It is at that time that Jesus startles them by telling them "'Do you not see all these things? Truly I say to you, not one stone here shall be left upon another, which will not be torn down'" (24:2). What Jesus says will be desolate, the Temple, in 23:38, is more precisely described in 24:2: both referring to the same thing—the Temple.

Finally, in Matthew 23, Jesus says, "For I say to you, from now on you shall not see Me until you say, 'Blessed is He who comes in the name of the Lord!'" (23:39). Not only does this verse hold out the certainty of soon judgment, but also the eventual promise of yet-to-come hope and blessing upon the Jewish nation. Alfred Edersheim, a son of the present remnant of Israel, wrote of this passage:

> Looking around on those Temple-buildings—that House, it shall be left to them desolate! And He quitted its courts with these words, that they of Israel should not see Him again till, the night of their unbelief past, they would welcome His return with a better Hosanna than that which had greeted His Royal Entry three days before. And this was the "Farewell" and the parting of Israel's Messiah from Israel and its Temple. Yet a Farewell which promised a coming again; and a parting which implied a welcome in the future from a believing people to a gracious, pardoning King.[3]

Thus, this verse (23:39) not only speaks of the judgment that surely came in A.D. 70, but looks to a future time of redemption for Israel because the passage contains the forward-looking word "until."

Luke 21:24 records another use of "until" by our Lord when He says, "and they will fall by the edge of the sword, and will be led captive into all the nations; and Jerusalem will be trampled underfoot by the Gentiles until the times of the Gentiles be fulfilled." Hebrew Christian Bible teacher, Arnold Fruchtenbaum, believes that Israel must call for the Lord to rescue them as a condition for the second coming, based upon Matthew 23:39.[4] Dr. Fruchtenbaum explains:

> But then He declares that they will not see Him again until they say, *Blessed is He that cometh in the name of the Lord*. This is a messianic greeting. It will mean their acceptance of the Messiahship of Jesus.
>
> So Jesus will not come back to the earth until the Jews and the Jewish leaders ask Him to come back. For just as the Jewish leaders lead the nation to the rejection of the Messiahship of Jesus, they must someday lead the nation to the acceptance of the Messiahship of Jesus.[5]

Biblical scholar David L. Cooper echoes Fruchtenbaum's understanding, writing: "Since Jesus came in the name of the Lord, and since He will not return until Israel says, 'Blessed is he that cometh in the name of the Lord,' it is clear that the people of Israel will see and recognize that Jesus was and is their true Messiah."[6] The last few verses of Matthew 23 teach that judgment was coming in the near future, but, beyond judgment, deliverance and redemption awaits the Jewish nation. Judgment did come in A.D. 70 and Matthew 24 speaks of the still-future redemption of Israel.

THE HISTORICAL SETTING FOR JESUS'S DISCOURSE

Matthew 24:1–3 identifies the setting for Jesus's delivery of His prophetic sermon. We see that Jesus is making His way from the Temple (24:1) to the Mount of Olives (24:3), which would mean that He most likely would travel down the Kidron Valley and on up to the Mount of Olives. The time would be two days before Jesus deliverd the Upper Room Discourse (John 13–17) the night before He is crucified. As He was leaving the Temple "His disciples came up to point out the temple buildings to Him" (24:1). This statement leads us to believe that they were talking to Jesus about the beauty of the Temple complex that Herod was still in the process of remodeling and refurbishing. Such an emphasis is borne out in the parallel references in Mark 13:1–2 and Luke 21:5–6 where the disciples speak of the beauty of the Temple buildings. The Lord must have startled His disciples by His response to their gloating over the beauty of the Temple complex when He said, "Do you not see all these things? Truly I say to you, not one stone here shall be left upon another, which will not be torn down" (24:2).

As 24:2 is completed with Christ's statement, there is a break in the narrative. The narrative picks back up in 24:3 when the text reads, "the disciples came to Him privately." Mark 13:3 tells us that the disciples who came to Him privately were Peter, James, John, and Andrew, and that they were sitting on the Mount of Olives looking at the Temple. This would be the same vista that may be seen today when one goes to the viewing point in modern Jerusalem on the Mount of Olives that overlooks the Temple Mount with the Dome of the Rock that is built upon it.

That the disciples came to Jesus privately fits the pattern that Jesus practices and Matthew records of teaching only His believing disciples once the nation rejected Him as their prophesied Messiah in Matthew 12. From Matthew 13 forward, Jesus speaks publicly to the rejecting nation only in parables (Matt. 13:10–17). "Therefore I speak to them in parables; because while seeing they do not see, and while hearing they do not hear, nor do they understand" (Matt. 13:13). However, many times He later would explain a public parable privately to His disciples (for example, Matt. 13:10–23). In the Olivet Discourse, we see Jesus following this pattern. This private explanation, which is the Olivet Discourse, means that Christ will provide His explanation of future history for the benefit of believers.

THE DISCIPLES' QUESTIONS

While sitting on the Mount of Olives these four disciples ask Jesus the following two questions: "Tell us, when will these things be, and what will be the sign of Your coming, and of the end of the age" (24:3)? Immediately, debate arises over whether these are two questions or three. If one takes the first option, then there is no doubt that the second question contains two parts to it. It is likely that there are two basic questions because of the grammar of the passage as explained by Dr. Craig Blomberg:

> "The sign of your coming and of the end of the age" in Greek reads, more literally, *the sign of your coming and end of the age*. By not repeating the definite article ("the") before "end of the age," Matthew's rendering of Jesus' words is most likely linking the coming of Christ and the end of the age together as one event (Granville Sharp's rule).[7]

This means that the two phrases are closely related to one another in the minds of the disciples who formulated the question. They believed the phases were linked closely together.

Clearly the first question relates to the destruction of the Temple, which was fulfilled in the Roman invasion and destruction of A.D. 70. It is equally clear that the two aspects of the second question have yet to occur in history, even though some want to see in this passage Christ's second coming (more on the errors of preterism as we progress through the passage).

It is likely that the disciples believed that all three aspects of their two questions would occur around the same event—the coming of Messiah.

Why would they have thought this way? Dr. Toussaint notes that the disciples were influenced by the prophet Zechariah:

> In their minds they had developed a chronology of events in the following sequence: (1) the departure of the King, (2) after a period of time the destruction of Jerusalem, and (3) 'immediately after Jerusalem's devastation the presence of the Messiah. They had good scriptural ground for this since Zechariah 14:1–2 describes the razing of Jerusalem. The same passage goes on to describe the coming of the Lord to destroy the nations which warred against Jerusalem (Zechariah 14:3–8). Following this the millennial kingdom is established (Zechariah 14:9–11).[8]

In other words, the disciples thought that all three events were related to a single event—the return of the Messiah as taught in Zechariah 14:4. As we shall see in the coming chapters, they were right to think of Zechariah 12–14 and Zechariah's teaching about Messiah's coming. However, they were wrong to relate the impending judgment of Jerusalem and the Temple with the return of Messiah.

ENDNOTES

1 Tim LaHaye and Thomas Ice, *Charting the End Times: A Visual Guide to Understanding Bible Prophecy* (Eugene, OR: Harvest House, 2001), 35.

2 Stanley D. Toussaint, *Behold The King: A Study of Matthew* (Portland: Multnomah Press, 1980), 264–65.

3 Alfred Edersheim, *The Life and Times of Jesus the Messiah*, 2 vols. (Grand Rapids: Eerdmans, 1974 [1883]), Vol. II, 414.

4 Arnold Fruchtenbaum, *The Footsteps of the Messiah: A Study of the Sequence of Prophetic Events* (San Antonio: Ariel Press, 1982), 212–15.

5 Fruchtenbaum, *Footsteps*, 215, emphasis original.

6 David L. Cooper, *Messiah: His Final Call to Israel* (Los Angeles: Biblical Research Society, 1962), 47.

7 Craig L. Blomberg, *Matthew*, Vol. 22 of The New American Commentary (Nashville: Broadman Press, 1992), 353, fn. 37.

8 Toussaint, *Behold The King*, 269.

2

THE FIRST QUESTION OF MATTHEW 24:3

The disciples' question in Matthew 24:3 is divided into two parts. The first half relates to the destruction of the Temple, which took place in A.D. 70. The second half is also composed of two parts but related to one another and refers to events that are still yet to come. The disciples apparently thought that all three items, destruction of the Temple, the sign of Christ's coming, and the end of the age would occur at the same time. However, this is not the case.

THE DISCIPLES' MISUNDERSTANDING

It was common for Jesus to correct the misunderstandings of the disciples that usually represented popular belief of their day.[1] Regarding their questions, Dr. J. Dwight Pentecost observed:

> The questions showed that they had arrived at certain conclusions.... To these men Christ's words concerning the destruction of Jerusalem was the destruction predicted by Zechariah that would precede the advent of the Messiah. In Jewish eschatology two ages were recognized: the first was this present age, the age in which Israel was waiting for the coming of the Messiah; the second was the age to come, the age in which all of Israel's covenants would be fulfilled and Israel would enter into her promised blessings as a result of Messiah's coming.[2]

Similarly, Stanley Toussaint echoes this notion:

> This sequence is so clearly in view that Luke records the question concerning the destruction of Jerusalem only (Luke 21:7). That is, the disciples took the destruction of Jerusalem to be completely eschatological. Therefore, Luke records this question only, as though Jerusalem's destruction would mark the coming of the King to reign. [A. B.] Bruce is correct when he asserts, "The questioners took for granted that all three things went together: destruction of temple, advent of Son of Man, end of the current age."[3]

Even though the disciples merged these three events, Jesus did not merge these events into a single time period.

In fact, Matthew and Mark do not deal with the destruction of Jerusalem in their accounts of the Olivet Discourse. Their focus is upon the future days of tribulation leading up to Christ's return. As will be noted below, only in Luke's account does Christ deal with the issue (21:20–24). But Luke also deals with future days of tribulation and Christ's return as well (21:25–36). For reasons not fully known to us, The entire focus of Matthew and Mark is upon the last question that speaks of "the sign of Your coming, and of the end of the age" (Matt. 24:3).

THE FIRST QUESTION

The first question by the disciples is, "Tell us, when will these things be" (Matt. 24:3)? Because Christ had been speaking about the Temple and a time when "not one stone here shall be left upon another, which will not be torn down" (Matt. 24:2), it is clear that Jesus prophesied the destruction of the Temple in Jerusalem by the Romans in A.D. 70. Jesus had predicted the destruction of Jerusalem and the Temple earlier in His ministry.

Jesus had spoken earlier of Israel's "house [Temple] is being left to you desolate" (Matt. 23:38). Luke records another prediction of judgment upon Israel, as in Matthew 23:37–39, preceded by Christ weeping over the city of Jerusalem (Luke 19:41). This prophecy occurred at the time of Christ's triumphal entry on Palm Sunday, based upon Israel's rejection of Jesus as their Messiah (Luke 19:42). Jesus prophesied in Luke 19:43–44, declaring:

> "For the days shall come upon you when your enemies will throw up a bank before you, and surround you, and hem you in on every side, and will level you to the ground and your children within you, and they will not leave in you one stone upon another, because you did not recognize the time of your visitation."

We learn a number of things from this prophecy. First, we learn that "your enemies" undoubtedly refers to the Romans who destroyed the city in A.D. 70. Second, "will throw up a bank before you, and surround you, and hem you in on every side," is a vivid description of the Roman siege used to defeat Jerusalem. Third, the Roman siege resulted in a total destruction of the city and of life within the city. Often in ancient warfare, if anyone is spared it might be the children, but even most of them were killed. Fourth, the very words of Christ from Matthew 24:2 were used by Him earlier in this passage when He said, "they will not leave in you one stone upon another." Fifth, the reason for the destruction of Jerusalem by the Romans will be because "you did not recognize the time of your visitation."

FULFILLMENT OF THE FIRST QUESTION

Because we will not be dealing specifically with Luke's version of the Olivet Discourse throughout this exposition, we will now briefly look at Luke 21:20–24, since it records the prophecy about the first question of the disciples. The passage reads:

> "But when you see *Jerusalem surrounded by armies*, then recognize that *her desolation is at hand*. Then let those who are in Judea flee to the mountains, and let those who are in the midst of the city depart, and let not those who are in the country enter the city; because *these are days of vengeance*, in order that all things which are written may

> be fulfilled. Woe to those who are with child and to those who nurse babes in those days; for *there will be great distress upon the land,* and *wrath to this people,* and *they will fall by the edge of the sword,* and *will be led captive into all the nations;* and *Jerusalem will be trampled under foot* by the Gentiles until the times of the Gentiles be fulfilled." (Luke 21:20–24, italics added)

Preterists (arguing that these prophecies were all fulfilled in the first century) and futurists do not agree on much when it comes to the Olivet Discourse. However, regarding the interpretation of Luke 21:20–24, both agree that it is a literal prophecy of the A.D. 70 judgment. Preterist Kenneth Gentry writes: "The context of Luke demands a literal Jerusalem (Luke 21:20) besieged by literal armies (Luke 21:20) in literal Judea (Luke 21:21)—which as a matter of indisputable historical record occurred in the events leading up to A.D. 70."[4] However, when expounding on Luke 21:25–28, preterists resort to massive amounts of *symbolic* interpretation in their attempt to give these verses a first-century fulfillment. The futurist does not need to make such adjustments and continues a *plain* or literal reading of the text. I believe that Luke 21:25–28 is a brief prophecy that parallels Matthew 24 and Mark 13, as we will see later in the book.

Luke 21:20–24 is an example of where preterists interpret prophecy literally when it is alleged to support their view, but if a passage would lead to a non-preterist view if interpreted literally, they allegorize it. On the other hand, futurists are able to take all parts of Christ's Olivet Discourse, and all prophecy literally.

It is clear that Luke 21:20–24 spoke of the first-century Roman invasion of Jerusalem. Note that above I have placed in italics the key phrases from Luke 21:20–24 that support the A.D. 70 fulfillment. The entire passage speaks repeatedly of judgment and wrath upon the Jewish people and their city just as Christ prophesied in Matthew 24:2 and the other passages noted earlier. Yet, when one searches prophecies of Matthew 24 and Mark 13, this language is missing. Instead of "great distress upon the land, and wrath to this people," Matthew 24 speaks of rescuing the Jewish people who are under great distress (Matt. 24:29–31).

CONTRASTS BETWEEN A.D. 70 AND A FUTURE TEMPLE

Preterists often misuse Luke 21:20–24, contending that all of Matthew 24 was a prophecy of the Roman conquest in A.D. 70. Yet, futurist Randall Price has noted six major differences between the A.D. 70 Temple and the Temple of the future tribulation period spoken of in Matthew 24. Price writes:

> During this time Jesus speaks of a signal event connected with the Temple—its desecration by an abomination which was prophesied by the Prophet Daniel (Matthew 24:15; Mark 13:14). What Temple is being spoken of here by Jesus? Was the Temple that was to be desecrated the same Temple as the one predicted to be destroyed? There are a number of contrasts within this text that indicate that Jesus was talking about *two different* Temples:
>
> (1) The Temple described in Matthew 24:15 is not said to be destroyed, only desecrated (see Revelation 11:2). By contrast, the Temple in Jesus' day (or Matthew 24:2) was to be completely leveled: "not one stone would be left standing on another" (Matthew 24:2; Mark 13:2; Luke 19:44).
>
> (2) The Temple's desecration would be a signal for Jews to escape destruction (Matthew 24:16–18), "be saved" (Matthew 24:22) and experience the promised "redemption" (Luke 21:28). By contrast the destruction of the Temple in Matthew 24:2 was a judgment "because you did not recognize the time of your visitation [Messiah's first advent]" (Luke 19:44b) and resulted in the Temple being level[ed] to the ground and your children [the Jews] within you" (Luke 19:44a).
>
> (3) The generation of Jews that are alive at the time that the Temple is desecrated will expect Messiah's coming "immediately after" (Matthew 24:29), and are predicted to not pass away until they have experienced it (Matthew 24:34). By contrast, the generation of Jews who saw the Temple destroyed would pass away and 2,000 years (to date) would pass without redemption.

(4) The text Jesus cited concerning the Temple's desecration, Daniel 9:27, predicts that the one who desecrates this Temple will himself be destroyed. By contrast, those who destroyed the Temple in A.D. 70 (in fulfillment of Jesus' prediction)—the Roman emperor Vespasian and his son Titus—were not destroyed but returned to Rome in triumph carrying vessels from the destroyed Temple.

(5) The time "immediately after" (Matthew 24:29) the time of the Temple's desecration would see Israel's repentance (Matthew 24:30), followed by, as Matthew 23:29 implies, a restoration of the Temple. By contrast, the time following the destruction of the Temple only saw a "hardening" happen "to Israel," which is to last "until the fullness of the Gentiles has come in" (Romans 11:25)—still 2,000 years and counting.

(6) For the Temple that is desecrated, the scope is of a worldwide tribulation "coming upon the world" (Luke 21:26; compare Matthew 24:21–22; Mark 13:19–20), a global regathering of the Jewish people "from one end of the sky to the other" (Matthew 24:31; Mark 13:27), and a universal revelation of the Messiah at Israel's rescue (Matthew 24:30–31; Mark 13:26; Luke 21:26–27). This scope accords with the prophesied end-time battle for Jerusalem recorded in Zechariah 12–14, where "all nations of the earth will be gathered against it" (Zechariah 12:3). By contrast the A.D. 70 assault on Jerusalem predicted in Luke 21:20 is by the armies of one empire (Rome). Therefore, if there are two different attacks on Jerusalem, separated by more than 2,000 years, then two distinct Temples are considered in Matthew 24:1–2 and Matthew 24:15.[5]

The above points demonstrate preterist problems that have no resolution in their attempt to compress still-future prophecy into a past mold. As we shall see, details of Matthew 24 cannot be made satisfactorily to fit into a first-century fulfillment scheme.

ENDNOTES

1 See the following passages for examples of Christ correcting the disciples beliefs: Matthew 5–7; 9:1–8; 12:1–8, 46–50; 13:10–23; 15:1–20; 16:13–26; 17:1–9; 18:1–6, 21–35; 19:3–12, 13–15, 27–30; 20:20–28; 21:33–46.

2 J. Dwight Pentecost, *The Words and Works of Jesus Christ: A Study of the Life of Christ* (Grand Rapids: Zondervan, 1981), 398.

3 Stanley D. Toussaint, *Behold The King: A Study of Matthew* (Portland: Multnomah Press, 1980), 269–70. Toussaint is quoting Alexander Balmain Bruce, "The Synoptic Gospels" in W. Robertson Nicoll, editor, *The Expositor's Greek Testament,* 5 vols. (Grand Rapids, Eerdmans, 1976), vol. I, 289.

4 Kenneth L. Gentry, Jr., *Before Jerusalem Fell: Dating the Book of Revelation* (Tyler, Texas: Institute for Christian Economics, 1989), 176.

5 Randall Price *Jerusalem in Prophecy: God's Stage for the Final Drama* (Eugene, OR.: Harvest House, 1998), 251–55, empahasis orginal.

3

THE TEMPLE'S DESTRUCTION

As we continue to consider the questions of the disciples in the Olivet Discourse (Matt. 24–25; Mark 13; Luke 21), we want to look more closely at the first question that is asked in the passage. After observing the Temple, Jesus said to the disciples, "Do you not see all these things? Truly I say to you, not one stone here shall be left upon another, which will not be torn down" (Matt. 24:2). The disciples ask Jesus, "Tell us, when will these things be,..." (Matt. 24:3). The first question relates to the destruction of the Temple in A.D. 70.

PRETERIST LITERALISM

As noted in the last chapter, referencing the Olivet Discourse as it is recorded in Luke 21, preterist Kenneth Gentry writes: "The context of Luke demands a literal Jerusalem (Luke 21:20) besieged by literal armies (Luke 21:20) in literal Judea (Luke 21:21)—which as a matter of indisputable historical record occurred in the events leading up to A.D. 70."[1] This demonstrates that preterists take Scripture literally, unless it contradicts their presupposed system of theology, at which time they present a more pliable, deeply spiritual meaning of the text. But because both preterist and futurists (like myself) believe that Luke 21:20–24 literally refers to Jerusalem in A.D. 70, then this can be used as a template to show how Scripture speaks of the destruction of Jerusalem in the first century.

CHRIST'S PROPHECY OF A.D. 70

Before we look at Luke 21:20–24, we will examine the prophecies that Jesus gave specifically referring to the destruction of Jerusalem and the Temple—prophecies that indeed were fulfilled in the first century. Note the following prophecies by Christ:

> "Truly I say to you, all these things shall come upon this generation. O Jerusalem, Jerusalem, who kills the prophets and stones those who are sent to her! How often I wanted to gather your children together, the way a hen gathers her chicks under her wings, and you were unwilling. Behold, your house is being left to you desolate!" (Matt. 23:36–38; see Luke 13:34–35 for parallel passage).

> And when He approached, He saw the city and wept over it, saying, "If you had known in this day, even you, the things which make for peace! But now they have been hidden from your eyes. For the days shall come upon you when your enemies will throw up a bank before you, and surround you, and hem you in on every side, and will level you to the ground and your children within you, and they will not leave in you one stone upon another, because you did not recognize the time of your visitation" (Luke 19:41–44).

Jesus speaks clearly about the coming Roman destruction of Jerusalem and the Temple in this prediction. Jesus clearly describes a siege in verses 43 and 44 because the nation of Israel "did not recognize the time of your visitation." They rejected Jesus as their Messiah. Notice that not once does Jesus describe this as a "judgment coming" as do preterists.[2] In fact, coming is not used in any of these prophecies relating to A.D. 70, as it is used of Christ's future return.

LUKE 21:20–24 AND A.D. 70

When we look at the words of Jesus's prophecy about the destruction of Jerusalem and the Second Temple, He uses words and phrases that clearly denote what the Romans did in A.D. 70 to Jerusalem and the Temple:

> "But when you see Jerusalem surrounded by armies, then recognize that her desolation is at hand. Then let those who are in Judea flee to the mountains, and let those who are in the midst of the city depart, and let not those who are in the country enter the city; because these are days of vengeance, in order that all things which are written may be fulfilled. Woe to those who are with child and to those who nurse babes in those days; for there will be great distress upon the land, and wrath to this people, and they will fall by the edge of the sword, and will be led captive into all the nations; and Jerusalem will be trampled underfoot by the Gentiles until the times of the Gentiles be fulfilled" (Luke 21:20–24).

Note how the following words and phrases support the notion of judgment upon Israel in the first century:

1) "Jerusalem surrounded by armies, then recognize that her desolation is at hand"
2) "flee to the mountains" (The admonition to flee would indicate that Jerusalem will be destroyed. If the Jews were to defeat the Romans, then the safe place to be would be inside the walled city.)
3) "these are days of vengeance"
4) "there will be great distress upon the land"
5) "wrath to this people" (Israel)
6) "they [Israel] will fall by the edge of the sword"
7) "[Israel] will be led captive into all the nations"
8) "Jerusalem will be trampled underfoot by the Gentiles"

There is not a single phrase in the above passage that suggests a future understanding beyond the A.D. 70 destruction of Jerusalem that was clearly a judgment upon the Jewish people for their national rejection of Jesus as their Messiah (Luke 19:44; Matt. 23:38). This passage is our Lord's undisputed answer to the disciples' first question about when there will not be one stone of the Temple left upon another. Yet when compared with other sections of the Olivet Discourse, this kind of language referenced above is totally missing (see Matt. 24:4–31; Mark 13:5–27; Luke 21:25–28). Instead, in general, the language of the Olivet Discourse, except for Luke 21:20–24, does not speak of Israel under God's judgment, but of Israel under threat from the Gentile nations and God's intervention that rescues the Jewish people. This overall thrust of the passage is even clearer when one looks at the parallel passage of Zechariah 12–14.

"UNTIL"

Luke 21:24 ends by stating that Jerusalem will be under Gentile domination "until the times of the Gentiles be fulfilled." The conjunction "until" clearly denotes that there will be a time when the current domination of Jerusalem by the Gentiles will come to an end. The current "times of the Gentiles" in which we currently live will indeed come to an end in the future. Thus, the end of verse 24 serves as a transitional period between the prophecy that refers to the past A.D. 70 event (Luke 21:20–24) and the prophecy that looks to a future fulfillment at Christ second coming (Luke 21:25–28). We now live in the "times of the Gentiles."

A clear connection is established between Luke 21:24 which speaks of the current era of "the times of the Gentiles" being fulfilled and coming to an end and Romans 11:25 which speaks of "the fullness of the Gentiles" having "come in." Both passages speak of Israel's redemption (Luke 21:28; Romans 11:26–27). When we consider that the Old Testament pattern which says that Israel will pass through the tribulation, repent toward the end when they recognize Jesus as the Messiah, experience conversion, and then the second coming will occur to rescue them from their enemies, it follows that "all Israel will be saved" (Romans 11:26) in connection with the tribulation. This is exactly the pattern of Luke 21:25–28. Preterist Ken

Gentry believes that Romans teaches a future conversion of Israel, yet he does not associate it with the Tribulation as does Scripture repeatedly. Dr. Gentry declares, "The future conversion of the Jews will conclude the fulfillment (Rom. 11:12–25)."[3] Yet only a futurist interpretation does justice to a harmonization of these passages that are so clearly connected to each other.

LUKE 21:25–28 AND THE FUTURE

> "And there will be signs in sun and moon and stars, and upon the earth dismay among nations, in perplexity at the roaring of the sea and the waves, men fainting from fear and the expectation of the things which are coming upon the world; for the powers of the heavens will be shaken. And then they will see the Son of Man coming in a cloud with power and great glory. But when these things begin to take place, straighten up and lift up your heads, because your redemption is drawing near" (Luke 21:25–28).

J. C. Ryle, a 19th-century English Anglican bishop, writes of this passage:

> The subject of this portion of our Lord's great prophecy is His own second coming to judge the world. The strong expressions of the passage appear inapplicable to any event less important than this. To confine the words before us, to the taking of Jerusalem by the Romans, is an unnatural straining of Scripture language.[4]

The focus of Luke 21:25–28 reveals a distinct shift from the first-century description of 21:20–24. The differences include the local focus of Jerusalem in the first century judgment verses the global perspective of the future tribulation.

The tribulation will involve heavenly and global events that did not literally occur in A.D. 70. If preterists such as Dr. Gentry would interpret verses 25–28 in the same way they did verses 20–24 then the events of 25–28 would be understood as global, and if global, then they did not occur in the first century. Because they did not occur in the first century, then they must take place in the future. These are future Tribulation events that are prophesied by our Lord in this section of the passage.

The basic thrust of Luke 21:25–28 is the opposite of God's judgment upon Israel as stated in Luke 21:20–24. Instead verse 28 tells Israel that, "your redemption is drawing near." This is all the difference of night (judgment) in verses 20–24 and day (salvation and deliverance) in verses 25–28. Plymouth Brethren expositor William Kelly describes some aspects of the differences:

> Hence, to, the reader may notice that, in spite of a considerable measure of analogy (for there will be a future siege, and even a twofold attack, one of which will be partially successful, the other to the ruin of their enemies, as we learn from Isaiah xxviii, xxix, and Zechariah xiv.), there are the strangest contrasts in the issue; for the future siege will be closed by Jehovah's deliverance and reign, as the past was in capture and destruction of the people dispersed ever since till the times of the Gentiles are full. Accordingly we hear nothing in this Gospel of the abomination of desolation, nor of the time of tribulation beyond all that was or shall be; we hear of both in Matthew and Mark, where the Spirit contemplates the last days.[5]

When one examines the Olivet Discourse as recorded in Matthew 24 and Mark 13, there is no reference to wrath or judgment upon the nation of Israel. Instead, Israel is delivered from its invader as noted in Matthew 24:31, "And He will send forth His angels with a great trumpet and they will gather together His elect from the four winds, from one end of the sky to the other" (see also Mark 13:27). The question arises, "When was Israel rescued in A.D. 70?" They were not! The events of Matthew 24 and Mark 13 (also Luke 21:25–28) will all be fulfilled in the tribulation, which will take place in the future.

Thus, the first question of the disciples to Christ in the Olivet Discourse relates to the destruction of Jerusalem in A.D. 70. The record of its fulfillment is recorded only in Luke 21. Matthew 24–25 and Mark 13 deal only with the last question, which are a prophecy of events that are still future to our era.

ENDNOTES

1 Kenneth L. Gentry, Jr., *Before Jerusalem Fell: Dating the Book of Revelation* (Tyler, Texas: Institute for Christian Economics, 1989), 176.

2 Gary DeMar, *Last Days Madness: Obsession of the Modern Church* (Powder Springs, GA: American Vision, 1999), 72.

3 Kenneth L. Gentry, Jr., *He Shall Have Dominion: A Postmillennial Eschatology* (Tyler, Texas: Institute for Christian Economics, 1992), 206.

4 J. C. Ryle, *Expository Thoughts on the Gospels: Luke,* 2 vols. (Cambridge: James Clarke & Co., [1858] n. d.), vol. II, 374.

5 William Kelly, *An Exposition of the Gospel of Luke* (Oak Park, IL: Bible Truth Publishers, 1971), 332–33.

4

THE TIMING OF MATTHEW 24:4–14

Because we have seen previously that Matthew 24 is a future, end-time prophecy, the next issue to tackle is: When will verses 4 through 14 come to pass?

There are two major views that futurists hold. First, some believe that verses 4–14 refer to the inter-advent age—that is the time between Christ's first coming and the beginning of the tribulation. Second, some hold that verses 4–14, especially verses 4–8, refer to the first part of the tribulation and correspond with the first four seal judgments of Revelation 6:1–8. I think that the second view is correct.

INTER-ADVENT AGE VIEW

Many futurist interpreters of the Olivet Discourse believe that verses 4–14 describe the general signs of the inter-advent age. Dr. John F. Walvoord, an advocate of this view says that verses 4–14 are:

> describing the general characteristics of the age leading up to the end, while at the same time recognizing that the prediction of difficulties, which will characterized the entire period between the first and second coming of Christ, are fulfilled in an intensified form as the age moves on to its conclusion.[1]

Dr. Walvoord believes that verses 15–26 are specific signs that describe the tribulation, while verses 27–31 relate to the second coming.[2]

Within the inter-advent age view, there is a variation of this perspective. Some think that verses 4–8 are general signs of the inter-advent age leading up to the tribulation, but verses 9–14 reference the first half of the tribulation. "The events concerning the first half of the tribulation are recorded in Matthew 24:9–14," writes Dr. Arnold Fruchtenbaum. This "passage begins with the word *then*, pointing out that what Christ is describing now will come *after* the event of nation rising against nation and kingdom against kingdom."[3]

If the inter-advent age view is the correct interpretation, then it would mean that wars, earthquakes, famines, and the appearance of false Christs would be constantly on the increase as we approach the tribulation period. However, if these items are references to the first half of the tribulation, then wars, earthquakes, famines, and false Christs during any part of the present church age would not constitute prophetic signs. This explains why some futurists believe that increasing wars, earthquakes, famines, etc., are prophetically significant, while others, do not think that they are prophetically significant, because these verses refer to global events during the seven-year tribulation.

TRIBULATION VIEW

I believe that Matthew 24:4–41 refers to the seven-year period (Dan. 9:24–27) that many commonly call the tribulation. The tribulation is divided in half by the abomination of desolation, mentioned by Jesus in verse 15. Thus, in this view, verses 4–14 refer to the first half of the tribulation and are parallel to the first five seal judgments found in Revelation 6.

"If our interpretation is the right one there must be perfect harmony between these three: Old Testament Prophecy: Matthew xxiv:4–44, and Revelation vi–xix." insists Arno Gaebelein.[4] I believe just such a harmony exists, especially between the Olivet Discourse and Revelation. This is what convinces me that verses 4–14 refer to the first half of the tribulation. Gaebelein continues:

> If this is the correct interpretation, if Matthew xxiv:4–14 refers to the beginning of that coming end of the age and if Revelation vi refers to the same beginning of the end and that which follows the sixth chapter leads us on into the great tribulation, then there must be a perfect harmony between that part of the Olivet discourse contained in Matthew xxiv and the part of Revelation beginning with the sixth chapter. *And such is indeed the case.*[5]

Similarly, "The acceptance of this view, in part," observes John McLean, "is dependent on how much weight is given to the parallels between the synoptics and Revelation."[6] Since all futurists understand the Olivet Discourse as being parallel to Revelation to some degree, it makes sense that these two portions of Scripture would be focused on the same basic time period—the tribulation. Dr. McLean has displayed these relationships in the following chart.[7]

PARALLELS BETWEEN THE OLIVET DISCOURSE AND THE SEAL JUDGMENTS OF REVELATION

	Revelation 6	Matthew 24	Mark 13	Luke 21
False Messiahs, False Prophets	2	5, 11	6	8
Wars	2–4	6–7	7	9
International Discord	3–4	7	8	10
Famines	5–8	7	8	11
Pestilences	8			11
Persecution, Martyrdom	9–11	9	9–13	12–17
Earthquakes	12	7	8	11
Cosmic Phenomena	12–14			11

BIRTH PANGS

Matthew 24:8 characterizes the events of verses 4–7 as "the beginning of birth-pangs." The Greek word *ôdinon* means "the pain of childbirth, travail-pain, birth-pang." It is said to be "intolerable anguish, in reference to the dire calamities which the Jews supposed would precede the advent of the Messiah."[8] Another lexical authority agrees and states, "of the 'Messianic woes', the terrors and torments that precede the coming of the Messianic Age."[9]

Most likely our Lord had in mind the Old Testament reference to birth pangs in Jeremiah 30:6–7, which states, "'Ask now, and see, if a male can give birth. Why do I see every man with his hands on his loins, as a woman in childbirth? And why have all faces turned pale? 'Alas! for that day is great, there is none like it; and it is the time of Jacob's distress, but he will be saved from it.' Dr. Randall Price explains the birth pangs of Messiah as follows:

> The birth pangs are significant in the timing of the Tribulation, as revealed by Jesus in the Olivet discourse (Matt. 24:8). Jesus' statement of the "birth pangs" is specifically that the events of the first half of the Tribulation (vv. 4–7) are merely the "beginning," with the expectation of greater birth pangs in the second half (the "Great Tribulation"). Based on this analogy, the entire period of the seventieth week is like birth pangs. As a woman must endure the entire period of labor before giving birth, so Israel must endure the entire seven-year Tribulation. The time divisions of Tribulation are also illustrated by the figure, for just as the natural process intensifies toward delivery after labor ends, so here the Tribulation moves progressively toward the second advent (vv. 30–31), which takes place "immediately after" the Tribulation ends (v. 29). As there are two phases of the birth pangs (beginning labor and full labor), so the seven years of Tribulation are divided between the less severe and more severe experiences of terrestrial and cosmic wrath, as revealed progressively in the Olivet discourse and the judgment section of Revelation 6–19.[10]

The Apostle Paul also uses the motif of birth pangs in 1 Thessalonians 5:3 where he says, "While they are saying, 'Peace and safety!' then destruction will come upon them suddenly like birth pangs upon a woman with child; and they shall not escape." The context of this passage relates to the tribulation period, which fits the other uses of birth pangs.

Raphael Patai in his helpful book *The Messiah Texts* has dozens of references to extra-biblical commentary from Jewish writings in a chapter entitled "The Pangs of Times."[11] Patai states that "the pangs of the Messianic times are imagined as having heavenly as well as earthly sources and expressions.... Things will come to such a head that people will despair of Redemption. This will last seven years. And then, unexpectedly, the Messiah will come."[12] This widespread Jewish idea fits exactly into the framework that Jesus expresses in the Olivet Discourse. The birth pangs of Messiah, also known as "the footprints of the Messiah,"[13] support the notion that Matthew 24:4–14 relate to the tribulation period leading up to the second advent of the Messiah since it is known as a time of great tribulation that results in Messiah's earthly arrival.

I have often been asked on radio talk shows if I believe that events like earthquakes, famines, wars, etc. mean that the end is near. I always say no. This usually surprises the host, because they so often hear from other prophecy teachers that these things have current prophetic significance. Yet, as you can see, if they don't refer to the church age, then they must have reference to the tribulation. Although it is likely that we stand on the verge of tribulation events, we are not yet in that time period. Because Matthew 24:4–14 cannot happen until after the rapture and the start of the tribulation, it is wrong to say that such events are prophetically significant in our own day. The birth pangs do not start until Israel faces her time of trouble.

ENDNOTES

1 John F. Walvoord, *Matthew: Thy Kingdom Come* (Chicago: Moody Press, 1974), 183.

2 Walvoord, *Matthew*, 183.

3 Arnold G. Fruchtenbaum, *The Footsteps of the Messiah: A Study of the Sequence of Prophetic Events* (San Antonio: Ariel Press, 1982), 439–40. For the most exhaustive presentation of this view that I have found so far, see David L. Cooper, *Future Events Revealed: According to Matthew 24 and 25*. Los Angeles: David L. Cooper, 1935.

4 Arno C. Gaebelein, *The Gospel of Matthew: An Exposition* (Neptune, NJ: Loizeaux Brothers, [1910] 1961), 476.

5 Gaebelein, *Matthew*, 481.

6 John McLean, "Chronology and Sequential Structure of John's Revelation," in Thomas Ice & Timothy Demy, *When the Trumpet Sounds: Today's Foremost Authorities Speak Out on End-Time Controversies* (Eugene, OR: Harvest House, 1995), 323.

7 McLean, "Chronology and Sequential Structure," 326.

8 Joseph Henry Thayer, *A Greek-English Lexicon of the New Testament* (New York: American Book Company, 1889), 679.

9 William F. Arndt and F. W. Gingrich, *A Greek-English Lexicon of the New Testament* (Chicago: University of Chicago Press, 1957), 904.

10 J. Randall Price, "Old Testament Tribulation Terms," in Thomas Ice & Timothy Demy, *When the Trumpet Sounds: Today's Foremost Authorities Speak Out on End-Time Controversies* (Eugene, OR: Harvest House, 1995), 72.

11 Raphael Patai, *The Messiah Texts: Jewish Legends of Three Thousand Years* (Detroit: Wayne State University Press, 1979), 95–103.

12 Patai, *Messiah Texts*, 95–96.

13 Price, "Tribulation Terms," 450, fn. 56.

5

FALSE CHRISTS OF MATTHEW 24:4–5

As seen in the previous chapter, Matthew 24:4–14 focuses on events of the first half of the seven-year tribulation period known as "the beginning of birth pangs" (Matt. 24:8). These events are parallel to the seal and trumpet judgments of Revelation 6, 8–9. I take it that in Christ's discourse "The disciples were the representatives of godly Jews, and were warned of what should befall their nation."[1] Thus, Matthew 24:4–5, which we now consider, will occur in the future, after the rapture of the church, at the time of the beginning of the tribulation.

DO NOT BE DECEIVED

Since the tribulation begins with the arrival of the Antichrist in global events (Dan. 7 & 9), it is not surprising that this section of the Olivet Discourse also begins with a warning to Christians regarding his arrival. Jesus begins answering the disciples' question with a warning about false messiahs: "And Jesus answered and said to them, 'See to it that no one misleads you. For many will come in My name, saying, 'I am the Christ,' and will mislead many'" (Matt. 24:4–5).

I think Brethren commentator William Kelly is correct to note that this passage is not referencing Christians during the current church age. He writes:

> In the epistles of Paul it is never exactly such a thought as warning persons against false Christs. For there the Holy Ghost addresses us as Christians; and a Christian could not be deceived by a man's pretensions to be Christ. It is most appropriate here, because the disciples are viewed in this chapter, as representatives, not of us Christians now, but of future godly Jews.[2]

The first thing Jesus tells the disciples is to make sure that no one misleads them. Spiritual deception will be the primary purpose of the Antichrist during the tribulation and thus is primary item to be avoided. Dr. Ed Glassock observes: "This warning was prompted by their eagerness for a sign. The danger of being misled was increased if one was too enthusiastic or anticipated some symbolic indication of the event."[3] Similarly, Dr. Stanley Toussaint writes of the potential of deception:

> The key to understanding the discourse is found in this first sentence. The disciples thought that the destruction of Jerusalem with its great temple would usher in the end of the age. The Lord separates the two ideas and warns the disciples against being deceived by the destruction of Jerusalem and other such catastrophes. The razing of the temple and the presence of wars and rumors of wars do not necessarily signify the nearness of the end.[4]

MANY FALSE CHRISTS

Why are the listeners to be on guard against deception? Vigilance will be needed because during the tribulation there will be a host of individuals claiming to be the Messiah and many people will be deceived and believe them. But the Jewish believers during the tribulation are not to fall prey to such deception.

The emphasis in verse 5 is upon "many." It is not just a single person who will come claiming to be the Messiah, but a whole host of individuals will make such claims. Multiple claims to messiahship are one of the reasons why this passage is not referring to events leading up to the A.D. 70 destruction of Jerusalem. Nineteenth-century biblical commentator A. H.

M'Neile writes, "No such definite claim to Messiahship is known till that of Barkokba in the reign of Hadrian."[5] The Bar-Kokhba Revolt, also known at the Second Jewish Rebellion, was put down by the Romans in A.D. 135 when Hadrian lead the Roman legions to once again destroy Jerusalem and the surrounding area, which resulted in the death of half a million Jews.[6] Robert Gundry notes the following:

> The lack of evidence that anyone claimed messiahship between Jesus and Bar-Kokhba a hundred years later militates against our seeing the discourse as a *vaticinium ex eventu* [a prophecy of an event] concerning the first Jewish revolt (A.D. 66–73). False prophets figured in that revolt (Josephus *J.W.* 6.5.2 §§285–87; 7.11.1 §§437–39; *Ant.* 20.5.1 §97); but one did not have to claim messiahship to be a false prophet. Cf. Acts 5:36; 8:9; 21:38.[7]

James R. Gray notes, "strict claims to the Messianic office in the strictest sense are almost nonexistent in history."[8] However, from this passage we learn that in the future, it will be rampant.

THE FIRST SEAL JUDGMENT

As noted previously in the book, the judgments of Matthew 24:4–11 parallel in order the first five seal judgments of Revelation 6:1–11. "The first seal depicts a false Messiah,"[9] as observed in Revelation 6:1–2:

> And I saw when the Lamb broke one of the seven seals, and I heard one of the four living creatures saying as with a voice of thunder, "Come." And I looked, and behold, a white horse, and he who sat on it had a bow; and a crown was given to him; and he went out conquering, and to conquer. (Rev. 6:1–2)

Arno Gaebelein, a well-known Bible teacher from the first half of the 20th century, writes of this similarity between Matthew 24 and Revelation 6:

> The rider upon the white horse under the first seal is a counterfeit. He is a false Christ, who goes forth to conquer. His conquest is a bloodless one, as he has only a bow. He will bring about a false peace among the nations, which for a time may have been alarmed by the supernatural removal of the church. The second rider "takes peace from the earth," from which we would conclude that the first rider upon the white horse (white emblem of peace) has established peace.
>
> And as we turn to Matthew xxiv we find that the first thing our Lord saith, is about the deceivers who will come with the beginning of the age ending saying: "I am Christ," and succeeding to lead away many.[10]

WHAT IS THE NATIONALITY OF THE ANTICHRIST?

A widely-held belief throughout the history of the church has been the notion that Antichrist will be of Jewish origin. This view remains popular in our own day. However, upon closer examination we find no real scriptural basis for such a view.

Arguments for a Jewish Origin

Three reasons are often given in support of the argument that Antichrist will be Jewish.[11] First, it is argued on an antisemitic premise that he will be a Jew because the Jews are responsible for the world's problems. Thus, according to this perspective, it follows that the greatest problem of history—Antichrist—will also be Jewish. This is the antisemitic reason. It should be clear that since antisemitism is unbiblical, so is any logic that reasons upon such a premise or perspective.

Dr. Arnold Fruchtenbaum offers a refutation of the second reason, which he calls "The Logical Reason." He writes:

> Stated in a syllogism, this argument goes as follows:

> MAJOR PREMISE: The Jews will accept the Antichrist as the Messiah
> MINOR PREMISE: The Jews will never accept a Gentile as the Messiah.
> CONCLUSION: The Antichrist will be a Jew.[12]

The difficulties of this argument are many, not the least of which are the two premises. Neither premise can be supported from the Bible. Just because the Jewish people make a covenant with the Antichrist (Dan. 9:27; Isa. 28:15), it does not follow either textually or logically that they accept him as Messiah (or Antichrist). Second, since they are not accepting him as Messiah, the fact that he is a Gentile peacemaker is irrelevant. Thus, the conclusion does not follow.

An attempt at a scriptural argument reasons that Antichrist will spring forth from the tribe of Dan. This has been a view that has been widely held throughout church history, from the earliest times to the present day. Support for this view is inappropriately derived from Genesis 49:17; Deuteronomy 33:22; Jeremiah 8:16; Daniel 11:37; and Revelation 7:4–8. Even though many passages are cited in support of this argument, none of them actually support the notion because they are all taken out of context. In reality, only Daniel 11:37 refers to the Antichrist. Even though some believe that the phrase in Daniel 11:37 "the God of his fathers" (KJV), implies a Jewish apostasy, the phrase is more accurately translated "the gods of his fathers" (NASB). As will be shown, because Antichrist will be a Gentile, the argument is unfounded. The NASB translation, not the KJV, supports the he original Hebrew; Antichrist's apostasy will be Christian and not Jewish.[13]

Arguments for a Gentile Origin

We have seen that the Bible does not teach that Antichrist will be Jewish; however, Scripture does teach that he will be of Gentile descent. This first can be seen from biblical typology. Most commentators agree that Daniel 11 speaks of Antiochus Epiphanes (reigned 175–164 B.C.), a Gentile, who typifies the future Antichrist. Since Antiochus was a Gentile, then so too will be Antichrist.

Second, biblical imagery supports a Gentile origin of Antichrist. Scripture pictures Antichrist as rising up out of the sea (Rev. 13:1; 17:15). In prophetic literature the sea is an image of the Gentile nations. Thus, Antichrist is seen as a Gentile progeny.

Third, the nature of the "Times of the Gentiles" (Luke 21:24) supports a Gentile Antichrist. Fruchtenbaum notes:

> It is agreed by all premillennialists that the period known as the Times of the Gentiles does not end until the second coming of Christ. It is further agreed that the Antichrist is the final ruler of the Times of the Gentiles....
>
> If this is so, how then can a Jew be the last ruler at a time when only Gentiles can have the preeminence? To say the Antichrist is to be a Jew would contradict the very nature of the Time of the Gentiles.[14]

Finally, the Bible not only teaches that Antichrist will be Gentile, but it also implies that he will be of Roman descent. This is understood from Daniel 9:27, where the one cutting a covenant with Israel is said to represent the revived Roman Empire because it was the Romans who destroyed Jerusalem and the Temple in A.D. 70. The revived Roman Empire comes from a second phase of the Roman Empire, i.e., "feet partly of iron and partly of clay" (Dan 2:33, 40–45).

The implications of the non-Jewishness of the Antichrist has significant implications as noted by Gray:

> Because the true Anti-Christ is not a Jew (cf. Daniel 7, 11, Revelation 13:1), therefore he will not claim to be a false Messiah. These false claimants will be contemporaneous with Antichrist and will likely oppose him. During this time Israel will have many options and opportunities to follow false Messiahs, yet, the Antichrist will not be one of them. He comes as a benefactor of Israel, a great world diplomat turned persecutor, but not a Messianic deliverer. He will be worshipped, not as Messiah, but as God.[15]

ENDNOTES

1 William Kelly, *Lectures on The Gospel of Matthew* (Sunbury, PA: Believers Bookshelf, 1971 [1868]), 479.

2 Kelly, *Matthew*, 479.

3 Ed Glasscock, *Matthew: Moody Gospel Commentary* (Chicago: Moody Press, 1997), 464.

4 Stanley D. Toussaint, *Behold The King: A Study of Matthew* (Portland: Multnomah Press, 1980), 270.

5 Alan Hugh M'Neile, *The Gospel According to St. Matthew* (London: MacMillan, 1915), 345.

6 Roman historian "Dio Cassius relates that the Romans demolished 50 fortresses, destroyed 985 villages, and killed 580,000 people in addition to those who died of hunger, disease, and fire." *Encyclopaedia Judaica*, 17 vols. (Jerusalem: Keter Publishing House, n.d.), vol. 4, 233.

7 Robert H. Gundry, *Matthew: A Commentary on His Handbook for a Mixed Church under Persecution*, second edition, (Grand Rapids: Eerdmans, 1994), 477.

8 James R. Gray, *Prophecy on The Mount: A Dispensational Study of the Olivet Discourse* (Chandler, AZ: Berean Advocate Ministries, 1991), 29. On false messiahs from a Jewish perspective and within Judaism, see Jerry Rabow. *50 Jewish Messiahs: The Untold Life Stories of 50 Jewish Messiahs Since Jesus and How They Changed the Jewish, Christian, and Muslim Worlds*. Jerusalem: Gefen Publishing House, 2002.

9 Thomas O. Figart, *The King of The Kingdom of Heaven: A Verse by Verse Commentary on the Gospel of Matthew* (Lancaster, PA: Eden Press, 1999), 438.

10 Arno C. Gaebelein, *The Gospel of Matthew: An Exposition* (Neptune, NJ: Loizeaux Brothers, [1910] 1961), 481–82.

11 These three reasons were gleaned from Arnold Fruchtenbaum, "The Nationality of the Anti-Christ" (Englewood, NJ: American Board of Missions To The Jews, n.d.).

12 Fruchtenbaum, "Nationality," 8.

13 Fruchtenbaum, "Nationality," 11–22.

14 Fruchtenbaum, "Nationality," 24, 26.

15 Gray, *Prophecy on The Mount*, 29.

6

FALSE MESSIAHS, WARS, AND FEAR IN MATTHEW 24:5

After Christ's primary warning about religious apostasy (Matt. 24:4–5), He turns His focus upon geopolitical events. Jesus says, "And you will be hearing of wars and rumors of wars; see that you are not frightened, for those things must take place, but that is not yet the end. For nation will rise against nation, and kingdom against kingdom, and in various places there will be famines and earthquakes. But all these things are merely the beginning of birth pangs" (Matt. 24:6–8). Since we have previously seen that verses 4–14 refer to the first half of the tribulation, it follows that these events will occur during that time, and will correspond with the seal judgments of Revelation 6.

FALSE MESSIAH'S

Before looking the next section I want to revisit the issue of false messiahs from verse 5. Preterists such as Gary DeMar like to say "False messiahs made regular appearances in Israel."[1] Kenneth Gentry is more careful in his statement, but nevertheless declares, "There are many examples of great pretenders who almost certainly make Messianic claims."[2] Gentry and DeMar are speaking of the first century and Gentry lists the following individuals as those whom he says made messianic claims: Theudas in Acts 5:36, Simon Magus in Acts 8:9–10, and "the Egyptian false prophet."[3] DeMar adds to the list with the following: "Josephus tells of 'a certain impostor named Theudas...' Dositheus, a Samaritan, 'pretended that he was the lawgiver prophesied of by Moses.'"[4] DeMar contends that all these individuals made claims to be the Messiah. However, when examined closely, none of these actually claimed to be Messiah.

Some of these people could be described as false prophets, but not false Messiahs. Preterists are playing fast and loose with the data because they have such a large investment in their view that all this took place in the first century. H. A. W. Meyer clarifies the issue when he notes,

> We possess no *historical* record of any false Messiahs having appeared *previous to the destruction of Jerusalem* (Barcochba did not make his appearance till the time of Hadrian); for Simon Magus (Acts viii. 9), Theudas (Acts v. 36), the Egyptian (Acts xxi. 38), Menander, Dositheus, who have been referred to as cases in point (Theophylact, Euthymius Zigabenus, Grotius, Calovius, Bengel), did not pretend to be the *Messiah*. (Comp. Joseph *Antt.* Xx. 5. 1; 8. 6; *Bell.* Ii. 13. 5.)[5]

Similarly, commentators Davis and Allison say, "The first and second centuries saw quite a few famous false prophets who made eschatological claims," as noted above. However, they continue, "That any of them (before Bar Kochba) said, in so many words, 'I am Messiah', is undemonstrated by the sources."[6] Finally, Leon Morris writes, "in this place the meaning is rather that they will claim for themselves the name *Messiah*, Jesus' own title." Morris explains:

> This will surely be a reference to the last days, for there is little evidence that any of the turbulent men so active preceding the fall of Jerusalem ever claimed to be the Messiah. Some claimed to be prophets, but that is not the same thing.[7]

Regarding the phrase "in my name," Donald Hagner notes:

> The statement that such persons will come, 'in my name," means either that they will come using the name of Jesus or that they will

> come assuming the messianic of Jesus, as is spelled out in the explicit claim that follows. The claim to be the Christ means here the claim to be the eschatological Messiah.[8]

Even if some first century individuals did claim to be the Messiah—but they did not—it would not fulfill this passage. This is one of the many reasons that it looks to the future tribulation and the coming of the beast of Revelation, popularly known down through Christendom as the Antichrist.

WARS AND RUMORS OF WARS

Verse 6 begins with an interesting Greek word—*mellô*—which is usually not translated into English, but it carries the idea of "about to." Because it is in the future tense, this opening phrase has the sense of "You are going to be about to hear..."[9] This indeed is the case!

The Greek word *polemos* is a general word for war and connotes the "whole course of hostilities" rather than just the individual battles that comprise the larger campaign or war.[10] This is a reference to wars that will be taking place in reference to the future Jewish people. Meyer says that this phrase is a "reference to wars near at hand, the din and tumult of which are actually heard, and to wars at a distance, of which nothing is known except from the reports that are brought home."[11]

Here we have the future parallel to Revelation 6:4 and the red horse judgment, which is said "to take peace from the earth, and that men should slay one another; and a great sword was given to him." The first seal judgment of Revelation 6:2 is the rider on a white horse, who is a counterfeit Christ, which corresponds to verses 4–5 of Matthew 24. This means that Antichrist begins the tribulation with a false peace that soon turns into multiple wars breaking out around the globe. There will be war that those in Jerusalem will experience and wars further away about which they will only hear.

To whom is the Lord addressing His comments in this discourse? I believe that it is not to the church, but "to the Jewish disciples as they then were, and as they will be."[12] William Kelly expounds upon this aspect:

> ...the Lord is predicting about the Jewish remnant,...And this, because many things must yet be accomplished before the Jews can come into their blessing. But for Christians, all things are ours in Christ even now; the blessing is never put off, though we await the crown at His coming. Again, many parts of scripture speak of scenes of anguish before the Lord's coming; others make Christians to be expecting Christ at any time. These scriptures cannot be broken, nor can they contradict one another; and yet they must do so, if they be applied to the same people.[13]

These wars of the tribulation are described in verse 7 as, nation against nation, and kingdom against kingdom. This description depicts multiple struggles taking place on various levels; international conflicts will be raging. Nations fighting nations, such as if the national entities of France and Germany fought one another. Kingdom against kingdom, such as if NATO were to fight the former Warsaw Pact nations. This is the kind of geopolitical conflicts depicted in Daniel and Revelation, which occur within the context of a future tribulation. This is not what took place in A.D. 70. Rome was an empire that fought against Israel—a single nation. Such a first-century single conflict does not resemble nation against nation and kingdom against kingdom. M'Neile notes, "The horrors described are not local disturbances, but are spread over the known world; nations and kingdoms are in hostility with one another."[14]

DO NOT BE FRIGHTENED

Jesus tells His disciples that they should not be frightened. The Greek word for frightened is only used here, in the parallel passage of Mark 8:15, and by Paul in 2 Thessalonians 2:2. New Testament Greek grammar expert A. T. Robertson says the word "means to cry aloud, to scream, and in the passive to be terrified by an outcry." He renders this passage as follows: "Look out for the wars and rumours of wars, but do not be sacred out of your wits by them."[15]

All three uses of this word are found within the context of the tribulation. Apparently, this is going to be a very scary and difficult time for those who do not understand that God is in control of these things. Paul makes a similar statement in 2 Thessalonians when he says, "that you may not be quickly shaken from your composure or be *disturbed* either by a spirit or a message or a letter as if from us, to the effect that the day of the Lord has come" (2:2). The Thessalonian Christians thought that they were in the day of the Lord or the tribulation. Paul tells them not to be disturbed, because they were not in the day of the Lord.

Twice, once by our Lord and once by Paul, are descriptions of a natural human reaction to thinking that one is in the tribulation as the temptation to cry out in pain. We can understand why one would think this way as we come to realize that the seal judgments of Revelation 6 describe this specific time as a time in which over a quarter of the earth's population will be killed (Rev. 6:8).

What is the antidote to this frightening knowledge? Simply to know that, "those things *must* take place" (verse 6). Meyer says, "The reflection that it is a matter of necessity in pursuance of the divine purpose (xxvi. 54), is referred to as calculated to inspire a calm and reassured frame of mind."[16] Believers are comforted to know that "if God says that something shall be, then it must be."[17] Morris explains: "They have one thing going for them that the general public has not: they know that God is over all and that his purpose will in the end be worked out. This is the significance of *it is necessary*."[18] This phrase lets us know that God is in control of what is seemingly out of control—His judgment.

Judgment is a necessary part of God's plan because there is evil in the world. Before the Lord can usher in His kingdom—because it will be a righteous kingdom—He must purge evil through judgment. This can be a scary thing if one does not know God and His plan. Knowing the predetermined plan of God is one of the comforting aspects that prophecy provides for the people of God during a time of global upheaval. Judgment must happen because God is a righteous God who has limits to His patience.

James R. Gray provides the following excellent summary of this passage:

> Matthew 24:6 and Revelation 6:3–4 are parallel. The red horse symbolizes war. The purpose of the rider is "to take peace from the earth,

> and that they should kill one another" (Rev. 6:3). Many perceive the first half of the Tribulation as a time of great peace. That is not so. The Antichrist will be perceived as a man of peace because of his great deceptive ability. The fact is he comes to power and stays in power because of war (Dan. 7:8, 24). The tribulation will bring war and more wars. The book of Revelation prophesies of many wars, not only in chapter 6, but also in 16:12–15, 17:14, 19:1 ff., and 20:8. These will not only be in invasions of Palestine (Daniel 9:26–27, 11:40–45, Zechariah 12:2–11, Revelation 12:9–17).[19]

A time of chaos and conflict is coming as part of God's judgment; even so, God remains in control.

ENDNOTES

1 Gary DeMar, *Last Days Madness: Obsession of the Modern Church*, (Power Springs, GA: American Vision, 1999), 73.

2 Kenneth L. Gentry, Jr., *Perilous Times: A Study in Eschatological Evil* (Texarkana, AR: Covenant Media Press, 1999), 46.

3 Gentry, *Perilous Times*, 46–47.

4 DeMar, *Last Days Madness*, 74.

5 Heinrich August Wilhelm Meyer, *Critical and Exegetical Handbook to The Gospel of Matthew*, 2 vols. (Edinburgh: T. & T. Clark, 1879), vol. 2, 128.

6 W. D. Davies and Dale C. Allison, Jr., *A Critical and Exegetical Commentary on The Gospel According to Saint Matthew*, 3 vols. (Edinburgh: T. & T. Clark, 1997), vol. 3, 338–39.

7 Leon Morris, *The Gospel According to Matthew* (Grand Rapids: Eerdmans, 1992), 597.

8 Donald A. Hagner, *Word Biblical Commentary: Matthew 14–28*, Vol. 33B (Dallas: Word Books, 1995), 690.

9 Randolph O. Yeager, *The Renaissance New Testament*, 18 vols. (Bowling Green, KY: Renaissance Press, 1978), vol. 3, 277.

10 Richard C. Trench, *Synonyms of the New Testament* (Grand Rapids: Eerdmans, [1880] 1953), 322.

11 Meyer, *Matthew*, vol. 2, 129.

12 William Kelly, *Lectures on The Gospel of Matthew* (Sunbury, PA: Believers Bookshelf, 1971 [1868]), 482.

13 Kelly, *Matthew*, 483.

14 Alan Hugh M'Neile, *The Gospel According to St. Matthew* (London: MacMillan, 1915), 346.

15 A. T. Robertson, *Word Pictures in the New Testament*, VI vols, (Nashville: Broadman Press, 1930), vol. I, 189.

16 Meyer, *Matthew*, vol. 2, 129.

17 Davies and Allison, *Matthew*, vol. 3, 349, fn. 81.

18 Morris, *Matthew*, 598.

19 James R. Gray, *Prophecy on The Mount: A Dispensational Study of the Olivet Discourse* (Chandler, AZ: Berean Advocate Ministries, 1991), 29–30.

7

EMPIRES AT WAR IN MATTHEW 24:6–24:27A

Jesus states in Matthew 24:6, "And you will be hearing of wars and rumors of wars; see that you are not frightened, for those things must take place, but that is not yet the end." Previously we looked at the first half of this verse, but the second half also makes an important statement.

"THAT IS NOT YET THE END"

Because wars and rumors of wars must take place, there would be a tendency for the disciples to think that the end was upon them, but such was not the case. In fact, this warning has been ignored down through church history. Too often many have thought that because of military conflicts that the end of the age has come.[1] With the current war against terrorism in which the United States, Israel, and others are currently engaged, as well as other conflicts and potential conflicts, some might be tempted to think that this is a sign of the end. While I do think that we might be near the end of the church age, it would not be for that reason.[2] If not, then to what does "that is not yet the end" refer?

Verses 4–31 of Matthew 24 cover the time period known as the seventieth-week of Daniel (Dan. 9:24–27), or more popularly called the tribulation period. Christ is telling His disciples that when one sees the beginning of the birth pangs—the first few seal judgments of Revelation 6—then that is not the end of the seven-year tribulation period, but just the beginning. Many more events must unfold before one can "straighten up and lift up your heads, because your redemption is drawing near" (Luke 21:28).

We are living in the church age, which will end when the rapture (I Thess. 4:15–18) takes place prior to the beginning of the tribulation. Yet, regardless of what happens in current events, they will not be specific events that are prophesied in the Bible; Scripture does not prophesy church age geopolitical events.

NATIONS AND KINGDOMS ON THE RISE

The first half of Matthew 24:7 reads, "For nation will rise against nation, and kingdom against kingdom." Immediately, we notice a difference between our Lord's use of "nation" and "kingdom." As we will see shortly, this is an important distinction.

First, we want to examine the usage of the conjunction "for." Does the Greek word *gar* refer to the preceding or following context? Dana and Mantey tell us in their Greek grammar that *gar* "may express: (a) a *ground* or *reason,* (b) an *explanation,* (c) a *confirmation* or *assurance*."[3] All nuances of the use of *gar* are what we might call resultant in scope. This would mean that verse 7 is "introducing a reason" or is "explanatory"[4] of the preceding statement from verse 6. M'Neile asserts that *gar* "links the verse with the preceding."[5] This means that Jesus is not introducing something totally new in verse 7. Rather, it means that the "wars and rumors of wars" of verse 6 are happening because of verse 7. So what is happening in verse 7?

The Greek word for "nation" is *ethnos*. It simply means "people" or if used of a national group of people it means "nation."[6] Our English word "ethnic" is derived from this Greek word. Because *ethnos* is set against *ethnos* in this context, it must mean a "nation," like Canada or Mexico. On the other hand, the Greek word for "kingdom" is *basileia*. This word simply means "the territory ruled over by a king."[7] Scottish cleric and biblical commentator James Morison writes, "Literally, *upon nation*. One nation shall rise in its anger to come *down upon* another."[8] But what is the relationship between nation and kingdom?

At the very least nation and kingdom are synonyms for national entities. However, it appears from the context that there is a progression from nation (*ethnos*) to a confederation of nations that form a kingdom (*basileia*). Morison says that the notion of kingdom could include "greater communities, or empire, embracing within one political sphere various distinct nationalities."[9] If this is the case, then the passage is saying that nations will be fighting against nations and groups of nations will also be fighting against each other. This would be similar to the alliance during the Cold War where NATO nations were aligned against the nations of the Warsaw Pact. M'Neile says, "The horrors described are not local disturbances, but are spread over the known world; nations and kingdoms are in hostility with one another (not divided against itself, as in xii. 25, Is. xix. 2)."[10]

PRETERIST DISTRACTION

Preterist Gary DeMar and other pretereists believe that this was fulfilled in the first century. He says the following:

> The *Annals of Tacitus*, covering the period from A.D. 14 to the death of Nero in A.D. 68, describes the tumult of the period with phrases such as "disturbances in Germany," "commotions in Africa," "commotions in Thrace," "insurrections in Gaul," "intrigues among the Parthians," "the war in Britain," and "the war in Armenia." Wars were fought from one end of the empire to the other. With this description we can see further fulfillment: "For nation will rise against nation, and kingdom against kingdom" (Matt. 24:7).[11]

Yet, as is often the case, when one examines the preterist view on a specific matter closely it does not correspond to what the passage is actually saying. Tacitus is describing internal conflict within the Roman Empire, not "nation against nation, and kingdom against kingdom." Craig Evans notes that this passage speaks of "the expectation of global warfare and chaos…However, there were no major wars prior to the Jewish revolt."[12] Meyer declares: "As for the Parthian wars and the risings that took place some ten years after in Gaul and Spain, they had no connection whatever with Jerusalem or Judea."[13] Biblical commentator, M. F. Sadler is on the mark when he notes the following about the parallel passage in Mark:

> If this verse is the sequence of the previous one, then it can hardly refer to the time before the destruction of Jerusalem; for then the Roman power kept the peace of the world. It is consequently explained by many commentators as fulfilled in various local tumults between the Jews who were scattered everywhere, and the various Gentile nations amongst whom they dwelt. But this by no means answers to such expressions as, "nation against nation," and "kingdom against kingdom." They seem rather to refer to such a time as the present, when the civilized world is divided into many separate nationalities.[14]

If this was the case more than one hundred twenty-five years ago, concerning the state of nationalism, how much more so are we in that condition in our own day? Sadler adds the following comment at the parallel passage in his commentary on Luke:

> I have noticed that these international conflicts seem to look rather to these latter times, when Europe and the adjacent part of Asia and Africa are divided into so many independent sovereignties, than to a time when there was but one great empire, which, as it were kept the peace amongst the smaller nationalities.[15]

FUTURE FULFILLMENT

Taking into account verses six and seven, this passage is describing future events that will take place during the first part of the tribulation. Because Matthew 24:6–7 is parallel to the second seal judgment in Revelation 6:3–4, it is further fixed within Scripture as part of the future time of tribulation. Revelation 6:4 states, "And another, a red horse, went out; and to him who sat on it, it was granted to take peace from the earth, and that men should slay one another; and a great sword was given to him." Thus, early in the tribulation the Antichrist is involved in warfare against nations and kingdoms (see also Dan. 7:8, 23–24; 9:36–45).

Interestingly senior British diplomat Robert Cooper, who helped shape former British Prime Minister Tony Blair's view of the world, wrote an article that provided insight as to why Blair was one of U. S. president George W.

Bush's strongest supporters for preemptive military action in Iraq.[16] Cooper's view of history holds that for the past few centuries the world has seen the rise of nationalism, which has led to international instability. He believes that we are now in the process of moving toward a time of postmodern internationalism, with global coalitions such as the European Union as the transitional stage. Cooper believes that military force is warranted by the international community when there are renegade states such as Iraq that refuse to enter into cooperation with this postmodern arrangement. Cooper explains:

> What is the origin of this basic change in the state system? The fundamental point is that "the world's grown honest". A large number of the most powerful states no longer want to fight or conquer. It is this that gives rise to both the pre-modern and postmodern worlds. Imperialism in the traditional sense is dead, at least among the Western powers.[17]

He continues, writing, "The EU is the most developed example of a postmodern system."[18]

Because we are in a transition from a premodern to a postmodern world, then "The challenge to the postmodern world is to get used to the idea of double standards."[19] What does he mean? Because there are nations like Iraq who will not come willingly into this wonderful new international community, then they have to be dealt with in the old-fashioned way—militarily. That is a very strong view. Thus, unlike old liberalism, which tends to be pacifistic, the new liberalism is selectively militant. Cooper calls for "a new kind of imperialism" that is built upon economic unity, while dealing militarily with dissent. This is why Cooper concludes his essay with a call for a "cooperative empire, like Rome."[20]

It is not surprising that as we see the world currently being set for post-rapture events that a European intellectual such as Robert Cooper would call for a revival of the Roman Empire, but with a new postmodern twist. How interesting that the Bible envisions a similar setup during the tribulation under the Antichrist. We can see from a proper interpretation of biblical passages that Scripture calls for a future time as described in Matthew 24:6–7. We should not be surprised that the same God who wrote that Scripture is moving to bring its fulfillment to pass, potentially in the near future.

ENDNOTES

1 For many examples see Francis X. Gumerlock, *The Day and the Hour: Christianity's Perennial Fascination with Predicting the End of the World*. Powder Springs, GA: American Vision, 2000.

2 See my views in Thomas Ice and Timothy Demy, *The Truth About The Signs of The Times*. Eugene, OR: Harvest House, 1997; or Thomas Ice and Timothy Demy, *Prophecy Watch: What to Expect in the Days to Come*. Eugene, OR: Harvest House, 1998, 9–76.

3 H. E. Dana and Julius R. Mantey, *A Manual Grammar of the Greek New Testament* (Toronto: The MacMillan Company, [1927] 1955), 242.

4 Dana and Mantey, *Grammar*, 243.

5 Alan Hugh M'Neile, *The Gospel According to St. Matthew* (London: MacMillan, 1915), 345.

6 William F. Arndt and F. W. Gingrich, *A Greek-English Lexicon of the New Testament* (Chicago: University of Chicago Press, 1957), 217.

7 Arndt and Gingrich. *Lexicon*, 134.

8 James Morison, *A Practical Commentary on the Gospel According to St. Mark* (Boston: N. J. Bartlett & Co., 1882), 355.

9 Morison, *Mark*, 355.

10 M'Neile, *Matthew*, 346.

11 Gary DeMar, *Last Days Madness: Obsession of the Modern Church*, (Power Springs, GA: American Vision, 1999), 79. For a similar view see also Kenneth L. Gentry, Jr., *Perilous Times: A Study in Eschatological Evil* (Texarkana, AR: Covenant Media Press, 1999), 47–49.

12 Craig A. Evans, *Word Biblical Commentary: Mark 8:27—16:20*, Vol. 34B (Dallas: Word Books, 2001), 307.

13 Heinrich August Wilhelm Meyer, *Critical and Exegetical Handbook to The Gospel of Matthew*, 2 vols. (Edinburgh: T. & T. Clark, 1879), vol. 2, 130.

14 M. F. Sadler, *The Gospel According to St. Mark: with Notes Critical and Practical* (London: George Bell and Sons, [1884] 1898), 298.

15 M. F. Sadler, *The Gospel According to St. Luke: with Notes Critical and Practical* (London: George Bell and Sons, [1886] 1911), 527–28.

16 Robert Cooper, "The New Liberal Imperialism," in the *Observer Worldview Extra* (London: April 7, 2002) at the following Internet address: www.observer.co.uk/international/story/0,6903,680094,00.html.

17 Cooper, "New Imperialism."

18 Cooper, "New Imperialism."

19 Cooper, "New Imperialism."

20 Cooper, "New Imperialism."

8

FAMINES AND EARTHQUAKES

Now that we have looked into the first half of Matthew 24:7, we will consider the second half of the verse. The passage reads, "For nation will rise against nation, and kingdom against kingdom, and in various places there will be famines and earthquakes. But all these things are merely the beginning of birth pangs" (Matt. 24:7–8). So what about famines and earthquakes?

FAMINES AND EARTHQUAKES

We previously have noted and defended the view that Matthew 24:4–14 covers the first half of the seven-year tribulation period. Because we know that the "abomination of desolation" (Matt. 24:15) occurs in the middle of the seven-year period (Dan. 9:24–27), we know that events prior to verse 15 will take place in the first half of the tribulation. This is further confirmed by the correlation of the major events of Matthew 24:4–8 with the first four seal judgments of Revelation 6:1–8. This then would mean that the famines and earthquakes of Matthew 24:7 speak of a future time, which Revelation 6:5–8 expounds upon, not of any events that have occurred during the last 2,000 years nor of anything in our present day.

There have been, no doubt, earthquakes and famines in the first century and during every generation since then. "It is hardly necessary to add to this that not only false Christs and false prophets, wars and rumors of war, earthquakes and famines occur in every age throughout the history of the church," declares William Hendriksen, "but so do also persecutions and defections, to which Jesus refers in verses 9, 10, 12, and 13."[1] The context of this passage is that of a time of future tribulation in which these events will occur as part of God's direct wrath and judgment. The earthquakes and famines of today and during the first century did not fulfill this prophecy because the context of this passage is of a still-future time period. Now, let us look further at the passage.

FAMINES

The Greek word for famine is *limos* and simply means "hunger," and, thus, when used of "dying of hunger," connotes "famine."[2] This word is also used in Revelation 6:8.

If Jesus is referencing a time during the first half of the tribulation, to what is He referring? I believe that Revelation 6:5–6 is a parallel passage. "And when He broke the third seal, I heard the third living creature saying, 'Come.' And I looked, and behold, a black horse; and he who sat on it had a pair of scales in his hand. And I heard as it were a voice in the center of the four living creatures saying, 'A quart of wheat for a denarius, and three quarts of barley for a denarius; and do not harm the oil and the wine.'" Even though the word "famine" is not used, the passage is an apt description of such and it is one of the earliest judgments of tribulation period. Arno C. Gaebelein says, "And the third seal reveals a rider upon a black horse and he has a balance in his hand and what he saith indicates clearly that he brings famines (Rev. vi:5–6)."[3]

Both the famines and earthquakes are governed by the phrase "in various places." R. C. H. Lenski says, "The distributive *kata* means, "from place to place."[4] Leon Morris also explains: "In many places means that the disasters in question will be widespread."[5] This global perspective fits a future understanding of the passage and cannot be limited to the first century and the area of Israel alone.

Robert Gundry notes, "The putting of famines before earthquakes may indicate that famines result from the ravages of the warfare just mentioned (cf. Rev. 6:3–6)."[6] If we follow the order from Revelation, then it is clear that famine is the result of war, as is usually the case.

Predictably, preterists believe that Christ's prophecy of famine was somehow fulfilled in A.D. 70 when the Romans destroyed the Temple and Jerusalem. Speaking of famines, Kenneth Gentry declares, "We may easily apply this also to the first century scene."[7] Fellow preterist, Gary DeMar cites the following as evidence for a first century fulfillment of famines:

> Beginning with the book of Acts, we see that famines were prevalent in the period prior to Jerusalem's destruction in A.D. 70:...The famine was dramatic evidence that Jesus' prophecy was coming to pass in their generation just like He said it would....
>
> Contemporary secular historians such as Tacitus, Suetonius, and Josephus mention other famines during the period prior to A.D. 70.[8]

Are preterist claims true? Because famines occur in every generation, one can find some examples of famines just as do those who believe that this is a prophecy for our own day cite numerous contemporary examples. Yet, Craig Evans writes, "Again, events in the decades immediately preceding the Jewish revolt only roughly parallel this part of Jesus' prophecy."[9] With famines always occurring, it seems to blur somewhat the precision of such events as a distinct fulfillment of past prophecy. Meyer rebuts the preterist notion writing:

> Nor, again, is this feature in the prediction to be restricted to some such special famine as that which occurred during the reign of Claudius (Acts xi.28), too early a date for our passage, and to one or two particular cases of earthquake which happened in remote countries, and with which history has made us familiar (such as that in the neighborhood of Colossae, Oros. *Hist.* vii. 7, Tacit. *Ann.* xiv. 27 and that at Pompeii).[10]

Like the details of the other items that we have examined in this context, the famines of Matthew 24 have yet to occur. They will take place during the first half of the tribulation. These famines will take place at various places all over the world, likely as a result of the preceding warfare.

EARTHQUAKES

Earthquake in the original Greek is *seismos*. The basic sense of the word is "shaking." It can refer to the shaking of a storm on a sea. However, it mostly occurs in the New Testament when speaking of an earthquake.[11] Our English word seismograph is derived from this Greek root.

For the same reasons noted earlier, I do not think that these earthquakes that will take place at various places around the world have already taken place in the past nor are they occurring today. Just like the famines that have preceded them, the earthquakes in this passage are parallel to the ones described as the fourth seal judgment in Revelation 6:7–8. "And when He broke the fourth seal, I heard the voice of the fourth living creature saying, 'Come.' And I looked, and behold, an ashen horse; and he who sat on it had the name Death; and Hades was following with him. And authority was given to them over a fourth of the earth, to kill with sword and with famine and with pestilence and by the wild beasts of the earth." Gaebelein further explains when he says, "The fourth rider of the fourth seal is upon a pale horse. His name is 'Death.' He takes the fourth part of the earth away. This corresponds to the Lord's announcement that there will be 'pestilences and earthquakes in divers places.'"[12]

Luke 21:11, a parallel passage to Matthew 24:7 states, "there will be great earthquakes." So these are not ordinary earthquakes that our Lord forecasts, but great or huge ones. So great, that they cause a great number of deaths worldwide.

Preterists Gentry and DeMar also believe that this sign was fulfilled in the first century. DeMar said, "The historical record of earthquakes that occurred before Jerusalem was destroyed in the first century fulfills Jesus' prophecy to the letter.... Three earthquakes are mentioned [in Acts] prior to the destruction of Jerusalem in A.D. 70."[13] Gentry adds:

> A particularly dreadful quake shakes Jerusalem in A.D. 67....
>
> Tacitus mentions earthquakes in Crete, Rome, Apamea, Phrygia, Campania, Laodicea (of Revelation fame) and Pompeii during the time just before Jerusalem's destruction."[14]

Once again, since there are these kinds of earthquakes mentioned by preterists that occur in the lifetime of every generation, it is only with great difficulty that one could cite this as a past fulfillment.

As we have been going through the early parts of the Olivet Discourse, we have found that there is little basis for many of the claims made by preterists. When taken together with the other signs of Matthew 24—earthquakes—as cited by the preterists, prove nothing. Morison notes the following:

> Scholars have busied themselves, and with wonderful success, in hunting up historical notices of the earthquakes that occurred before the destruction of Jerusalem, just as they have laboured to find out records of famines and wars.... But there is no special significance in such records, or in the occurrences recorded. The role of wars and famines and earthquakes is not yet finished.[15]

THE BEGINNING OF BIRTH PANGS

I have already dealt with this passage (vs. 8) in a previous chapter. Based upon the Old Testament use of birth pangs in Jeremiah 30:6–7, it appears that Jesus picks up on that theme in Matthew 24, as does Paul in 1 Thessalonians 5:3. Birth pangs were a clear expression in rabbinic Judaism for the tribulation. Thus, the time of birth pangs commences with the beginning of tribulation period and culminates with the second coming of Christ. Therefore, the events of Matthew 24:4–7 are described as events that will take place during the first part of the tribulation and do not signal the end, which is the second coming of Jesus (Matt. 24:27–31).

CONCLUSION

Two important characteristics of the first part of the tribulation will be the occurrence of famines and earthquakes, which will likely follow a time of global wars between nations and kingdoms. These cannot be references to past or present events. As Gaebelein notes:

> Fearful have been the famines, pestilences and earthquakes of the last twenty-five years. But these are insignificant in comparison with those to which our Lord refers here, the mighty events which tell all the earth that the day of wrath is rapidly approaching.[16]

John MacArthur echoes Gaebelein's sentiment writing, "The world has witnessed many earthquakes, famines, plagues, and even some heavenly signs, but those will be nothing compared to the calamities of the end times. They will occur **in various places** and apparently simultaneously."[17]

Even though there have been famines and earthquakes in the past, they are just a warm-up for what God will bring about during the future time of tribulation. When these miraculous events occur, there will be no doubt about the fulfillment of the details of Matthew 24. We are building toward that day when God will judge and remove evil so that He can establish His righteous rule for a thousand years.

ENDNOTES

1 William Hendricksen, *The Gospel of Matthew* (Grand Rapids: Baker Book House, 1973), 853.

2 William F. Arndt and F. W. Gingrich, *A Greek-English Lexicon of the New Testament* (Chicago: University of Chicago Press, 1957), 476.

3 Arno C. Gaebelein, *The Gospel of Matthew: An Exposition* (Neptune, NJ: Loizeaux Brothers, [1910] 1961), 483.

4 R. C. H. Lenski, *The Interpretation of St. Matthew's Gospel* (Minneapolis: Augsburg Publishing House, 1943), 931.

5 Leon Morris, *The Gospel According to Matthew* (Grand Rapids: Eerdmans, 1992),598.

6 Robert H. Gundry, *Matthew: A Commentary on His Handbook for a Mixed Church under Persecution*, second edition, (Grand Rapids: Eerdmans, 1994), 478.

7 Kenneth L. Gentry, Jr., *Perilous Times: A Study in Eschatological Evil* (Texarkana, AR: Covenant Media Press, 1999), 49.

8 Gary DeMar, *Last Days Madness: Obsession of the Modern Church* (Powder Springs, GA: American Vision, 1999), 79.

9 Craig A. Evans, *Word Biblical Commentary: Mark 8:27–16:20*, Vol. 34B (Dallas: Word Books, 2001), 308.

10 Heinrich August Wilhelm Meyer, *Critical and Exegetical Handbook to The Gospel of Matthew*, 2 vols. (Edinburgh: T. & T. Clark, 1879), vol. 2, 131.

11 Arndt and Gingrich. *Lexicon*, 753.

12 Gaebelein, *Matthew*, 483.

13 DeMar, *Last Days Madness*, 80.

14 Gentry, *Perilous Times*, 50.

15 James Morison, *A Practical Commentary on the Gospel According to St. Matthew* (London: Hodder and Stoughton, 1883), 459.

16 Gaebelein, *Matthew*, 483.

17 John MacArthur, *The New Testament Commentary: Matthew 24–28* (Chicago: Moody Press, 1989), 21.

9

A TIME OF PERSECUTION

"Then they will deliver you to tribulation, and will kill you, and you will be hated by all nations on account of My name."

—Matthew 24:9

After painting a global scenario of future tribulation, Jesus turns in verse 9 to the personal consequences that will take place during the seventieth-week of Daniel, known as the tribulation. In fact, Christ uses the word "tribulation" for the first time in His discourse. There are a number of issues that arise from this passage as it relates to the different interpretative approaches to our Lord's discourse.

JEWISH ORIENTATION

Verse 9 provides further explanation of the suffering and the tribulation that will be directed toward the Jewish remnant. "The temporal adverb *tote* links the persecution, killing and hatred with the famines, earthquakes and wars."[1] James R. Gray explains the significance of the word "then" and its impact upon the immediate passage as follows:

> Matthew uses the word *"then"* throughout the discourse (24:9,10,14,16,21,23,30,40). The Greek word is *toute*. Matthew uses this word 90 times in his gospel, more than the rest of the New

> Testament writers combined. The word is "a demonstrative adverb of time, denoting at that time."[2] The word then in verse 9 means simultaneously as the events that occur in verses 4–8. Matthew places this persecution with the beginning of sorrows. This presents a problem for those who believe that the church age separates Matthew 24:8 and 9. They look upon Matthew 24:4–8 as historical, and verse 9 as future. However, the word "*then*" makes it difficult to hold such a view. The word does not mean after the beginning of sorrows, but at the same time or simultaneously with the beginning of sorrows. Thus, verse 9, cannot be projected into the second half of the Tribulation. There is no sequence here, for this persecution will take place during or at the same time, as the beginning of sorrows. And as we have seen, the beginning of sorrows refers to the early tribulation period, and corresponds to the events of Revelation 6.[3]

Because the focus of the Olivet Discourse is Jerusalem-centered, most likely Jesus has in view Jewish persecution. However, there is no doubt that Christians of all types will receive similar harsh treatment during this time of tribulation. Robert Govett writes: "The persons addressed in this division, are, as I suppose, Jewish believers in Jesus: holding in spiritual things, the place which 'the twelve' of that day held."[4] This sentence regarding tribulation and hatred appears only in Matthew's account of the Olivet Discourse, perhaps because of his Jewish orientation.

The "they" must refer to those described in verse 10, which reads as follows: "And at that time many will fall away and will deliver up one another and hate one another." "They" are the traitors who betray their brethren and deliver them up to death. "They" will be judged for their actions at the "sheep and goat" judgment as recorded in Matthew 25:31–46.

Preterists believe that because the second person plural "you" is used here in verse 9, these events must have happened in the first century. Gary DeMar says, "notice how many times Jesus uses the plural *you* in Matthew 24 and in the parallel passages in Mark 13 and Luke 21."[5] Yet, the plural you, in this context, is a corperate expression, for the Jewish people as a whole, which includes multiple generations. James Morison explains, "When the Saviour says *you* He is not confining His attention *specifically* to Peter, James, John and the other apostles, as individuals. He is speaking to them *generically*, as representatives of the entire body of His disciples. If this fact be overlooked, nothing will be understood."[6] Morison's point can be well applied to the preterists' persepctive, who misjudge the timing of Christ's discourse, with the result that from their perspective "nothing will be understood."

Preterist, Gary DeMar states, "'Tacitus says that Nero, for the conflagration of Rome, persecuted the Christians,'...But between A.D. 30 and 70, the tribulation of the church experienced was a fulfillment of the specific prophecy outlined in Matthew 24:9."[7] However, such could not be the case as noted by H. A. W. Meyer who writes, "It is a mistake to suppose that we have here a reference to Nero's persecution (proceeding upon an erroneous interpretation of the well-known 'odio humani generis' in Tacit. *Ann.* xv. 44, see Orelli on the passage)."[8] M. F. Sadler also speaks against DeMar's notion when he writes, "Do not such words look to a far more world-wide hatred from without, and a far more generally diffused declension within the church, than was possible before the year 72?"[9] Further, William Hendriksen notes the following: "The very expression 'all nations' clearly shows that Jesus is not thinking solely of what happens during the life-time of the apostles."[10]

The Old Testament teaches that the tribulation will be a time of great persecution toward the Jewish people specifically (Jer. 30:7, 11, 23–24; Ezek. 20:33–44; 22:17–22; Dan. 7:25; 12:1–3; Hosea 5:15; Zeph. 1:7—2:3). The New Testament echoes this teaching as well (Matt. 10:17–22; 24:9, 15–24; Mark 13:9–20; Luke 21:12–19; Rev. 13:7a; 18:24). The entire chapter of Revelation 12 is devoted to depicting the future persecution of the Jewish remnant during the second half of the seven-year tribulation period by Satan himself and his partner in crime—the Antichrist known also as the beast.

TRIBULATION

The timing of this passage is the first half of the seven-year tribulation. Gray explains the timing of these events observing:

> Matthew writes in precise chronological language so that we may know the time of the events spoken of.... *First,* in the progression of terms used to show movement of thought. This progression is seen in the term tribulation. Notice that Matthew moves from "*tribulation*" (v. 9, KJV "to be afflicted"), to "*great tribulation*" (v. 21), to "*after the tribulation*" (v. 29). This progression of thought falls naturally into the periods of Daniels' Seventieth Week. Daniel saw the week as divided into two halves. The dividing factor is when the Antichrist breaks the covenant with Israel in the middle of the week. The terminology of the discourse suggests that Jesus was using Daniels' prophecy as a point of reference for this discourse. Both Daniel and Jesus divide the week with the same event: the abomination of desolation (v. 15). Matthew refers to the first half of the week referred to by the term "tribulation" (vv. 9–14), the last half of the week referred to by the term "great tribulation" (vv. 15–28); and then the events after the events after the week by the phrase "after the tribulation" (vv. 29–31).[11]

However, it is not only preterists who distort the passage and the timing presented by futurists such as Gray above.

Pre-wrath rapturist[12] Marvin Rosenthal declares, "Of the four times the Lord spoke of *tribulation* in a prophetic context, He was speaking of the Great Tribulation which begins in the middle of Daniel's seventieth week—precisely three and one-half years into it."[13] The four passages he mentions are Matthew 24:21, 29, and Mark 13:19, 24.[14] Rosenthal conveniently excludes Matthew 24:9. Certainly Matthew 24:9 is given in a prophetic context. Davies and Allison classify it as such.[15] It seems obvious that because Matthew 24:9 occurs in the first half of the tribulation, Rosenthal had to exclude verse 9 in order to make his statement fit the erroneous theory he advocates. Clearly the word "tribulation," in Matthew 24:9, appears in a context that references the first half of the tribulation.

MARTYRDOM

The persecution, which Matthew notes here, is a future one that will take place in the first half of the tribulation. The verb, "deliver" is the same one used of the betrayal of Jesus by Judas (Matt. 26:15) and supports the notion that this future deliverance unto death will be a similar betrayal of the Lord's people. John MacArthur says, "*Paradidômi* (**will deliver**) has the basic meaning of giving over and was often used in a technical sense for arrest by the police or military (see Matt. 4:12)."[16]

The martyrdom described in this passage, that occurs in the first half of the tribulation, is to be seen as a parallel passage to the fifth seal in Revelation 6:9–11. Revelation 6:9 says, "And when He broke the fifth seal, I saw underneath the altar the souls of those who had been slain because of the word of God, and because of the testimony which they had maintained." Arno Gaebelein explains the parallel as follows:

> And now under the fifth seal we do not behold another rider, but instead of it we hear the souls underneath the altar, that had been slain for the Word of God, and for the testimony which they gave, crying out with a loud voice, saying, How long? (Rev. vi:9–11.) Who are these? Not the saints of the church.... They are such of the remnant of the Jews who began to give their witness for the Word of God after the church had departed and they suffered martyrdom in consequence of their faithful testimony. It is exactly that of which our Lord speaks next in His discourse. "Then shall they deliver you up to tribulation and shall kill you; ye will be hated of all the nations for my names sake."[17]

This parallel continues to sustain the notion that verses 4–14 of Matthew 24 are parallel to the seal judgments of Revelation 6. Such a parallel supports my contention that verses 4–14 describe the first half of the tribulation, which is also known as the seventieth week of Daniel. Thus, wars, earthquakes, famines, and persecution of believers in our own day are not signs that relate to the end-times. These prophetically-significant events will take place during the first half of the coming tribulation.

The motive for the martyrdom of Christ's disciples during the tribulation will be "on account of My name." Just as we see in Revelation 12 that the dragon (Satan himself) will pour out his wrath on the Jewish remnant in the second half of the tribulation because of His hatred of God, so will these disciples of the Lord be killed "on account of My name." Because unbelievers will not be able to get at the Lord Himself, they will go after the Lord's disciples.

CONCLUSION

We see from an examination of Matthew 24:9 that more reasons are provided for the futurist understanding of the Olivet Discourse, as against the preterist perspective. We also see that our understanding of this verse provides further reasons to understand that the birth pangs of Matthew 24:4–14 refer to the first half of the seven-year tribulation. Further coordination between the events of Matthew 24:4–14 are seen in the parallel of verse 9 with the fifth seal judgment of Revelation 6:9–11.

ENDNOTES

1 Randolph O. Yeager, *The Renaissance New Testament,* 18 vols. (Bowling Green, KY: Renaissance Press, 1978), vol. 3., 281.

2 W. E. Vine, *Expository Dictionary of New Testament Words,* (Fleming H. Revell Co,: Old Tappan, NJ, n.d.), 123.

3 James R. Gray, *Prophecy on The Mount: A Dispensational Study of the Olivet Discourse* (Chandler, AZ: Berean Advocate Ministries, 1991), 54.

4 Robert Govett, *The Prophecy on Olivet* (Miami Springs, FL: Conley & Schoettle Publishing Co., [1881] 1985), 22.

5 Gary DeMar, *Last Days Madness: Obsession of the Modern Church* (Powder Springs, GA: American Vision, 1999), 58.

6 James Morison, *A Practical Commentary on the Gospel According to St. Matthew* (London: Hodder and Stoughton, 1883), 460.

7 DeMar, *Last Days Madness,* 83.

8 Heinrich August Wilhelm Meyer, *Critical and Exegetical Handbook to The Gospel of Matthew,* 2 vols. (Edinburgh: T. & T. Clark, 1879), vol. 2, 132.

9 M. F. Sadler, *The Gospel According to St. Matthew: with Notes Critical and Practical* (London: George Bell and Sons, 1898), 356.

10 William Hendricksen, *The Gospel of Matthew* (Grand Rapids: Baker Book House, 1973), 853.

11 Gray, *Prophecy on The Mount,* 53–54.

12 I hesitate to use the term "pre-wrath rapture" of Rosenthal's view, since the pre-trib position is certainly pre-wrath as well. Other rapture nomenclature refers to when the rapture will take place in relation to the seven-year tribulation. Thus, Rosenthal's view would more aptly be titled the three-quarters rapture view.

13 Marvin Rosenthal, *The Pre-Wrath Rapture of The Church* (Nashville: Thomas Nelson Publishers, 1990), 105.

14 Rosenthal, *Pre-Wrath Rapture,* pp. 104–05.

15 W. D. Davies and Dale C. Allison, Jr., *A Critical and Exegetical Commentary on The Gospel According to Saint Matthew,* 3 vols. (Edinburgh: T. & T. Clark, 1997), vol. 3, 341.

16 John MacArthur, *The New Testament Commentary: Matthew 24–28* (Chicago: Moody Press, 1989), 23.

17 Arno C. Gaebelein, *The Gospel of Matthew: An Exposition* (Neptune, NJ: Loizeaux Brothers, [1910] 1961), 483–84.

10

HATRED AND FALSE PROPHETS

"And at that time many will fall away and will deliver up one another and hate one another. And many false prophets will arise, and will mislead many. And because lawlessness is increased, most people's love will grow cold. But the one who endures to the end, he shall be saved."

—Matthew 24:10–13

Jesus is progressing through His description of the first half of the tribulation, building toward the middle of the seven-year period of verse 15. In this section our Lord describes the spiritual state of the Jews within the land of Israel (Matt. 24:10–13). From God's perspective their spirituality is not good.

THE HATRED OF JEWISH BELIEVERS

In verse 9 Jesus predicts that all the nations of the world will hate the Jewish believers living in Israel during the tribulation. Why? Because the nations hate Jesus, the Messiah! This section of Christ's discourse (verse 9–13) is parallel to Revelation 6:9–11 and the fifth seal judgment. Many who professed faith in Jesus as the Messiah in easier times, will deny Him and cooperate in exposing those who are true believers in Jesus. Such an understanding of this passage coordinates well with the sheep and goats judgment of Matthew 25:31–46. "Brothers" in Matthew 25 are the persecuted Jewish believers during the tribulation that are being spoken of here in Matthew 24. Only Gentile genuine believers will be willing to risk their lives in order to help the Jewish remnant. While this speaks of persecution of believers, especially Jewish believers during the first half of the tribulation, the entire seven-year tribulation will be a time of great persecution.

The external hatred from the world (verse 9) puts all who profess the name of Christ under pressure. This in turn produces internal hatred among the professing Christian community during the tribulation due to false professors of Christ. "And at that time" locates the events of verses 10–13 to be the time of tribulation mentioned in verse 9. It is clear that all these things will take place during the same time period. When the pressure comes, those who are not genuine believers will do three things at this time: 1) fall away, 2) deliver up one another, and 3) hate one another.

Fall Away

The verb "fall away" carries the idea of "to cause to sin," and in the passive use, as we have in this instance, it means to "let oneself be led into sin," thus "fall away" from the truth.[1] This word is the verbal form of the noun "stumbling block" that is used often in Matthew (5:29f; 6:3; 11:6; 13:21, 57; 15:12; 17:27; 18:6, 8f; 26:13,33), although that is not the nuance here. Thomas Figart says that this word "refers to a stick-trap used to catch animals. Such entrapped persons could hardly be classed as true believers; rather, they arte exactly like the seed which fell on stony ground in 13:21:... This leads to betrayal of one another, which is engendered by hatred."[2] Matthew 10:16–23 is a parallel passage, which also speaks of the persecution described in this passage in greater detail. All of these things occur during the tribulation.

Deliver Up One Another

Look at Matthew's wording in 10:21–22: "And brother will deliver up brother to death, and a father his child; and children will rise up against parents, and cause them to be put to death. And you will be hated by all on account of My name, but it is the one who has endured to the end who will be saved." This is exactly the same thing that is going on here in

Matthew 24. Because of the global reach of the Antichrist and his regime during the tribulation, the pressure will be so great that even fellow family members will turn against one another rather than face the consequences of not following the instructions of the global leader. "The greatest expression of apostasy was betraying others who intended to remain faithful,"[3] notes Craig Keener.

Hate One Another

The hatred by all the nations (verse 9) against believers, especially Jewish believers (the remnant) in this context, will create such external pressure that it will result in hatred within the believing community among themselves. That is, false professors will turn against and hate the true believers. "The repeated reciprocal 'one another,' thus refers to betrayal ('they will betray'; cf. v. 9) and hostility ('they will hate'; cf. v. 9) within the ranks of the followers of Jesus."[4] There will be virtually nowhere to turn for the remnant of Jewish believers. The only place where they will be able to turn for any kind of help will be Gentile believers. This explains the rationale of Matthew 25:31–46 and why there will be the judgment of the Gentiles at the second coming for how they treated the Jewish believers during the tribulation.

PAST OR FUTURE?

Although weaker on this verse than others, it is not surprising to find that preterists believe that verse 10 has already occurred in the past.[5] "The pagan Roman historian Tacitus speaks of Christians in the era of Nero as universally 'hated for their crimes,'"[6] declares Kenneth Gentry. He continues, "In verses 10 and 12 we discover a consequence of the persecution."[7] Yet, Tacitus describes what is happening in Rome, not Jerusalem, as does Matthew 24. How does this quote in any way relate to Matthew 24:10? In fact, Tacitus says in the same section that "there arose a feeling of compassion,"[8] for the persecuted Christians in Rome. This hardly fits the context of Matthew 24:10.

Further, it has been noted above that verse 9 is linked to verse 10. Verse 9 states, "Then they will deliver **you** to tribulation, and will kill **you**, and **you** will be hated by all nations on account of My name." Those whom Jesus calls "you" in verse 9, are referred to as the "many" and "one another" (2x) in verse 10. Because our Lord speaks of the same group of people (the saved remnant) in both verses, whatever happens to them in verse 10 must be the same people referenced by the plural "you" in verse 9. If, as preterists believe, verses 9 and 10 happened to the disciples to whom Jesus was specifically addressing in the passage, instead of a still future group of Jewish believers in Jerusalem, then those events did not happen in the first century. When did *many* of the apostles fall away?[9] When did *many* of the apostles betray one another? When did *many* of the apostles hate one another? They did not ever do so. Instead, they loved one another.

This verse, like all verses in Matthew 24:4–14, does not reference a past event. Instead, the verses look forward to a future time and a global event that will take place in literal Jerusalem.

MANY FALSE PROPHETS

In conjunction with the events of the preceding verses, "many false prophets will arise, and will mislead many." This did not occur in the first century, to the extent that fulfilled the language of this passage, as taught by preterists like Gentry and DeMar.[10] False prophets are not the same as false teachers, as some suppose. The use of the term "false prophets" reinforces our understanding of the Jewish orientation of this passage. Bruce Ware notes:

> Here [2 Pet. 2:1] false prophets are distinguished from pseudodidaskalos, "false teachers." The implication is clear: False prophets were Israel's trouble; false teachers are the church's problem. Jesus' use of pesudoprophetes, then, in the Olivet Discourse calls for a Jewish understanding of the term unless some contrary internal contextual evidence can be advanced to show that the word has taken on some different and rare meaning. Since there is no such evidence contextually, it is best to understand the word to refer to false prophets in

> Judaism. Again this "Jewish element" in the discourse remains Jewish and does not relate to the church.[11]

Arno Gaebelein echoes Ware's understanding of this passage when writes:

> The Jewish age has false prophets; the Christian age has *false teachers*. "But there were false prophets also among the people, as there shall be also among you false teachers, who shall bring in by the bye destructive heresies, etc." (2 Pet. ii:1). These false prophets who come in the end of the Jewish age will be possessed by evil spirits. Such was the case during the great apostasy of Israel under the reign of Ahab. The Lord permitted then a lying spirit to take possession of the false prophets as revealed by the prophet Micaiah (2 Chronicles xviii:18–22).[12]

The tribulation will be a time in which prophecy will be restored to Israel during the seventieth week of Daniel. Thus, Jesus provides instruction warning the nation of Israel to exercise discernment concerning this matter. Ware further explains:

> Whom then could Jesus be warning? Obviously the warning is to Israel through the Apostles (who represent their nation Israel—this nation that anxiously looks for her Messiah). Jesus warned Jews in the tribulation not to be deceived by false Christs no matter what signs and wonders they perform. *Israel* is in danger of following false Christs because she has not yet recognized the true Christ. Unquestionably this is another example of exclusively Jewish element in the context of the Olivet Discourse which proves, along with the other contextual items not handled by Gundry, that Jesus addressed the nation Israel and its future in accordance with the intent of His Apostles' questions.[13]

CONCLUSION

This passage lays out a future time of great persecution and hatred. Robert Gundy writes: "Throughout, we see a logical progression: persecution by outsiders causes many in the church to avoid persecution by betraying fellows disciples to the persecutors; and through failure to condemn this woeful loss of brotherly love, easygoing false prophets exacerbate the problem of treachery in the brotherhood."[14] The events described by our Lord will occur during the future tribulation period and this era will require great perseverance on the part of the Jewish remnant.

ENDNOTES

1 William F. Arndt and F. W. Gingrich, *A Greek-English Lexicon of the New Testament* (Chicago: University of Chicago Press, 1957), 760.

2 Thomas Figart, *The King of The Kingdom of Heaven: A Commentary of Matthew* (no publisher given, 1999), 438–39.

3 Craig S. Keener, *A Commentary on The Gospel of Matthew* (Grand Rapids: Eerdmans, 1999), 571.

4 Donald A. Hagner, *Word Biblical Commentary: Matthew 14–28,* Vol. 33B (Dallas: Word Books, 1995), 694–95.

5 See for example, Gary DeMar, *Last Days Madness: Obsession of the Modern Church,* (Power Springs, GA: American Vision, 1999), 82–85. Kenneth L. Gentry, Jr., *Perilous Times: A Study in Eschatological Evil* (Texarkana, AR: Covenant Media Press, 1999), 52–53. R. C. Sproul, *The Last Days According To Jesus* (Grand Rapids: Baker, 1998), 35.

6 Tacitus, *Annals* 15.44.

7 Gentry, *Perilous Times,* 52.

8 Tacitus, *Annals* 15.44.

9 This cannot be fulfilled through Judas, since he was a single individual and the text says "many." Also, Judas' defection was at least 40 years before the Romans destroyed Jerusalem in A.D. 70.

10 See Gentry, *Perilous Times,* 53–54 and *DeMar, Last Days Madness,* 84–85.

11 Bruce A. Ware, "Is the Church in View in Matthew 24–25?" *Bibliotheca Sacra* (April–June 1981; Vol. 138, No. 550), 169.

12 Arno C. Gaebelein, *The Gospel of Matthew: An Exposition* (Neptune, NJ: Loizeaux Brothers, [1910] 1961), 484.

13 Ware, "Is the Church in View?" 169.

14 Robert H. Gundry, *Matthew: A Commentary on His Handbook for a Mixed Church under Persecution,* 2nd ed. (Grand Rapids: Eerdmans, 1994), 479.

11

INCREASED LAWLESSNESS

"And because lawlessness is increased, most people's love will grow cold. But the one who endures to the end, he shall be saved."

—Matthew 24:12–13

In Matthew 24:9–14, Jesus is talking about the spiritual condition of people during the first half of the seven-year tribulation period. It is not a pretty sight. Because believers will be persecuted and put to death for their faith, extreme pressure will be on them, especially Jewish believers to fall away from serving Jesus the Messiah.

INCREASED LAWLESSNESS

The Greek word *anomia* is usually translated as "lawless" or "iniquity." It carries with it the idea of deliberately disobeying a specific standard. In the context of this passage—it is disobedience of God's standard. Often the word "lawless" is used in apposition to "righteousness" or "good deeds" (Matt. 23:28; Rom. 6:19; 2 Cor. 6:14; Titus 2:14; Heb. 1:9). Arno Gaebelein explains:

> "*Lawlessness shall prevail;*" that is, complete anarchy will hold sway. This too is clearly seen in the breaking of the sixth seal (Rev. vi:12–17). The earthquake, the darkened sun, the blood-red moon, the

> falling stars, the rolled up heavens and the removal of mountains and island are all great symbols of starling political events, which will take place in the first three and one-half years.... the reign of terror and anarchy, worse than that of the French revolution and the Russian revolution of today, all classes of men, the kings, the wealthy, the rich and the poor, the bondman and the free, will be seized with terror.... This is the sixth seal, and it is precisely what the Lord saith: "Lawlessness shall prevail!"[1]

This time of lawlessness is surely an unusual time in all human history. Leon Morris says that it is "a way of life that refuses to recognize any divine law, which is identical for Matthew with a way of life in which one's neighbor no longer has any legal claim."[2]

Our Lord has been expounding upon the qualitative nature of the spiritual condition of unbelievers that will characterize the tribulation period, especially the first half. This description of lawlessness strikes a parallel to Paul's description of the "man of lawless" in 2 Thessalonians 2:3. This passage (Matt. 24) is building toward the abomination of desolation (24:15), which will be committed by Antichrist in the middle of the tribulation. Paul, in 2 Thessalonians 2, combines the man of lawlessness with the abomination of desolation when he says, "the man of lawlessness is revealed, the son of destruction, who opposes and exalts himself above every so-called god or object of worship, so that he takes his seat in the temple of God, displaying himself as being God" (2 Thess. 2:3b–4). Robert Govett tells us: "It is this abounding of lawlessness which gives to Antichrist his power both against the Jew and the temple."[3]

What does the phrase "is increased" mean in this context? Commentators are in agreement that it means unusually rapid or exponential increase. Morris notes that "the thought is that in the days of which Jesus is speaking lawlessness will not simply increase a little: it will be multiplied."[4] James Morison observes that "all other passages where the verb (*pléthuno*) occurs, it is translated *multiply*."[5] This clearly fits the idea of future tribulation period when lawlessness will reach the highest levels in all of human history. We think it is bad today or in previous times; it will be even worse during this unique seven-year period of history.

LOVE WILL GROW COLD

The result of lawlessness increasing will be that "most people's love will grow cold." There is a cause-and-effect relationship in this passage. The phrase "most people" is literally "the many." Morris tells us that in this context, "'the many,' indicates the majority;...'most of you.'"[6] This is one of the reasons I think it is speaking of the unbelieving world, as opposed to believers. The rest of Scripture does not support the notion that most believers will be characterized by apostasy during the tribulation; instead, this is the state in which the world in general is characterized. "This seems more related to the general condition of the world," writes Ed Glasscock, "than to the followers of Jesus."[7]

What does Jesus mean when he says, "love will grow cold." The expression itself is clear: loss of love. The main significance is to see the cause/effect relationship between lawlessness and loss of love. Morris explains it well:

> But real love is impossible for the lawless person. By definition the lawless person is motivated by personal, selfish concerns, not by any regard for others or for the rules that govern our intercourse with one another. So with the upsurge of lawlessness there is a cooling off of love. The one necessarily involves the other.[8]

It is in just such an environment that will facilitate the man of lawlessness of 2 Thessalonians 2 to set up his image in God's rebuilt Temple in Jerusalem. And, it is to just such an act that Jesus's current discourse is moving (24:15).

END-TIME ENDURANCE

The exact meaning and implications of "the one who endures to the end, he shall be saved," is a hotly-debated passage. Some use this passage to teach a Christian doctrine known as the "perseverance of the saints." Others believe that it refers to a physical deliverance. I hold to the latter position, primarily because it is the only view that makes sense in this specific context.

The first issue that must be dealt with in this matter is the meaning of the term "saved." Because the word "saved" is used in the New Testament to refer to the time when one becomes a Christian (the moment of justification), many readers just plug that meaning into this passage. The leading Greek lexicon of our days says that the basic meaning of this word is "save, keep from harm, preserve, rescue."[9] This word can be used in relation to the doctrine of salvation (Matt. 1:21; Acts 16:31; 1 Cor. 1:18; Eph. 2:8–9; Phil. 1:19; Titus 3:5, etc.), or it can simply refer to physical deliverance or rescue (Matt. 8:25; 14:30; 27:49; Acts 27:31; Heb. 5:7; Jude 5, etc.). The exact nuance is determined by its context. "The problem begins with the superficial hermeneutic of giving 'saved' the same meaning in every context, which is not true of any word," declares Glasscock. "Words have no specific meaning apart from context. Here, 'saved' (*sozo*) means basically to 'deliver' or to 'rescue'—from what and in what manner is dependent upon the context."[10]

Many commentaries on this passage fail to consider the contextual factors before they start sermonizing on endurance in the Christian life. They make this into a passage that teaches the Christian doctrine of endurance, even though it is not supported by the specific factors in the text.[11] Truly, there is a Christian doctrine of endurance taught in the Epistles (Rom. 12:12; 1 Cor. 13:7; 2 Tim. 2:10, 12; Heb. 12:3, 7; James 1:12; 5:11; 1 Pet. 2:20). This doctrine teaches that one of the many character qualities that believer is to have is endurance. Why is this so? It is true because endurance under suffering produces character (Rom. 5:3–4). Yet, none of those references to the Christian doctrine of endurance speak of "enduring to the end." Instead, passages that speak of enduring to the end all occur within the same context—the tribulation (Matt. 10:22; 24:13; Mark 13:13; Luke 21:19; Rev. 13:10; 14:12). John Walvoord explains:

> The age in general, climaxing with the second coming of Christ, has the promise that those that endure to the end (Mt 24:13), that is, survive the tribulation and are still alive, will be saved, or delivered, by Christ at His second coming. This is not a reference to salvation from sin, but rather the deliverance of survivors at the end of the age as stated, for instance, in Romans 11:26, where the Deliverer will save the nation Israel from its persecutors.[12]

Specifically this section is referring to the Jewish remnant, who, if they endure to the end, will be physically rescued by Christ at His second advent and they will go into the millennial kingdom in their mortal bodies (Matt. 25:21, 34). William Kelly explains: "It is evident that the language is only applicable in its full force to Jews—believing ones, no doubt, but still Jews in the midst of a nation judicially chastised for their apostacy from God and rejection of their own Messiah.... Thus there is a certain, defined period of endurance—an end to come, as truly as there was a beginning of sorrows."[13]

PARALLEL PASSAGES

There are a number of parallel passages to Matthew 24:13 that support the understanding of this text as presented in the above paragraphs. First, Daniel 12:1 says, "Now at that time Michael, the great prince who stands guard over the sons of your people, will arise. And there will be a time of distress such as never occurred since there was a nation until that time; and at that time your people, everyone who is found written in the book, will be rescued." Michael tells Daniel that this will be the time of tribulation in which the elect Jews will be rescued, which is the Hebrew word for saved.

Second, Mark 13:13, a direct parallel passage to Matthew 24:13 and says, "And you will be hated by all on account of My name, but the one who endures to the end, he shall be saved." The first half of Mark 13:13 is a summary statement of Matthew 24:9–12, which is followed by the endurance statement in both passages. Luke 21:18–19, also parallel says, "Yet not a hair of your head will perish. By your endurance you will gain your lives." This is the clearest of all when it reads: "you will gain your lives." "Lives" is the normal word for physical life.

Third, Matthew 10:22, also within the context of the future tribulation says, "And you will be hated by all on account of My name, but it is the one who has endured to the end who will be saved." Once again we see an emphasis upon the physical deliverance of Jews during the tribulation after a time of persecution.

Finally, the two passages in Revelation (13:10 and 14:12) that speak of the "perseverance of the saints" also are references to physical deliverance.

Both references are clearly within a tribulational context and speak of physical deliverance when one endures to the end.

CONCLUSION

With Matthew 24:12–13 we have come to an end of a section in Christ's discourse. Speaking specifically to Jewish believers during the tribulation (the remnant), Jesus alerts them to the many dangers that will confront them during this unique period of history. Having told them of the great trials of this time, Christ promises that the ones who physically make it to the time of His second coming will be delivered into the millennial kingdom which will come at the end of the tribulation period.

ENDNOTES

1 Arno C. Gaebelein, *The Gospel of Matthew: An Exposition* (Neptune, NJ: Loizeaux Brothers, [1910] 1961), 484–85.

2 Leon Morris, *The Gospel According to Matthew* (Grand Rapids: Eerdmans, 1992), fn., 23, 600–01.

3 Robert Govett, *The Prophecy on Olivet* (Miami Springs, FL: Conley & Schoettle Publishing Co., [1881] 1985), 29.

4 Morris, *Matthew*, fn. 22, 600.

5 James Morison, *A Practical Commentary on the Gospel According to St. Matthew* (London: Hodder and Stoughton, 1883), 461.

6 Morris, *Matthew*, fn. 24, 601.

7 Ed Glasscock, *Moody Gospel Commentary: Matthew* (Chicago: Moody Press, 1997), 466.

8 Morris, *Matthew*, 601.

9 William F. Arndt and F. W. Gingrich, *A Greek-English Lexicon of the New Testament* (Chicago: University of Chicago Press, 1957), 805.

10 Glasscock, *Matthew*, 466.

11 An example of one who turns this passage into a sermon on Christian endurance is found in John MacArthur, *The New Testament Commentary: Matthew* 24–28 (Chicago: Moody Press, 1989), 28–29.

12 John F. Walvoord, *Matthew: Thy Kingdom Come* (Chicago: Moody Press, 1974), 184.

13 William Kelly, *Lectures on The Gospel of Matthew* (Sunbury, PA: Believers Bookshelf, 1971 [1868]), 484.

12

THE KINGDOM GOSPEL

"And this gospel of the kingdom shall be preached in the whole world for a witness to all the nations, and then the end shall come."

—Matthew 24:14

As our Lord's discourse approaches the mid-point of the seven-year tribulation, verse 14 raises a number of interpretive issues. What exactly is meant by "the gospel of the kingdom?" Is this proclamation still a future event? What does "a witness to all nations" mean? What is meant by "then the end shall come?"

THE GOSPEL OF THE KINGDOM

Simply put, some believe that "gospel of the kingdom" is the gospel or the message about forgiveness of sins through faith in Christ, as preached in the New Testament epistles. Others, like myself, believe that it is more of a technical term that describes the coming of Christ's kingdom, which we know as the millennium.

The Greek word "gospel" is a compound word made up of "good" and "message." "It meant originally the reward given to the messenger, but came to be used for the good news he brought."[1] The word by itself simply means "good news." Good news about what? Well, that depends upon what is being discussed. Here the phrase would mean good news about the kingdom.[2] Dr. J. Dwight Pentecost explains:

> During the time that the politico-religious system of the beast is in absolute control, the gospel of the kingdom will be preached throughout the whole world (Matt. 24:14). The gospel of the kingdom was preached by both Jesus and John (Matt. 3:2; 4:17). This was the announcement of the good news that the kingdom was near. This message had both a soteriological and an eschatological emphasis.... The gospel of the kingdom as preached in theTribulation will have two emphases. On the one hand it will announce the good news that Messiah's advent is near, at which time He will introduce the messianic age of blessing. On the other hand it will also offer men salvation by grace through faith based upon the blood of Christ.[3]

The preaching of the kingdom during this terrible time will be "good news" indeed.

The word "kingdom" is used 51 times in Matthew. It is a major theme in Matthew's Jewish-oriented gospel. Dr. Stanley Toussaint has done an exhaustive study of how "kingdom" is used in Matthew and has concluded as follows: "Every time the term *kingdom* is used theologically in Matthew it refers to the same thing, the kingdom yet to come on this earth inaugurated and governed by the Messiah."[4] Specifically, Dr. Toussaint has the following comments on Matthew 24:14:

> What is this "gospel of the kingdom?" It must be the same good news as was described in 3:2; 4:17, 23; and 9:35. Entrance into the coming kingdom was based on repentance; that was and is the gospel of the kingdom. In the context, however, it would also portray the nearness of the kingdom during the Tribulation period.[5]

FULFILLMENT TIMING

There are three basic views of when this passage will be fulfilled. They are past, present, and future. Preterists believe that the passage was fulfilled by A.D. 70. Historicists believe that this passage relates to the fulfillment of the Great Commission during our current church age. Futurists believe that it will be fulfilled during the seven-years of the tribulation.

Preterist

"Matthew 24:14 clearly shows that the gospel would be preached throughout the Roman Empire before Jesus returned in judgment upon Jerusalem,"[6] insists preterist Gary DeMar. He further claims:

> The word translated "world" in 24:14 is the Greek word *oikoumene*... It is best translated as "inhabited earth," "known world," or the "Roman Empire" (Acts 11:28; 17:6).... This translation helps us understand that Jesus was saying the gospel would be preached throughout the Roman Empire before He would return in judgment upon Jerusalem. In fact, this is exactly what happened, and that is what the Bible says happened.[7]

This passage has not been fulfilled in the past,[8] because the context of Matthew 24 is futuristic, as we have seen throughout the exposition of Matthew 24.

Historicist

The historicist understands Matthew 24:14 as fulfillment of the Great Commission during our present church age. A. Lukyn Williams says, "So in the present age we are not to expect more than that Christian missions shall reach the uttermost parts of the earth, and that all nations shall have the offer of salvation, before the final appearance of Christ. The success of these efforts at universal evangelization is a mournful problem."[9] This verse is often used at missions conferences as a motivation for becoming a missionary. But that is an incorrect usage. The Great Commission is sufficient, because this passage relates to evangelism during the tribulation, not for our current church age.

Futurist

I believe that this passage will be fulfilled in the future, not during the current church age, but during the tribulation. The context supports a future fulfillment, since Christ's discourse has not yet been fulfilled.

THE MEANING OF WORLD

Although it is true that "world" *oikoumenê* is used in the New Testament to refer to "the Roman Empire of the first century," its basic meaning is that of "the inhabited earth."[10] This compound word contains the prefix from *oikos* that means "house," thus the "inhabited" or "lived-in" part of the world. The inhabited world could refer to the Roman Empire if supported by the context (for example Luke 2:1) since Roman arrogance thought that nothing of significance existed outside of their realm. However, this word was earlier "used of the Greek cultural world."[11]

Because the core meaning of *oikoumenê* is "inhabited world," the scope of its meaning has multiple possibilities depending upon the referent. If the contextual referent is Roman, then it will mean the Roman Empire as in Luke 2:1. However, if its referent is global, then it must include the entire world as in Acts 17:31, which says, "He has fixed a day in which He will judge the world in righteousness." Surely this speaks of the entire globe since not a single individual will escape God's judgment. Clearly *oikoumenê* can be used globally, even though it may have a more restricted use. The deciding factor is the context. Thus, if Matthew 24:24 was fulfilled in A.D. 70 then it would have a localized meaning as noted by DeMar. However, if it will be fulfilled in the future, then it has the meaning of the entire inhabited world at some future date, which would clearly include much more than the old Roman Empire.

ANGELIC EVANGELISM

I believe that Revelation 14:6–7 is a parallel passage to Matthew 24:14. Both speak of global evangelization during the seven-year tribulation, leading up to the second coming of Christ to planet earth. John MacArthur writes:,

> Just before the bowl judgments are poured out and the final great holocaust begins, and just before the increasingly rapid birth pains issue in the kingdom, God will supernaturally present the gospel to every person on earth. He will send an angel with "an eternal gospel to preach to those who live on the earth, and to every nation and

> tribe and tongue and people," saying, "Fear God, and give Him glory, because the hour of His judgment has come; and worship Him who made the heaven and the earth and sea and springs of waters" (Rev. 14:6-7).[12]

Interestingly both passages are referring to the period around the middle of the tribulation. This will likely occur at that time because it is at the mid-point of the seven years that the beast will require the number—six hundred, sixty-six—on either the right hand or forehead of every human being in order to buy or sell (Rev. 13:16–18). Thus, it is important to know that the witness of the gospel is given to every individual in which they are given the opportunity to trust Christ before they take the number. In addition to that, the third angel announces to each individual in the world that there are consequences to taking the number of the beast. "If anyone worships the beast and his image, and receives a mark on his forehead or upon his hand, he also will drink of the wine of the wrath of God, which is mixed in full strength in the cup of His anger; and he will be tormented with fire and brimstone…forever and ever" (Rev. 14:9–11).

It appears that the tribulation period will be the greatest time of evangelization the world will ever see. There will be normal evangelism, like that which we have today. Then there will be the evangelism of the 144,000 Jewish witnesses (Rev. 7:3–10; 14:1–5), the two witnesses (Rev. 11:3–13), and the angelic evangelism already mentioned. David Cooper explains: "The purpose of preaching the gospel during the Great Tribulation is twofold: first, to give all honest-hearted truth-seekers an opportunity of accepting the Lord Jesus Christ and salvation through Him; secondly, to prepare for judgment those who will not receive a love of the truth in order that God might be just in bringing upon them the terrific plagues foretold in Revelation."[13]

THEN THE END SHALL COME

Earlier Jesus said, "for these things must take place, but that is not yet the end" (Matt. 24:6). Now He says, that after the successful preaching of the gospel of the kingdom to the entire planet, "then the end shall come." "In the background is the Old Testament motif of the nations' end-time conversion to Yahweh (cf. Isa. 2:2–4; 45:20–22; 49:6; 55:5; 56:6–8; Mic. 4:1–3). Here that conversion heralds the end."[14] The end spoken of here is not the end of the end. It means the end of the age of the tribulation through the second coming of Christ (Matt. 24:27–31). The final end will occur one thousand years later as the millennial kingdom of Christ comes to its end.

Because Matthew 24:14 is a future event, the gospel will be preached across the globe as described in Revelation 14:6–7. Both passages are set in contexts that tell us that this global evangelization will take place just before the middle of the seven-year tribulation. Craig Kenner says, "Jesus' claim in 24:14 does not imply that all peoples will be converted, but that the kingdom will not come in its fullness until all peoples have had the opportunity to embrace or reject the King who will be their judge (25:31–32)."[15] This passage was no more fulfilled during the early decades of Christianity than was the Great Commission. The prophecy of Matthew 24:14, like all of those in that context, awaits a future fulfilment, specifically during the future tribulation.

ENDNOTES

1 Leon Morris, *The Gospel According to Matthew* (Grand Rapids: Eerdmans, 1992), 88, fn. 67.

2 The exact phrase, "gospel of the kingdom," is only found in Matthew's Gospel in the entire New Testament (4:23; 9:35; 24:14).

3 J. Dwight Pentecost, *The Words and Works of Jesus Christ: A Study of the Life of Christ* (Grand Rapids: Zondervan, 1981), 400–01.

4 Stanley D. Toussaint, "The Kingdom and Matthew's Gospel," in Stanley D. Toussaint and Charles H. Dyer, *Essays in Honor of J. Dwight Pentecost* (Chicago: Moody Press, 1986), 19–20.

5 Toussaint, "The Kingdom and Matthew's Gospel," 33.

6 Gary DeMar, *Last Days Madness: Obsession of the Modern Church* (Powder Springs, GA: American Vision, 1999), 88.

7 Gary DeMar, *End Times Fiction: A Biblical Consideration of the Left Behind Theology* (Nashville: Thomas Nelson, 2001), 82–83.

8 I have dealt more extensively with this matter in Thomas Ice, "The Global Proclamation of the Gospel," *Pre-Trib Perspectives* (March 2002), 4–5, available at https://www.pre-trib.org/tom-s-perspectives/message/the-global-proclamation-of-the-gospel/read.

9 A. Lukyn Williams, "St. Matthew" in H. D. M. Spence and Joseph S. Exell, ed., *The Pulpit Commentary*, 23 vols, (Grand Rapids: Eerdmans, 1974), vol. 15, 434.

10 William F. Arndt and F. W. Gingrich, *A Greek English Lexicon of the New Testament* (Chicago: University of Chicago Press, 1957), 563.

11 Horst Balz and Gerhard Schneider, editors, *Exegetical Dictionary of the New Testament*, 3 vols. (Grand Rapids: Eerdmans, 1991), vol. 2, 503.

12 John MacArthur, *The New Testament Commentary: Matthew 24–28* (Chicago: Moody Press, 1989), p. 29.

13 David L. Cooper, *Future Events Revealed: According to Matthew 24 and 25* (Los Angeles: David L. Cooper Publishing, 1935), 63.

14 W. D. Davies and Dale C. Allison, Jr., *A Critical and Exegetical Commentary on The Gospel According to Saint Matthew*, 3 vols. (Edinburgh: T. & T. Clark, 1997), vol. 3, 344.

15 Craig S. Keener, *A Commentary on the Gospel of Matthew* (Grand Rapids: Eerdmans, 1999), 572.

13

THE ABOMINATION OF DESOLATION

"Therefore when you see the abomination of desolation which was spoken of through Daniel the prophet, standing in the holy place (let the reader understand),"

—Matthew 24:15

We have now reached the midpoint of the tribulation in the chronological progress of this passage. Christ mentions the key event upon which the entire passage turns when He speaks of the abomination of desolation. What is He speaking about here?

THE ABOMINATION OF DESOLATION

The key passages in Daniel that mention the term "abomination of desolation" are Daniel 9:27, 11:31 and 12:11. The phrase is a technical term having a precise and consistent meaning in all three passages. It refers to an act of abomination that renders something unclean. In this case, the Temple. Daniel 11:31 speaks of an act that was fulfilled in history before the first coming of Christ. Dr. John Walvoord explains:

> In Daniel 11:31, a prophecy was written by Daniel in the sixth century B. C. about a future Syrian ruler by name of Antiochus Epiphanes who reigned over Syria 175–164 B. C., about 400 years after Daniel.

> History, of course, has recorded the reign of this man. In verse 31, Daniel prophesied about his activity: "… they shall pollute the sanctuary of strength, and shall take away the daily sacrifice, and they shall place the abomination that maketh desolate." This would be very difficult to understand if it were not for the fact that it has already been fulfilled. Anyone can go back to the history of Antiochus Epiphanes and discover what he did as recorded in the apocryphal books of 1 and 2 Maccabees. He was a great persecutor of the children of Israel and did his best to stamp out the Jewish religion and wanted to place in its stead a worship of Greek pagan gods….
>
> One of the things he did was to stop animal sacrifices in the temple. He offered a sow, an unclean animal, on the altar in a deliberate attempt to desecrate and render it unholy for Jewish worship (cf. 1 Macc. 1:48). First Maccabees 1:54 specifically records that the abomination of desolation was set up, fulfilling Daniel 11:31. In the holy of holies Antiochus set up a statue of a Greek god…. In keeping with the prophecy the daily sacrifices were stopped, the sanctuary was polluted, desolated and made an abomination.[1]

Old Testament scholar Dr. Randall Price agrees: "In my own study of the phrase in the context of Temple desecration I discovered the phrase served as a technical reference to the introduction of an idolatrous image or an act of pagan sacrilege within the Sanctuary that produces the highest level a of ceremonial impurity, Temple profanation."[2]

This passage sets the pattern and provides details about what the abomination of desolation consists of. The Daniel 9:27 passage says that this abomination is to take place in the middle of a seven year period. The passage says, "in the middle of the week he will put a stop to sacrifice and grain offering; and on the wing of abominations will come one who makes desolate." "In other words, the future prince will do at that time exactly what Antiochus did in the second century B.C."[3] But Daniel goes on to say that the one who commits this act will be destroyed three and a half years later. Daniel 12:11 provides "the precise chronology."[4] The text says, "And from the time that the regular sacrifice is abolished, and the abomination of desolation is *set up*, there will be 1,290 days."

In addition to the three passages in Daniel, the two references by our Lord in Matthew and Luke, 2 Thessalonians 2:4 and Revelation 13:14–15 also have this event in view. Therefore, the abomination of desolation, which the reader is to understand, includes the following elements:

1. It occurs in the Jewish Temple in Jerusalem (Daniel 11:31; 2 Thessalonians 2:4).
2. It involves a person setting up a statue in place of the regular sacrifice in the holy of holies (Daniel 11:31; 12:11; Revelation 13:14–14).
3. This results in the cessation of the regular sacrifice (Daniel 9:27; 11:31; 12:11).
4. There will be a time of about three-and-a-half years between this event and another event and the end of the time period (Daniel 9:27; 12:11).
5. It involves an individual setting up a statue or image of himself so that he may be worshipped in place of God (Daniel 11:31; 2 Thessalonians 2:4; Revelation 13:14–15).
6. The image is made to come to life (Revelation 13:14).
7. A worship system of this false god is thus inaugurated (2 Thessalonians 2:4; Revelation 13:14–15).
8. At the end of this time period the individual who commits the act will himself be cut off (Daniel 9:27).

PRETERIST MISINTERPRETATION

Not surprisingly, perterists such as Dr. Kenneth Gentry believe that the famous "abomination of desolation" in Matthew 24:15 (cf. Mark 13:14) was fulfilled in the first-century destruction of Jerusalem.[5] Even though there are similarities between the past destruction of Jerusalem and a future siege, there are enough differences to distinguish the two events.

Despite this specific information about the abomination of desolation, Dr. Gentry identifies it as simply the Roman invasion and destruction of Jerusalem and the Temple in A.D. 70.[6] Rather than going to Daniel for an understanding of what our Lord wanted the reader to understand, Gentry goes to Luke 21:20–22, with a little help from Josephus, to conclude that Christ is warning of Jerusalem's devastation by military assault, not just the temple's desecration by profane acts".[7] Let's see if this interpretation measures up to the Biblical explanation concerning the abomination of desolation.

AN ANSWER TO PRETERISM

Luke 21:20–24 does refer to the A. D. 70 destruction of Jerusalem. Therefore, when verse 20 says, "when you see Jerusalem surrounded by armies, then recognize that her desolation is at hand," it is describing in clear language the destruction of Jerusalem. This is vindicated by the language of the rest of the passage, especially verse 24: "and they will fall by the edge of the sword, and will be led captive into all the nations; and Jerusalem will be trampled underfoot." In context, the desolation is the destruction of Jerusalem; it is not a technical term relating to the Temple, as Dr. Gentry suggests.

In contrast, the Matthew 24:15 passage has a context of its own which differs from the Luke account. Matthew records, "when you see the abomination of desolation which was spoken of through Daniel the prophet (not Luke), *standing in the holy place*." Comparison of the description in Matthew and Daniel with the passage in Luke yields differences, which prove that they are two separate events.

In the A.D. 70 destruction of Jerusalem there was...

- no image set up in the holy place.
- no worship of the image was required.
- no three-and-a-half year period of time between that event and the coming of Christ. This is especially true since the destruction

of Jerusalem occurred at the end of the siege by Rome. It was over in a matter of days. D. A. Carson notes, "By the time the Romans had actually desecrated the temple in A.D. 70, it was too late for anyone in the city to flee."[8]

- no image came to life and beckoned men to worship it.

First-century historian Flavius Josephus tells us that Titus did not want the Temple burned. However, the Roman solders were so upset with the Jews that they disobeyed his orders and burned the temple anyway. All Titus was able to do was to go in and tour the holy place shortly before it burned.[9] This does not comport with the biblical picture of the image to be set up on the altar in the middle of Daniel's seventieth week, resulting in cessation of the regular sacrifice and a rival worship system set up in its place for three-and-a-half years. Dr. Stanley Toussaint writes:

> Because Christ specifically related the prophecy of the abomination of desolation to Daniel's prophecy, it seems best to see some correspondence between the abomination of desolation committed by Antiochus Epiphanes and that predicted by Christ. If this is so it would entail not only defilement on the altar by sacrifices offered with impure hearts, but also an actual worship of another god using the Temple as a means for such a dastardly act. Those preterists who agree with this take it to be the worship of the Roman standards in the Temple precincts. However, if this interpretation is taken, Matthew 24:16–20 is difficult if not impossible to explain. By then it would be too late for the followers of the Lord Jesus to escape; the Romans had already taken the city by this time.
>
> If the abomination of desolation spoken of by Daniel 9:27 and 12:11 is foreshadowed by Antiochus Epiphanes (11:31), it would be best to say it is a desecration carried out by a person who sacrilegiously uses the Temple to promote the worship of a god other than Jehovah. This is what is anticipated in 2 Thessalonians 2.[10]

Another major dissimilarity between Gentry's preterism and Matthew 24 is that according to Matthew, "neither the city nor the temple are destroyed, and thus the two situations stand in sharp contrast."[11] The Luke 21:20–24 reference does record the "days of vengeance" which befell Jerusalem. Let us look at some other details related to the fact that the future fulfillment of Matthew 24 is one in which Christ delivers the Jews, rather than destroying them, as in A.D. 70.

First, as Luke shifts from the A.D. 70 destruction of Jerusalem in 21:20–24 to the second coming of Christ in 21:25–28, Jesus tells them in verse 28 to "straighten up and lift up your heads, because your redemption is drawing near." This is the language of deliverance from the threat of the nations, not destruction. This language of deliverance is reflected in Zechariah 12–14.[12] These three chapters include three important factors: 1) Jerusalem surrounded by the nations who are seeking to destroy it (12:2–9; 14:2–7); 2) the Lord will fight for Israel and Jerusalem and defeat the nations who have come up to lay siege against the city (14:1–8); 3) at this same time the Lord will also save Israel from her sins and she will be converted to Messiah—Jesus (12:9–14).

ENDNOTES

1 John F. Walvoord, "Christ's Olivet Discourse on the Time of the End: Signs of the End of the Age." *Bibliotheca Sacra* (Vol. 128, Num. 512, Oct–Dec, 1971), 318–19.

2 J. Randall Price, "Historical Problems with a First-Century Fulfillment of the Olivet Discourse," in Tim LaHaye and Thomas Ice, editors, *The End Times Controversy: The Second Coming Under Attack* (Eugene, OR: Harvest House, 2003), 387.

3 Walvoord., "Olivet Discourse," 319.

4 Walvoord., "Olivet Discourse," 319.

5 Kenneth L. Gentry, Jr., *Perilous Times: A Study in Eschatological Evil* (Texarkana, AR: Covenant Media Press, 1999), 22–26.

6 Gentry in Thomas Ice and Kenneth L. Gentry, Jr., *The Great Tribulation: Past or Future?* (Grand Rapids: Kregel, 1999), 47–48.

7 Gentry in Ice and Gentry, *Great Tribulation*, 47.

8 D. A. Carson, "Matthew," *The Expositor's Bible Commentary*, Vol. 8 (Grand Rapids: Zondervan Publishing House, 1984), 500.

9 See David Chilton, *Paradise Restored: An Eschatology of Dominion* (Tyler, TX: Reconstruction Press, 1985), 274–76.

10 Stanley D. Toussaint, "A Critique Of The Preterist View Of The Olivet Discourse," an unpublished paper presented to the Pre-Trib Study Group, Dallas, Texas, 1996, n.p.

11 Walvoord, "Olivet Discourse," 317.

12 For more on Zechariah 12–14 and the fact that it will be fulfilled in the future see Arnold G Fruchtenbaum, "The Little Apocalypse," in LaHaye and Ice, editors, *The End Times Controversy*, 251–81.

14

FLEEING TO SAFETY

> *"then let those who are in Judea flee to the mountains; let him who is on the housetop not go down to get the things out that are in his house; and let him who is in the field not turn back to get his cloak. But woe to those who are with child and to those who nurse babes in those days! But pray that your flight may not be in the winter, or on a Sabbath;"*
>
> —Matthew 24:16–20

Previously, we saw that verse 15 describes an event that fixes the chronological mid-point of the seven-year tribulation. Verses 16–20 describe the recommended response of the faithful who see the abomination of desolation in Jerusalem. As said in western movies, they are to get out of Dodge as fast as they can! They need to leave Jerusalem. Why? It is because the second-half of the tribulation will be a time of persecution and great tribulation for the Jewish remnant.

THE COMMAND TO FLEE

This passage says that the moment the Jewish Remnant (the elect in verses 22, 24 and 31) sees the watershed event of the abomination of desolation they are to flee to the Judean hills. Why are they to flee instantly? It is because with the instantaneous event of the beast (Antichrist) setting up the abomination of desolation in the rebuilt Jewish Temple, he goes from protecting Israel to persecuting her. Therefore, the sooner that the Remnant can get out of town, then the less likely it will be that Antichrist will be able to persecute the Jews. Another reason why they will be able to flee instantly is because they will be miraculously provided for and protected as they make their way to Petra for three and a half years of safekeeping.

Matthew 24:16–20 provides a set of instructions for the Remnant. Christ tells them where to go: the Judean mountains. Jesus says to flee instantly. Don't even take a few minutes to collect a few personal belongings such as your cloak in the field or a few items from your house for the journey. He warns that it will be difficult to navigate the mountainous terrain if pregnant or nursing a newborn. Jesus does not say that it will be impossible, but it will be difficult. The difficulty will be compounded if this event occurs in winter or on a Sabbath because of the added restrictions that these times pose. The winter in Israel is the rainy season which increases the hazards of travel in the Judean hills because the creeks and rivers provide an obstacle that is not there during other seasons. The Sabbath imposes a travel restriction that is not in force on the other six days of the week and that poses a real problem to the observant Jew. So why is the Jewish Remnant supposed to be aware of a special event which triggers their escape into the Judea wilderness, yet they are not told to make any preparations for that day?

MIRACULOUS PROVISION

While Matthew 24:16–20 focuses upon the divinely-suggested response to the abomination of desolation by the Jewish Remnant, other passages provide a more complete picture of this three-and-a-half year wilderness sojourn. The parallel passage of Revelation 12 provides further details of this mid-tribulational escape. Revelation 12:6 says, "And the woman [Israel] fled into the wilderness where she had a place prepared by God, so that there she might be nourished for one thousand two hundred and sixty days." The key word in this verse is "nourished." This explains why the Jewish Remnant is told to flee without consideration for any provisions, because God has prepared a place where Israel will be nourished and taken care of for three and a half years (the second-half of the tribulation).

Notice some of the Old Testament passages that describe God's provision for His people during this three and a half year period:

> The afflicted and needy are seeking water, but there is none, and their tongue is parched with thirst; I, the LORD, will answer them Myself, as the God of Israel I will not forsake them. I will open rivers on the bare heights, and springs in the midst of the valleys; I will make the wilderness a pool of water, and the dry land fountains of water. I will put the cedar in the wilderness, the acacia, and the myrtle, and the olive tree; I will place the juniper in the desert, together with the box tree and the cypress, that they may see and recognize, and consider and gain insight as well, that the hand of the LORD has done this, and the Holy One of Israel has created it.
>
> —Isaiah 41:17–20

> "I will surely assemble all of you, Jacob, I will surely gather the remnant of Israel. I will put them together like *sheep in the fold* [Hebrew word is *basrah*]; like a flock in the midst of its pasture they will be noisy with men."
>
> —Micah 2:12

The drama is further explained in Revelation 12:12–13, in which we read:

> For this reason, rejoice, O heavens and you who dwell in them. Woe to the earth and the sea, because the devil has come down to you, having great wrath, knowing that he has only a short time. And when the dragon saw that he was thrown down to the earth, he persecuted the woman who gave birth to the male child.

Satan's wrath is directed toward the Jewish Remnant at the middle of the tribulation. This requires Divine protection. There is a cause-and-effect relationship between the heavenly (the casting of Satan from heaven to earth) and earthly (the abomination of desolation) events. At the mid-point of the tribulation, Satan indwells the human Antichrist and commences his campaign of antisemitism against the Jews with all haste. Thus, the need for a hasty retreat by Israel as advocated by Jesus.

Next, Revelation 12:14 says, "And the two wings of the great eagle were given to the woman, in order that she might fly into the wilderness to her place, where she was nourished for a time and times and half a time, from the presence of the serpent." The "two wings of the great eagle," do not refer to the Israeli or American or any other air forces as some sensationalists have argued. Instead, it is a figure of speech denoting Divine assistance, like that which was given to Israel during the Exodus and for her forty-year wonderings. That very same language was used in Exodus 19:4 of God's miraculous provision for the nation: "You yourselves have seen what I did to the Egyptians, and how I bore you on eagles' wings, and brought you to Myself." Deuteronomy 32:10–12 speaks of a similar miraculous provision at the Exodus in relationship to eagles' wings.

Putting the pieces of the puzzle together, it appears that the Jewish Remnant can flee Jerusalem without concern for provisions, because God will nurture and care for them through miraculous means as He did for the Exodus generation. Very likely the Lord will provide food (perhaps manna), water, and clothing for His Remnant that will be on the run and in hiding so as to escape the persecution of the dragon during the final half of the tribulation.

PRETERIST OBJECTIONS

It should come as no surprise that preterists do not agree with this interpretation. Predictably, they believe Matthew 24:16–20 was fulfilled in the first century. Gary DeMar says, "Matthew 24:16–20 clearly presents first-century-Israel living conditions."[1] But such conditions present no problem at all for a future fulfillment. In fact, I have been to Jerusalem a number of times over the years. In the old city, many of the houses are very old and have retained many of the features of "first-century-Israel," including the fact that the top of one's roof is still part of modern living in Jerusalem. In fact, one of the best ways to navigate across the old city is to walk on the roofs. I have done it many times. DeMar needs a good tour of "modern" Jerusalem. The points he makes in his attempt to argue that this passage requires a first-century setting have no traction and does not at all render a modern fulfillment unlikely.

Dr. Kenneth Gentry speaks of "Christ's dire warning to flee without turning back (Matt. 24:16–18). Once Titus begins encircling the city, it will not take him long to seal it off from the outer world (Matt. 24:16–20)."[2] There are a number of problems with trying to make Dr. Gentry's position fit the A.D. 70 event. Dr. Randall Price provides the following objections to Dr. Gentry's misguided assertion:

> According to the fourth-century Church historian Eusebius, Christians fled to Pella in A.D. 61–62, many years before the beginning of the Jewish Revolt in A.D. 66, and many more years before the "abomination of desolation" (according to the preterist's interpretation) occurred with the Roman army surrounding Jerusalem or entering the Temple precincts in A.D. 70. To this problem should be added the fact that the Romans controlled the Judean countryside (to which Jerusalem belongs) as well as its immediate environs for some time prior to their siege of the city, which would have made it practically impossible for either Jerusalemites or those in fields outside the city, to make an escape. Neither Jesus could have meant that a flight should take place once the siege began, for any escaping at this time would have run into the hands of the enemy! Moreover, as many commentators have observed, the biblical command to "flee to the *mountains*" (Matt. 24:16; Mk. 13:14; cf. Lk. 21:21) hardly agrees with the geographical setting of Pella in the low-lying foothills of the Transjordan valley on the other side of the River Jordan. Since Jerusalem is called "the Holy Mountain" (Psa. 48:1; cf. 87:1–2), "Mount Zion" (Psa. 74:2; 78:68–69), and is situated and surrounded by "mountains" (Psa. 125:1–2; cf. 48:2) "fleeing to the mountains" could not be interpreted as descending to a lower elevation and it is far more reasonable that "the mountains" of Jesus' reference would be those that immediately surrounded the city (i.e., the Judean hills, cf. Ezek. 7:15–16), since Jesus' command was not to flee *from* Judea but *within* it.[3]

CONCLUSION

It is clear that the Jewish Remnant will be fleeing to the Judean wilderness where Old Testament passages teach (along with Revelation 12) that she will be miraculously protected for the latter half of the tribulation. The place of her protection is said in the Old Testament to be Bozrah. "'For I have sworn by Myself,' declares the LORD, 'that Bozrah will become an object of horror, a reproach, a ruin and a curse; and all its cities will become perpetual ruins. I have heard a message from the LORD, and an envoy is sent among the nations, saying, 'Gather yourselves together and come against her, and rise up for battle!'" (Jeremiah 49:13–14) Bozrah is a region in southwest Jordan, where the ancient fortress city of Petra is located. Isaiah 63:1–3 asks:

"Who is this who comes from Edom, with garments of glowing colors from Bozrah, this One who is majestic in His apparel, marching in the greatness of His strength? It is I who speak in righteousness, mighty to save. Why is Your apparel red, and Your garments like the one who treads in the wine press? I have trodden the wine trough alone, and from the peoples there was no man with Me. I also trod them in My anger, and trampled them in My wrath; and their lifeblood is sprinkled on My garments, and I stained all My raiment."

Bozrah (Petra) is the place where up to a couple of million Jews will have been hidden away since the middle of the tribulation when they fled from Judea. The Lord has nourished them for those three and a half years and now He defends this Jewish Remnant that by the time of the second coming has converted in mass to Jesus as their Messiah. Christ has blood on His garments from defending the Jews against the army of the Antichrist, who have gathered themselves to attack the Jews at Armageddon. Such a force arrayed against the Lord's people requires His personal intervention. This He does first at Petra.

ENDNOTES

1 Gary DeMar, *Last Days Madness: Obsession of the Modern Church* (Powder Springs, GA: American Vision, 1999), 111.

2 Kenneth L. Gentry, Jr., *Perilous Times: A Study in Eschatological Evil* (Texarkana, AR: Covenant Media Press, 1999), 61.

3 J. Randall Price, "Historical Problems with a First-Century Fulfillment of the Olivet Discourse," in Tim LaHaye and Thomas Ice, editors, *The End Times Controversy: The Second Coming Under Attack* (Eugene, OR: Harvest House, 2003), 394.

15

THE GREATEST TIME OF TRIBULATION

"For then there will be a great tribulation, such as has not occurred since the beginning of the world until now, nor ever shall."

—Matthew 24:21

In Matthew 24:21, our Lord's prophetic discourse continues dealing with mid-tribulational events. He says that the second three-and-a-half year period will not only be "tribulation," as noted of the first half (Matt. 24:9), but a time of "great tribulation." In fact, it will be the greatest time of tribulation since the beginning of creation (cf. Mark 13:19), or that will ever be on earth. The focus of this time of tribulation will revolve around the Jewish people and their land of Israel.

THE TRIBULATION

The verse starts with a reference back to the preceding section. Ed Glasscock explains: "Verse 21 offers an explanation (*gar*) for the illustrations of urgency just presented and uses the temporal adverb *tote* ("then") to connect the previous statements with the prediction of the worst tribulation ever."[1] This tells the Jewish remnant in Jerusalem and Judea why they need to immediately head for the hills when they learn that the abomination of desolation event (Matt. 24:15) has taken place. "Evidently, this will be the last possible moment for escape," notes James Gray, for, "if they do not escape, they will be caught in this great and terrible trouble. It will come so suddenly that they do not have time to get their things together to get out."[2]

Previously, we have seen that the word "tribulation" was used to refer to the first half of Daniel's seventieth week (Matt. 24:9). Dr. J. Dwight Pentecost provides an excellent statement of the usage of "tribulation" in the Bible:

> The term *tribulation* is used in several different ways in Scripture. It is used in a non-technical, non-eschatological sense in reference to any time of suffering or testing into which one goes. It is so used in Matthew 13:21; Mark 4:17; John 16:33; Romans 5:3; 12:12; 2 Corinthians 1:4; 2 Thessalonians 1:4; Revelation 1:9. It is used in its technical or eschatological sense in reference to the whole period of the seven years of tribulation, as in Revelation 2:22 or Matthew 24:29. It is also used in reference to the last half of this seven year period, as in Matthew 24:21.[3]

The tribulation period is not exclusively a New Testament doctrine. The tribulation period is a topic that has a rich Old Testament background and the events of this time are directed toward and involve the nation of Israel.

The Old Testament speaks of a time of tribulation that Israel is destined to endure (in the latter days); but when this period is past, it will result in national repentance and the nation in a right relationship with the Lord. Note some of the following key passages:

- "When you are in *distress* [i.e., tribulation] and all these things have come upon you, in the latter days, you will return to the LORD your God and listen to His voice." (Deut. 4:30)

- "Alas! for that day is great, there is none like it; and it is the time of Jacob's *distress* [i.e., tribulation], but he will be saved from it." (Jer. 30:7)

- "Now at that time Michael, the great prince who stands guard over the sons of your people, will arise. And there will be a time

> of *distress* [i.e., tribulation] such as never occurred since there was a nation until that time; and at that time your people, everyone who is found written in the book, will be rescued." (Dan. 12:1)

In addition to these specific tribulation passages noted above, there is the general theme that is dominant in the Old Testament of individuals and the nation crying out to the Lord when in a time of distress and tribulation. For example, this is a major theme in Psalm 107. Verse 6 reads, "Then they cried out to the LORD in their *trouble* [i.e., tribulation]; He delivered them out of their distresses." Note the following passages that have a similar pattern: Gen. 35:3; 1 Sam. 10:19; 26:24; 2 Sam. 4:9; 1 Ki. 1:29; 2 Chron. 15:4; Psa. 20:1; 25:22; 34:17; 46:1; 50:15; 81:7; 86:7; 107:6, 13, 19, 28; 116:3; 120:1; Isa. 33:2; Jer. 14:8; 16:19; Jonah 2:2; Nahum 1:7.

In fact, Paul writes about Israel's deliverance from tribulation in Romans 9–11. Romans 10:11–15 tells us that one day Israel will call upon the name of the Lord and be saved. This redemption will occur one day to national Israel, but it will come during the tribulation period—the great tribulation.

GREAT TRIBULATION

Matthew 24:21 speaks about the great tribulation. What is the great tribulation? The great tribulation is the last three-and-a-half year period of the tribulation, which will culminate in the second advent of Christ. Dr. John Walvoord writes:

> The great tribulation, accordingly, is a specific period of time beginning with the abomination of desolation and closing with the second coming of Christ, in the light of Daniel's prophecies and confirmed by reference to forty-two months. In Revelation 11:2 and 13:5 the great tribulation is a specific three-and-a-half-year period leading up to the second coming...
>
> That the period would be a time of unprecedented trouble is brought out clearly in Revelation 6–19.... Putting all these Scriptures together,

> it indicates that the great tribulation will mark the death of hundreds of millions of people in a comparatively short period of time.[4]

The New Testament uses the term "great tribulation" in three other places in addition to Matthew 24:21. While Acts 7:11 does not refer to the last half of a future seven-year period, the other two do:

- "Behold, I will cast her upon a bed of sickness, and those who commit adultery with her into *great tribulation,* unless they repent of her deeds." (Rev. 2:22)

- "And I said to him, 'My lord, you know.' And he said to me, 'These are the ones who come out of the *great tribulation,* and they have washed their robes and made them white in the blood of the Lamb.'" (Rev. 7:14)

The "great tribulation" is said by Jesus in Matthew to be the greatest since the world began, or ever will be for the Jewish people. Mark 13:19 is even clearer where our Lord says, "For those days will be a time of tribulation such as has not occurred since the beginning of the creation which God created, until now, and never shall." "Since the beginning of the creation" makes it very clear that this time period will be the greatest time of tribulation for the Jewish people in all history. John MacArthur writes:

> No time or event in the history of Israel fits the description of the holocaust Jesus is here speaking of. The horrifying time is further described in some detail in Revelation 6–16, where the seal, trumpet, and bowl judgments exhibit the escalating intensity of God's wrath upon sinful, rebellious mankind. Both the books of Revelation and of Daniel make clear that the Antichrist will tyrannize the world for "a time, times, and half a time" (Dan. 7:25; 12:7; Rev. 12:14), that is, a year, two years, and a half year, or three and one half years (Rev. 11:2; 13:5). Clearly, the events described by our Lord, by Daniel, and by John must refer to the same great holocaust at the end time, just before the millennial kingdom is established on earth.[5]

Christ is clearly using the language of Daniel 12:1, which says, "And there will be a time of *distress* [i.e., tribulation] such as never occurred since there was a nation until that time; and at that time your people shall be delivered, everyone found written in the book." Joel 2:2 also employs similar language when it says, "A day of darkness and gloom, a day of clouds and thick darkness. As the dawn is spread over the mountains, so there is a great and mighty people; there has never been anything like it, nor will there be again after it to the years of many generations."

It is significant that in both of these passages, the time of tribulation results in the redemption of the Jewish remnant. Just such a redemption is described in Matthew 24:29–31 where it says, "But immediately after the tribulation of those days... And He will send forth His angels with a great trumpet, and they will gather together His elect from the four winds, from one end of the sky to the other."

PURGING THE REBELS

As I have been saying, the purpose of the tribulation, especially the great tribulation, in relation to the nation of Israel is to prepare her for final redemption. This is taught in the passages cited above about her deliverance from tribulation. We also find in passages, like Ezekiel 20 and 22, the Lord providing an overview of Israel's entire history. Often the prophet recounts the nation's past history of disobedience and then predicts that there will come a time in the future when the nation will finally become obedient to the Lord. Usually this will come after the nation has gone through a time of great trial and tribulation as we see in Ezekiel 20:33–38. But the significant thing is that at the end of this process the nation is brought into "the bond of the covenant." Note the words in Ezekiel:

- "As I live," declares the Lord God, "surely with a mighty hand and with an outstretched arm and with wrath poured out, I shall be king over you. And I shall bring you out from the peoples and gather you from the lands where you are scattered, with a mighty hand and with an outstretched arm and with wrath poured out; and I shall bring you into the wilderness of the peoples, and there

> I shall enter into judgment with you face to face. As I entered into judgment with your fathers in the wilderness of the land of Egypt, so I will enter into judgment with you," declares the Lord God. "And I shall make you pass under the rod, and I shall bring you into the bond of the covenant; and I shall purge from you the rebels and those who transgress against Me; I shall bring them out of the land where they sojourn, but they will not enter the land of Israel. Thus you will know that I am the Lord." (Ezek. 20:33–38)

Zechariah 13–14 records a similar scenario as we have seen in many of the Old Testament passages noted above. This passage speaks of all the nations of the world sending armies to surround Jerusalem, yet through this time of tribulation Israel is converted and rescued through the personal return of Christ. The following passage from Zechariah 13 speaks of God purging out two-thirds of Israel, but saving the remaining third. Note:

- "And it will come about in all the land," declares the Lord, "that two parts in it will be cut off and perish; but the third will be left in it. And I will bring the third part through the fire, refine them as silver is refined, and test them as gold is tested. They will call on My name, and I will answer them; I will say, 'They are My people,' and they will say, 'the Lord is my God.'" (Zech. 13:8–9)

CONCLUSION

Matthew 24 is similar to these Old Testament passages in that Christ predicts the nation will pass through the time of great tribulation (verse 21), but when these events have transpired, Jesus will return and rescue the elect remnant (verses 29–31). Christ's prophetic sermon as recorded in Matthew follows the well-established pattern found in the Old Testament. Since Matthew 24 speaks of tribulation followed immediately by rescue (verse 29), then His prophecy has to be future to our time since the Jewish people have never gone through anything like that in past history.

ENDNOTES

1 Ed Glasscock, *Matthew: Moody Gospel Commentary* (Chicago: Moody Press, 1997), 470–71.

2 James R. Gray, *Prophecy on The Mount: A Dispensational Study of the Olivet Discourse* (Chandler, AZ: Berean Advocate Ministries, 1991), 78.

3 J. Dwight Pentecost, *Things To Come: A Study in Biblical Eschatology* (Grand Rapids: Zondervan, 1958), 170.

4 John F. Walvoord, *Matthew: Thy Kingdom Come* (Chicago: Moody Press, 1974), 188.

5 John MacArthur, Jr., *The MacArthur New Testament Commentary: Matthew 24–28* (Chicago: Moody Press, 1989), 44.

16

TRIBULATION AND CONTEXT

"... for then there will be a great tribulation, such as has not occurred since the beginning of the world until now, nor ever shall."

—Matthew 24:21

In the previous chapter I surveyed some of the biblical teaching on the great tribulation. It will not come as a surprise that many interpreters do not understand the tribulation to be a yet-future time. Historicists and preterists believe that much, if not all of the tribulation has already occurred. Therefore, if one denies the futurity of the tribulation then it produces a great distortion of biblical prophecy.

HISTORICISM

Historicism teaches that the events of the tribulation, as recorded in the book of Revelation, have been occurring throughout the entire 2,000 years of the current church age. Historicist, Steve Wohlberg, says, "Historicism is the belief that the prophecies of Daniel and Revelation find fulfillment *throughout the history of Christianity*."[1] They usually teach that the six seal, six trumpet and seven bowl judgments are cyclical of seven major judgments throughout the history of the church. Generally, they believe that we are awaiting the breaking of the seventh seal, which will complete the judgments of revelation (i.e., the tribulation), lead to the events of Armageddon, and then to the second coming. According to historicism, the time of the tribulation is equated with what has been thus far about 2,000 years of Christian history, with only Armageddon and the second coming still in the future.

The historicist scheme will not work if the prophetic events of the tribulation are taken literally. Historicists have to allegorize many details of biblical prophecy in order to make their system appear to explain Scripture. For example, they turn 1260 days (Rev. 11:3; 12:6) into 1260-years, the Antichrist is not a person but the papal system of Roman Catholicism and entities such as angels (the three angelic witnesses of Revelation 14) turn out to be humans what have lived in the past during the current church age. Historicists generally regard the belief that the tribulation and most Bible prophecy still awaits a future fulfillment as a Roman Catholic plot implemented by the Jesuits in the sixteenth century.[2] Historicism contends that we are in the tribulation now, even though most of it has already passed. Such a view is not supported by Christ's explanation of the great tribulation in Matthew 24.

PRETERISM

Modern preterists go even further than historicists and contend that the entire time of the tribulation is totally in the past and that it was entirely completed by A.D. 70. Preterist, Dr. Kenneth Gentry says, "I hold that the Tribulation occurs in our distant past in the first century;...I hold that the Tribulation closes out the Jewish-based, old covenant order, and establishes the new covenant (Christian) order as the conclusive redemptive-historical reality."[3] Again, "This statement of Christ is indisputably clear—and absolutely demanding of a first-century fulfillment of the events in the preceding verses, including the Great Tribulation (v. 21),"[4] declares Dr. Gentry. So how does Dr. Gentry take Matthew 24:21? He says, "This is prophetic hyperbole." He further explains: "Clearly, the unique-event language is common parlance in prophetic literature. We must not interpret it in a woodenly literal manner."[5]

What does he mean by "prophetic hyperbole"? Dr. Gentry cites Exodus 11:6, Ezekiel 5:9; 7:5–6, and Daniel 9:12[6] as examples of other passages using similar language. Further, Dr. Gentry argues that the flood of Noah was a worse judgment than described in Matthew 24 since it "destroys the entire world except one family."[7] I believe there are a number of errors in Dr. Gentry and preterist thinking at this point. First, they generalize many of the specifics of a given text that limit the scope of these absolute descriptions. These passages that preterists cite are all limited in scope, not simply the greatest disaster of any time, place, or thing. A few years ago I wrote Hebrew Christian scholar, Dr. Arnold Fruchtenbaum and presented these same arguments made by Dr. Gentry's fellow preterist Gary DeMar. Below is Dr. Fruchtenbaum's able response:

> As for Exodus 11:6, the focus here is specifically on one country, which is the nation of Egypt. Furthermore, the verse is not saying that what happened with the ten plagues was the worst judgment that Egypt will ever experience and, therefore, the correlation between 14 million and 55 million is irrelevant. The text is saying that there was not such a great cry in all the land of Egypt in the past, nor will there be such a great cry in the land of Egypt in the future. The emphasis is not on the judgment itself but on the Egyptian response to the judgment. The first-born son of every Egyptian family died, but the remainder of the family was spared, so every single family was affected. In the tribulation, there is no need to assume that every family will be affected and, furthermore, rather than merely one or two members of the family, whole families might be destroyed; and if whole families are destroyed, there will be no one to mourn for that particular family. Another point is the Bible says that one quarter of the world's population will be destroyed, but mentions the world population in general and does not apply that exactly twenty-five percent of the Egyptian population will be destroyed. In other words, whether we speak of twenty-five percent or seventy-five percent of the earth's population destroyed, most of it is among the nations outside of the Middle East and, therefore, will not effect Egypt to the same degree as it would affect, let's say North America or Europe. Therefore, there might be a lot less death in Egypt than there would be elsewhere, and it still might be less than those who died in the

tenth plague. In other words, Exodus 11:6 simply does not present such a great problem.

Finally, concerning Ezekiel 5:9–10,...There are two implications. The first implication is that what happened in A.D. 70 was far more severe than what happened in 586 B.C. That point is true. But the point of Ezekiel 5:9 is that God, in this case, is going to perform a judgment of the type that He has not done before and will not do again, and the type of judgment was that one third will die by plague and famine, one third will die by the sword, and one third will be scattered to the four winds. It did not happen that way in A.D. 70, and it will not happen that way in the tribulation. What Ezekiel is describing is something that happened uniquely in the Babylonian destruction of Jerusalem when the inhabitants were equally divided into thirds with two thirds dying in two different ways, and one third surviving but under divine judgment were scattered. No such three-fold division equally happened in A.D. 70. Even the tribulation where it does mention in Zechariah 13:8–9 that two thirds will die and one third will survive, it does not say that the two thirds will die in an equal two halves by sword and by famine. Furthermore, the remaining surviving third is not under divine judgment and remaining surviving third is not under divine judgment and scattered, but rather, they are saved and regathered. So, Ezekiel's words can be taken as literally true; what he said did happen to Jerusalem and was unique to the Babylonian destruction.

The second implication is his statement under point 4: "The flood was obviously a greater tribulation." This is true as far as tribulation in general. However, here we are dealing specifically with the Jewish people and Jerusalem. The focus of the flood was not on the Jewish people, since Jewish history had not begun as yet. Nor was the focus on Jerusalem since that city had not existed yet. The Noahic flood destroyed the world in general and was the worst flood that ever was or will be. But Ezekiel's prophecy focuses specifically on the Jewish people and Jerusalem which was not or will not be destroyed by flood.

> And while God will once again destroy the mass of humanity, according to Isaiah 24, it will no be by means of water but by means of fire.
>
> So, none of these "problems" that Gary DeMar is presenting are in any sense a great problem. They are all solvable if we remain with their own context and we move carefully through the actual words and to what they are referring.[8]

These issues are not a problem if one follows the context that governs the words of these passages. It is quite clear that if the plain meaning of the text is allowed to stand then a first century interpretation is precluded. Preterists must revert to sophistry in order to say why the text does not mean what it says so they can suggest a meaning in support of their view. Interestingly, they tend to only take this approach with given passages that do not appear to support their thesis, but take verses plainly that appear to support their views, even when figures of speech are embedded in the text. No, the great tribulation has not yet happened, but the world is now being prepared for this future time (2 Thess. 2:6–7).

THE BOOK OF DANIEL

In Matthew 24:21 Christ speaks of a yet future time that will be the worst time in the history of the world for the Jewish people. Nevertheless, He will deliver those who come to faith in Him as their Messiah from this terrible time (Matt. 24:31). These things must take place in order that God's plan for history to work out issues of good and evil. How do we know this? Matthew 24:21 is a quote by Jesus from Daniel 12:1.

The entire context of Daniel 12 provides further information about what Christ has said in Matthew 24:21. Daniel's response is not surprising to the revelation of the tribulation as we see in Daniel 12:8: "As for me, I heard but could not understand; so I said, 'My lord, what will be the outcome of these events?'" This is often a question that comes into our mind when we read of the events of the tribulation. God's answer through the angel is as follows: "And he said, 'Go your way, Daniel, for these words are concealed and sealed up until the end time. Many will be purged, purified and refined; but the wicked will act wickedly, and none of the wicked will understand, but those who have insight will understand.'" (Dan. 12:9–10)

God's purpose of the tribulation, especially the great tribulation (last three and a half years), is to purge those unbelieving Jews through the events of this time and to bring to faith the elect Jewish remnant. We know that the events described in both Matthew and Daniel have not yet in the past lead to the mass conversion of the Jews as these passages indicate. That the conversion of the Jews is yet to occur, no Christian would doubt. Since the tribulation precedes and gives rise to their conversion, there is no doubt that it too lies in a time future to our own day.

ENDNOTES

1 Steve Wohlberg, *The Antichrist Chronicles: What Prophecy Teachers Aren't Telling You!* (Fort Worth: Texas Media Center, 2001), 86. (Italics original)

2 See Steve Wohlberg's chapter called "The Evil Empire of Jesuit Futurism," in *The Left Behind Deception: Revealing Dangerous Errors About The Rapture And The Antichrist* (Coldwater, MI: Remnant Publications, 2001), 58–74.

3 Kenneth L. Gentry Jr. in Thomas Ice and Kenneth L. Gentry Jr., *The Great Tribulation: Past or Future?* (Grand Rapids: Kregel, 1999), 12. This is a book in which Dr. Gentry and I debate whether the tribulation is past or future. For a more extensive rebuttal of many aspects of the preterist position see Tim LaHaye and Thomas Ice, editors, *The End Times Controversy: The Second Coming Under Attack* (Eugene, OR: Harvest House, 2003).

4 Gentry, *Great Tribulation*, 26–27.

5 Gentry, *Great Tribulation*, 52.

6 Gentry, *Great Tribulation*, 55–56.

7 Gentry, *Great Tribulation*, 56.

8 Arnold Fruchtenbaum, personal letter to Thomas Ice, dated September 16, 1994, cited with permission.

17

DAYS CUT SHORT

"And unless those days had been cut short, no life would have been saved; but for the sake of the elect those days shall be cut short."

—Matthew 24:22

In our journey through the Olivet Discourse, the passage at hand has a number of interesting issues for our consideration. They include: the cutting short of days, no life being saved, and the question of who are the elect.

THE CUTTING SHORT OF DAYS

Partial or three-quarters rapture advocate, Marvin Rosenthal, says "The Lord is teaching that the Great Tribulation will be cut short."[1] He continues: "The shortening of the Great Tribulation to less than three and one-half years is one of the most important truths to be grasped if the chronology of end-time events is to be understood."[2] Does this text teach that the Lord will cut short the number of days prophesied elsewhere from 1260 days (Rev. 11:3; 12:6)? Will the Great Tribulation be less than 1260 days? Simply put, no! What does it teach?

First, only Mark (13:20) has a parallel passage to Matthew, while Luke does not. Luke's omission of this verse is perhaps due to the fact that his focus is upon A.D. 70,[3] thus this statement relating to the future tribulation would not be appropriate. Mark states specially that it is "the Lord" who had cut short those days. Otherwise, there is no significant difference in the two passages.

The Greek word for "cut short" has the core meaning "to cut off," or, when applied to time, "to cut short."[4] Dr. Randolph Yeager notes that the verb used both in Matthew and Mark means "'lopped off', 'mutilated.' To shorten. Always in the New Testament in a chronological sense—Mt. 24:22, 22 Mk. 13:20, 20."[5] It is significant to note that both verbs (in Matthew and Mark) "are all in the aorist tense and indicative mood with the augment," declares Dr. Renald Showers. "Aorist tense verbs have no time significance except when they are in the indicative mood with the augment. That form is used to express past time.[6]"[7] What does this mean?

Dr. Showers states that "a number of scholars have concluded that since the two verbs in Mark 13:20 are in that form, they are expressing action in the past and therefore have significant bearing on the meaning of Jesus' statement."[8] What is that bearing? It is that the "aorist tenses are prophetic pasts: God has already decided about the future,"[9] as one scholar explains. Another says, "The future tense interprets the preceding 'had been shortened' as having a future reference (like the Hebrew 'prophetic perfect')."[10] This means that the cutting short, spoken of by our Lord in both Matthew and Mark, is something that has already taken place in the past when God's plan for history was put forth before the creation of the world. "The aor. Tenses put this action in the past," concludes Ezra Gould. "The language is proleptic, stating the event as it already existed in the Divine decree."[11]

Marvin Rosenthal's conjecture that these passages support his mistaken view that the Great Tribulation will be cut short of its Divinely decreed 1260 days does not hold up under scrutiny of the biblical text. Dr. Showers explains as follows:

> Jesus was teaching that God in the past had already shortened the Great Tribulation. He did so in the sense that in the past He determined to cut it off at a specific time rather than let it continue indefinitely. In His omniscience, God knew that if the Great Tribulation were to continue indefinitely, all flesh would perish from the earth. To prevent that from happening, in the past God sovereignly set a specific time for the Great Tribulation to end.[12]

Said another way, God, in His omniscience, knew that if He let the Great Tribulation go 1320 days (an arbitrary number for the sake of illustration), then all flesh would be wiped out. Therefore, in eternity past when God was planning this time of history, He cut it short to 1260 days, so that the elect would in fact be saved.

NO LIFE WOULD HAVE BEEN SAVED

We have already seen previously that for Satan and the Antichrist their goal for these events is to destroy the Jewish people. Why does the Devil want to do that? He believes that if he can destroy the Jews, then He will be able to prevent the second coming, since Christ's return is a response to the converted Jewish remnant's request for physical deliverance. Satan believes that if he can prevent a key event in God's predestined plan for history from occurring then he will have defamed God and proven his slander that God is not worthy of His exalted position. He cannot succeed because God is faithful to fulfill His word.

So what does the phrase "no life would have been saved" (lit. "all flesh would not be saved") mean in light of Christ's prophetic sermon? There are two views that I think are worthy of consideration and they revolved around the meaning of the term "no life." Does it refer to the Jewish remnant, which is destined for salvation during this time, or does Christ have in mind all humanity? First, I agree with the general consensus among commentators that salvation in this context refers to physical deliverance and not salvation from one's sins (i.e., justification), because the danger in this context is physical, not spiritual.[13]

Before studying and writing this current commentary, I held the view that "no life," or "no flesh" was a reference to Israel. I have changed my mind and now think that this phrase refers to all humanity. Why have I changed? I have changed my mind primarily because of the lexical data (i.e., how a word or phrase is used in other instances). Dr. Stanley Toussaint explains:

> BAG[14] take *pasa sarx* to mean *every person, everyone*. With the negative they take it to mean *no person, nobody* and list Matthew 24:22 and Mark 13:20 as instances of this meaning. The expression *pasa*

> *sarx* comes from the Septuagint which in turn looks at the Hebraism *kol basar* "all flesh." Gesenius[15] says this Hebrew construction means "all living creatures…especially *all men*, the whole human race…" Therefore, to interpret "all flesh" in Matthew 24:22 and Mark 13:20 as referring to Jews living in Judea in A. D. 70 is too limiting. "All flesh" describes all humanity.[16]

Dr. Craig Evans concurs:

> reflects Semitic idiom (e.g., Gen 9:11: "never again shall all flesh be cut off by the waters of a flood", Isa 40:5: "all flesh shall see it together").… the warning that the period of tribulation will be so severe that unless shortened it will extinguish human life argues that the prophecy portends more than the Jewish war.… but the fate of the whole of humanity did not hang in the balance.[17]

It appears that Satan's effort to destroy the Jews would result in the total annihilation of all humanity, were not for Christ's intervention at the second advent. This fact provides us with further insight into the purposes of Christ's return.

WHO ARE THE ELECT?

The term "the elect" is uttered three times by Jesus in the Olivet Discourse (Matt. 14:22, 24, 31; also in Mark 13:20, 22, 27). I believe that all three uses must refer to the same entity in each instance. They clearly refer, in context, to some group of believers during the tribulation. Since the church has been raptured, it cannot refer to her. Thus, does "the elect" reference saved Jews and Gentiles, or only the Jewish remnant? I believe that this term refers to the Jewish remnant, primarily because of contextual factors.

While it is true that the term "the elect" is used in the New Testament Epistles of church age believers (i.e., both Jews and Gentiles) (see Rom. 8:33; Col. 3:12; 2 Tim. 2:10; Titus 1:1), it is also true that this term is used in a variety of other ways. Note multiple uses as follows: Rufus, a choice man (Rom. 16:13); elect angels (1 Tim. 5:21); of Jewish believers (1 Pet.

1:1; 2:9); Christ a choice building stone (1 Pet. 2:4, 6); a chosen lady (2 John 1); a chosen sister (2 John 13). In the Old Testament the term "elect" is used in the following references to Israel: Isaiah 42:1; 43:20; 45:4; 65:9; 65:15; 65:22; Psalm 89:3; 105:6, 43; 106:5; 1 Chronicles 16:13. The verbal form of "to choose" is used dozens of times in relation to Israel in the Old Testament (i.e., Deut. 7:6). Even though a majority of the biblical occurrences refer to Israel, usage must always be determined by how it is used in a specific context. "In this context, it is most likely used regarding the nation," concludes Dr. Ed Glasscock. "Daniel identifies this time as 'decreed for your people and your holy city,' indicating that Israel, not the church or mankind in general, will be the center of the Tribulation suffering."[18]

We have seen that the term "elect" has a fairly wide range of usage. "Out of every dispensation there will be some gathered of God's mere mercy and sovereignty. These are 'the elect' of that dispensation," explains Robert Govett. "Therefore the term has as many special meanings as there are dispensations."[19] But since the focus of this passage is upon Israel it is not a mystery that Christ has them in mind. William Kelly says, "the evidence unmistakably points to a converted body of Jews in the latter day, not standing in church light and privilege, but having Jewish hopes, and while awaiting the Messiah."[20] The term "the elect" is most likely used because Christ looks forward to those belonging to the Jewish remnant, though not yet saved, they are chosen to such a destiny—the elect.

ENDNOTES

1 Marvin Rosenthal, *The Pre-Wrath Rapture of the Church* (Nashville: Thomas Nelson Publishers, 1990), 108–09.

2 Rosenthal, *Pre-Wrath Rapture*, 111.

3 See Alan Hugh M'Neile, *The Gospel According to St. Matthew* (London: MacMillan, 1915), 350.

4 Walter Bauer, *A Greek-English Lexicon of the New Testament and Other Early Christian Literature*, a translation and adaptation by William F. Arndt & F. Wilbur Gingrich (Chicago: The University of Chicago Press, 1957), 442.

5 Randolph O. Yeager, *The Renaissance New Testament*, 18 Vols. (Bowling Green, Ken.: Renaissance Press, 1978), vol. 3, 301.

6 H. E. Dana and Julius R. Mantey, *A Manual Grammar of the Greek New Testament* (New York: The Macmillan Company, 1927), 193.

7 Renald Showers, *Maranatha: Our Lord, Come! A Definitive Study of the Rapture of the Church* (Bellmawr, NJ: The Friends of Israel Gospel Ministry, Inc., 1995), 51.

8 Showers, *Maranatha*, 51

9 W. D. Davies and Dale C. Allison, Jr., *A Critical and Exegetical Commentary on The Gospel According to Saint Matthew*, 3 vols. (Edinburgh: T. & T. Clark, 1997), vol. 3, 351.

10 Robert H. Gundry, *Matthew: A Commentary on His Handbook for a Mixed Church under Persecution*, second edition, (Grand Rapids: Eerdmans, 1994), 484.

11 Ezra P. Gould, *A Critical and Exegetical Commentary on The Gospel According to St. Mark*, (Edinburgh: T. & T. Clark, 1896), 247–48.

12 Showers, *Maranatha*, 51.

13 See Morna D. Hooker, *The Gospel According to Saint Mark* (Peabody, MA: Hendrickson Publishers, 1991), 316.

14 Walter Bauer, *A Greek-English Lexicon of the New Testament and Other Early Christian Literature*, a translation and adaptation by William F. Arndt & F. Wilbur Gingrich. Chicago: The University of Chicago Press, 1957.

15 William Gesenius, *A Hebrew and English Lexicon of the Old Testament, including the Biblical Chaldee*, 13th. Edition, Translated from Latin by Edward Robinson. Boston: Houghton, Mifflin and Company, 1882.

16 Stanley D. Toussaint, "A Critique Of The Preterist View Of The Olivet Discourse," unpublished paper presented at The Pre-Trib Study Group, Dec. 1995, n.p.

17 Craig A. Evans, *Mark 8:27–16:20* in Word Biblical Commentary, 34b (Nashville: Thomas Nelson, 2001), 322.

18 Ed Glasscock, *Moody Gospel Commentary: Matthew* (Chicago: Moody Press, 1997), 472.

19 Robert Govett, *The Prophecy on Olivet* (Miami Springs, FL: Conley & Schoettle Publishing Co., [1881] 1985), 54.

20 William Kelly, *Lectures on The Gospel of Matthew* (Sunbury, PA: Believers Bookshelf [1868] 1971), 492.

18

BEWARE OF FALSE CHRISTS AND FALSE PROPHETS

"Then if anyone says to you, 'behold, here is the Christ,' or 'there He is,' do not believe him. For false Christs and false prophets will arise and will show great signs and wonders, so as to mislead, if possible, even the elect, I have told you in advance."

—Matthew 24:23–25

In the midst of what Jesus says will be the greatest time of upheaval and chaos in the history of the world, Jesus reminds his disciples that even then, the most important thing in life is one's relationship with Christ. As this passage moves into the events of the second half of the tribulation, the number one priority is to avoid deception.

It is important to avoid deception during the latter half of the tribulation because this is the time in which Antichrist (also known as the beast in Revelation) begins his global rule and requires all to take the mark of the beast in order to by or sell (Rev. 13:17). This is such an important time in history that God sends angelic messengers to specifically preach the gospel to the entire world and warn them of the consequences of accepting the mark of the beast (Rev. 14:6–13). This is an important time because individuals alive at this time will determine their eternal destiny on the basis of their response to the gospel and Antichrist's appeal to take his mark.

Matthew 24 and Mark 13 are generally parallel to one another on this passage, while Luke 21 totally omits this text. Matthew and Mark speak of a future tribulation, while Luke's focus is primarily on events of the first century. What is Jesus saying?

He is speaking in verses 23–25 of two major points about false Messiahs. First, the false Messiah will not be visible and out in the open. Second, the false Messiah will do miracles in order to mislead and deceive many.

LOOKING FOR MESSIAH IN ALL THE WRONG PLACES

Verse 23 reports on hearsay about the impending appearance of the Messiah. Here, our Lord is setting up a contrast between the false and the true. The false program of Antichrist will be laden with rumor and innuendo, but the genuine coming of Messiah will be clear to all (see verse 27). Why does Jesus come back to a warning about deception in this passage after having already addressed the issue in verses 4, 5, and 11? I think that the answer is in the wording of His warning. Dr. Thomas Figart explains:

> Following the evacuation of Judea, the false messengers of Satan will find it necessary to attempt to infiltrate those who have fled to the mountains. First, they will claim that Christ has already appeared, saying *"Lo, here is Christ, or there"* (24:23). In order to bolster such claims, they *"shall show great signs (semeia) and wonders" (terata)*, two words that are used of Christ's miracles in Acts 2:22; so that their counterfeit ministry *"if possible"* might deceive the very elect. Obviously this will fail, yet the attempt will be made.[1]

Robert Mounce notes: "The central point in verses 23–28 is that believers are not to be deceived by false prophets who claim to have special information about the whereabouts of the Christ."[2]

Such an understanding fits into the flow of the passage. In verse 15 Jesus tells his disciples to head for the hills when they see the abomination of desolation take place in Jerusalem's rebuilt Temple. It is shortly after this that Antichrist requires the mark of the beast during the second half of the tribulation. As events unfold during the second half of the tribulation, the Antichrist (i.e., the beast in Revelation) attempts to entice the elect, Jewish remnant out of their wilderness hiding by saying that the Messiah is clandestinely in Jerusalem, thus, they should come and see Him. However, Jesus has warned his disciples in advance not listen to such propaganda.

This passage is parallel to Paul's writings in 2 Thessalonians 2 and John's words in Revelation 13. Both passages speak of Antichrist's deceptions. While Matthew 24:26 says that the elect will not be deceived, 2 Thessalonians 2:9–12 says that the non-elect will be deceived. "The one whose coming is in accord with the activity of Satan, with all power and signs and false wonders, and with all the deception of wickedness for those who perish, because they did not receive the love of the truth so as to be saved. And for this reason God will send upon them a deluding influence so that they might believe what is false, in order that they all may be judged who did not believe the truth, but took pleasure in wickedness" (2 Thess. 2:9–12). "Not alone will the apostate part of the Jewish people be deceived by theses lying wonders," explains Arno Gaebelein. "But also the apostate part of Christendom, left behind after the rapture of the church has taken place, will be deceived and swept away in the great judgments of that coming day."[3] Interestingly Jesus says concerning these false announcements: "Do not believe!" This demonstrates that a Believer should not just believe anything that comes down the pike, but it does matter what you believe.

FALSE CHRISTS AND FALSE PROPHETS

Just as there are true prophets who prepare the way for the true Messiah, so also, Satan will have false prophets to prepare the way for his false Messiah often known as the Antichrist. In fact, it is often said that the term "antichrist" only appears in 1 John (2:18; 4:3). This is true. However, the use of "false Christs" in verse 24 is similar to the language for antichrist in 1 John. Robert Govett says, "From the word 'false Christ' being equivalent to 'Antichrist' (1 John ii.18; iv.3), we see the meaning of the preposition *anti*. By 'Antichrist' is not meant 'one in opposition to Christ,' but *'a false Messiah resembling the true.'*"[4] This is expounded upon in Revelation 13, where the first part of the chapter (1–10) describes the first beast or the Antichrist, while the second part (11– 18) explains the role of the false prophet. Here we see the traditional marriage of religion being used to support the political. It is the false prophet who uses his religious office to advocate loyalty to the beast and to take his mark of allegiance on the right hand or forehead. This is why Jesus warns of false signs and wonders in Matthew 24.

The "false Christs" clearly is a reference to the Antichrist, who is also known as the beast (Dan. and Rev), the man of sin and the man of lawlessness (2 Thess. 2). The reference to "false prophets" would certainly include the false prophet of Revelation 13:11–18. Revelation 19:20 summarizes the career and destiny of the false prophet as follows: "And the beast was seized, and with him the false prophet who performed the signs in his presence, by which he deceived those who had received the mark of the beast and those who worshiped his image; these two were thrown alive into the lake of fire which burns with brimstone."

Preterists contend that these verses were fulfilled through events leading up to, and including, the destruction of Jerusalem and the Temple by the Romans in A.D. 70.[5] They can cite a few examples of false prophets, since there have been false prophets since the writing of the New Testament (2 Pet. 2:1). However, there is consensus that there were not false Messiahs or Christs until till around A.D. 130. In fact, preterists do not even attempt to cite examples of false Christs. Apparently there were none in the first century to reference. H. A. W. Meyer explains:

> We possess no *historical* record of any false Messiahs having appeared *previous to the destruction of Jerusalem* (Barcochba did not make his appearance till the time of Hadrian); for Simon Magus (Acts viii. 9), Theudas (Acts v. 36), the Egyptian (Acts xxi. 38), Menander, Dositheus, who have been referred to as cases in point (Theophylact, Euthymius Zigabenus, Grotius, Calovinus, Bengel), did not pretend to be the *Messiah*. Comp. Joseph *Antt*. Xx. 5. 1; 8. 6; *Bell*. Ii. 13. 5.[6]

Jesus is looking toward a time that has not yet taken place in history. He is looking forward to the time of the tribulation where the Jewish remnant will have fled to the hills at the site of the abomination of desolation. The false prophets and Messiahs attempt to draw them out of their hiding, but true believers (the elect) will not fall for it, because Jesus is warning them ahead of time about this tactic.

FALSE SIGNS AND WONDERS

Here we have the same words (great signs and wonders) that are used to describe the miracles of Christ and His apostles, however, these works are preformed by false prophets and false Messiahs. Does this mean that Satan is merely deceptive, in that, "he makes men think that they see a genuine miracle?"[7] Or, should this be understood as "happenings that cannot be understood on the basis of merely human powers?"[8] I prefer the second view; that these are genuine miracles. I favor that view because every time there are statements about these false miracles the language used is that they actually do these things, as we have in this passage "will show great signs and wonders." I don't know of an instance where the language of appearance is used to describe these miracles. In other words, if they were just tricking people into thinking that they were doing miracles with smoke and mirrors, it would seem to me that scripture would have used language that indicates this. Instead it uses words and phrases that say that they are actually doing these things.

For example, look at some of the satanic miracles performed by the false prophet in Revelation 13. "And he performs great signs, so that he even makes fire come down out of heaven to the earth in the presence of men" (verse 13). "And he deceives those who dwell on the earth because of the signs which it was given him to perform in the presence of the beast, telling those who dwell on the earth to make an image to the beast who had the wound of the sword and has come to life" (verse 14). "And there was given to him to give breath to the image of the beast, that the image of the beast might even speak and cause as many as do not worship the image of the beast to be killed" (verse 15). These are the words of actual events, not slight of hand.

It appears that God grants temporary power to these false prophets and Messiahs so that they will be used of God to attract all unbelievers to themselves in unbelief. This is what is meant in 2 Thessalonians 2:9–12 when it says, "the one whose coming is in accord with the activity of Satan, with all power and signs and false wonders, and with all the deception of wickedness for those who perish, because they did not receive the love of the truth so as to be saved" (verses 9–10). Paul tells us the reason is that "God will send upon them a deluding influence so that they might believe what is false, in order that they all may be judged who did not believe the truth, but took pleasure in wickedness." However, His elect will not be deceived, because Jesus has warned them in advance to watch out for these false miracles.

ENDNOTES

1 Thomas O. Figart, *The King of The Kingdom of Heaven: A Commentary of Matthew* (Lancaster, PA: Eden Press, 1999), 446.

2 Robert H. Mounce, *New International Biblical Commentary: Matthew* (Peabody, MA: Hendrickson Publishing, 1991), 225.

3 Arno C. Gaebelein, *The Gospel of Matthew: An Exposition* (Neptune, NJ: Loizeaux Brothers, 1961), 505.

4 Robert Govett, *The Prophecy on Olivet* (Miami Spring, FL: Conley & Schoettle Publishing, [1881] 1985), 56.

5 Gary DeMar, *Last Days Madness: Obsession of the Modern Church* (Powder Springs, GA: American Vision, 1999), pp. 122–23; and *End Times Fiction: A Biblical Consideration of the Left Behind Theology* (Nashville: Nelson, 2001), 89–91.

6 Heinrich August Wilhelm Meyer, *Critical and Exegetical Handbook to The Gospel of Matthew*, 2 vols. (Edinburgh: T. & T. Clark, 1879), vol. 2, 128.

7 R. C. H. Lenski, *The Interpretation of St. Matthew's Gospel* (Minneapolis: Augsburg Publishing House, 1943), 944.

8 Leon Morris, *The Gospel According to Matthew* (Grand Rapids: Eerdmans, 1992), 607.

19

A PUBLIC APPEARING

"If therefore they say to you, 'Behold, He is in the wilderness,' do not go forth, or, 'Behold, He is in the inner rooms,' do not believe them. For just as the lightning comes from the east, and flashes even to the west, so shall the coming of the Son of Man be."

—Matthew 24:26–27

Previously, Jesus has been warning the Jewish remnant during the second half of the seven-year tribulation to watch out for spiritual deception. Jesus referenced "the elect" (verse 24) for the second of three times in which that term is used in this passage—a term that refers to the Jewish remnant who will come to Christ during the tribulation. Jesus continues His instruction and warnings to "the elect" in verses 26–28.

WATCH WHERE YOU LOOK

This passage (verses 26–28) from Christ's Olivet Discourse is largely found only in Matthew's account. Jesus is continuing His warning to the elect about how to not be misled. In essence, He is saying that if someone comes to you during the tribulation and says that the Messiah is hidden away somewhere, then do not believe anyone's account of this. Why? The reason for scepticism is because when the Messiah does return it will be of such a public nature that there will not be any doubt that He has arrived. It will be the false Christs and false prophets who will attempt clandestine, backroom appearances for the purpose of deceiving people. Nevertheless, if the passage says anything, it shouts that the return to which Jesus speaks will be a bodily, physical, and public advent.

It is interesting that the preterist view of how Christ comes in this passage is closer to the kind to which Jesus warns the elect to beware. If you want to see an example of obfuscation and sophistry at work, note two examples First, preterist Dr. Kenneth Gentry says the following about this passage:

> Quite emphatically the Lord warns his disciples he will not come in a visible, bodily manner in those days. He twice states that any report of his physical presence would be erroneous:...Clearly these statements discourage their expecting any visible return in that day; he expressly declares that any command to look for Him in some limited particular location would be a mistake.
>
> Yet there will be a "coming" of Christ in that day:...This, however, is a spiritual judgment-coming, rather than a bodily coming.[1]

Second, fellow preterist Gary DeMar also adopts an anti-bodily coming view of Jesus' predicted coming in this passage when he says the following:

> Jesus would come "just as the lightning comes from the east," that is, quickly and without warning.... What the people saw was the manifestation of the Lord's coming even though they did not actually see Him.... Was God physically present? He was not. Did He come? Most certainly!...
>
> Matthew 24:27 reveals that Jesus is somehow participating in Jerusalem's destruction. This is exactly the point....
>
> Jesus came "like lightning" to set Jerusalem "aflame all around." If you recall, it was Titus, as God's representative agent, who set the temple on fire and leveled the edifice....

> In A.D. 70 Rome was sent by God to fulfill a similar task. "Our Lord forewarns His disciples that His coming to that judgment-scene would be conspicuous and sudden as the lightning-flash which reveals itself and seems to be everywhere at the same moment."[2]

The statements of these two preterists are examples of the kind of propaganda that Jesus is warning the elect to avoid during the tribulation. Matthew 24:27–31 clearly is a reference to a still future second advent. We next look at reasons why verse 27 does indeed reference Christ second coming.

A FUTURE EVENT

Both Gentry and DeMar interpret this passage as if it were not teaching a bodily, physical return of Christ. This preterist view is one that few interpreters have taken on this passage down through church history. That Jesus speaks here of his bodily return is supported by the context. In contrast to Christ's coming in verse 27 are the false Christs and false prophets of verses 23–24, who are clearly individuals that can be physically seen. Christ's return is juxtaposed to them. Christ will not return and hide out in some back room in which an undercover agent will lead people to meet the Messiah. No, Christ's return will be public and obvious to all. This cannot fit some "judgment-coming" through the Roman army. Regardless of what other biblical passages may teach in other contexts, the context of Matthew 24 only supports a bodily coming by Jesus, which has to be the future second coming.

Jesus specifically compares His coming in verse 27 to a lightning strike. I agree with DeMar that included in Christ's imagery is the idea of suddeness. However, because the force of the context (verse 26) is whether He will appear privately (i.e. "inner rooms") or publicly (i.e. like a "lightning" flash) it clearly argues for an emphasis upon appearance. Further, the Greek word for "flashes" has the core meaning of "to appear, to make visible, or to reveal."[3] Thus, when speaking of lightening that appears, it would be translated idiomatically as "flashes." When referring to people it is always rendered "appear." This is how it is used in verse 30: "then the sign of the

Son of Man will appear." In fact, "Wycliffe renders it appeareth"[4] in verse 27. When this detail is combined with the fact that in both verse 27 and 30 the one appearing is called "the Son of Man," which always emphasizes the human aspect of Christ, the clear conclusion is that Jesus is communicating His bodily return. Even preterists agree that He did not return bodily in A.D. 70. If the text intended to speak of an invisible return through the Roman army then Christ's Deity would have been emphasized, not His humanity. Meyer says the following:

> The advent of the Messiah will not be of such a nature that you will require to be directed to look here or look there in order to see him; but it will be as the lightning, which as soon as it appears, suddenly announces its presence *everywhere*;...what is meant is, that when it takes place, it will all of a sudden openly display itself in a glorious fashion *over the whole world*. Ebrard (comp. Schott) is wrong in supposing that the point of comparison lies only in the circumstance that the event comes *suddenly and without any premonition*. For certainly this would not tend to show, as Jesus means to do, that the assertion: he is in the wilderness, etc. is an *unwarrantable* pretence.[5]

In all his effort to say why "the coming of the Son of Man" in Matthew 24:27 was not a literal coming of Christ, Gentry fails to tell his readers that the Greek word *parousia* is used in this verse. Three of the four times that *parousia* is used in Matthew 24, Gentry admits that it refers to the yet future second coming.[6] The Greek lexicon, *BAG* says that *parousia* means "presence;" "coming, advent," and "of Christ, and nearly always of his Messianic Advent in glory to judge the world at the end of this age."[7] *BAG* cites all four uses of *parousia* in Matthew 24 as a reference to Christ second advent. In fact, *BAG* does not even recognize Gentry or DeMar's stated meaning as a possible category. It appears that the preterist mother is the necessity of invention in this instance. The mother of all Greek word study tools, Kittel's dictionary, in concert with *BAG*, tells us that the core idea of the word means "to be present," "denotes esp. active presence," "appearing."[8] Kittel's describes *parousia* as a technical term "for the 'coming' of Christ in Messianic glory."[9] Thus, *parousia* carries the idea of a "presence coming," contra the preterist notion of a "non-presence coming," an invisible coming. Our Lord's use of *parousia* demands His physical, bodily presence.

Toussaint provides further reasoning for the futurist understanding of *parousia* in this passage:

> ..."What will be the sign of your coming?" (Matt. 24:3). What does "coming" (*parousia*) mean? That term is filled with significance. This noun occurs four times in the Olivet discourse (the only times Matthew uses *parousia* and the only occurrence in the Gospels). The first occurrence is in the question asked by the disciples. Very interestingly, the remaining three are in identical clauses, "thus, shall be the coming of the Son of Man"...(Matthew 24:27, 37, 39).
>
> ...The problem with this interpretation is the meaning of parousia before verse 36 and after. If the coming of the Son of Man in Matthew 24:37, 39 is the Second Advent, one would expect *the identical clause* in 24:27 to refer to the same event. The word would also have the same meaning in 24:3. It must be the Second Advent in each case.
>
> Furthermore, the word *parousia* as found in the New Testament is always used of an actual presence. It may be employed of the presence of persons as in 1 Corinthians 16:17; 2 Corinthians 7:6–7; 10:10; Philippians 1:26; 2:12 and 2 Thessalonians 2:9. In each of these above cases the person is *bodily* present. In all the other cases *parousia* is used of the Lord's presence at His second coming, cf. 1 Corinthians 15:23; 1 Thessalonians 2:19; 3:13; 4:15; 5:23; 2 Thessalonians 2:1, 8; James 5:7, 9; 2 Peter 1:16; 3:4, 12; 1 John 2:28. The only occurrences in the Gospel of *parousia* are in Matthew 24. It would seem that they, too, refer to a yet future coming of Christ.[10]

Gentry believes that the "lightning" description in Matthew 24:27 "reflects the Roman armies marching toward Jerusalem from an easterly direction."[11] It is hard to imagine that the time-consuming march of the Roman armies is the true interpretation of this passage. Once again, I follow Toussaint's explanation of the text. He states:

What then is Matthew 24:27 saying? It is simply saying people should not be misled by false teachers or counterfeit messiahs who make their deceptive claims in some wilderness or inner sanctum (24:26). They may even fortify their pretensions by fantastic miracles (24:24). The reason the Lord's followers should not be drawn aside is because the coming of the Lord Jesus will be so spectacular no one will miss seeing it. It will be like a bolt of lightning that streaks from one horizon to the other. This is why the Lord used the correlatives *hosper... . houtos*; He is simply using an analogy or comparison. His Second Advent will be as obvious as a brilliant sky-spanning bolt of lightning. So will be the unmistakable and actual presence of the Lord Jesus Christ in His second coming to earth.[12]

ENDNOTES

1 Kenneth L. Gentry, Jr., *Perilous Times: A Study in Eschatological Evil* (Texarkana, AR: Covenant Media Press, 1999), 71.

2 Gary DeMar, *Last Days Madness: Obsession of the Modern Church* (Powder Springs, GA: American Vision, 1999), 123–25.

3 William F. Arndt and F. W. Gingrich, *A Greek-English Lexicon of the New Testament* (Chicago: University of Chicago Press, 1957), 859.

4 James Morison, *A Practical Commentary on the Gospel According to St. Matthew* (London: Hodder and Stoughton, 1883), p. 475.

5 Heinrich August Wilhelm Meyer, *Critical and Exegetical Handbook to The Gospel of Matthew*, 2 vols. (Edinburgh: T. & T. Clark, 1879), vol. 2, 143.

6 Gentry in Thomas Ice and Kenneth L. Gentry, Jr., *The Great Tribulation: Past or Future* (Grand Rapids: Kregel, 1999), 53.

7 Arndt and Gingrich, *Greek-English Lexicon*, 635.

8 Gerhard Kittel and Gerhard Friedrich, eds., *Theological Dictionary of The New Testament*, X vols., (Grand Rapids: Eerdmans, 1967), vol. V, 859.

9 Kittel and Friedrich, *Theological Dictionary*, vol. V, 865.

10 Stanley D. Toussaint, "A Critique Of The Preterist View Of The Olivet Discourse," an unpublished paper presented to the Pre-Trib Study Group, Dallas, Texas, 1996, n.p.

11 Gentry in Ice and Gentry, *Great Tribulation*, 54.

12 Toussaint, "Critique," n.p.

20

A PROVERB OF WARNING

"Wherever the corpse is, there the vultures will gather. But immediately after the tribulation of those days the sun will be darkened, and the moon will not give its light, and the stars will fall from the sky, and the powers of the heavens will be shaken."

—Matthew 24:28–29

After speaking of the suddeness and public visibility of His return in verses 26–27, our Lord now adds a proverb in verse 28. He says, "Wherever the corpse is, there the vultures will gather." The phrase is also found in a similar context in Luke 17:37. What does this mean and to whom does it refer? However, before that question is answered, I want to make a final point concerning verse 27.

GLOBAL, NOT LOCAL

We have seen in verse 27, which says, "For just as the lightning comes from the east, and flashes even to the west, so shall the coming of the Son of Man be," that it emphasizes a global coming. This verse is set in contrast to the false teachers of verse 26 who say that the Messiah has appeared locally; in a back room somewhere. Preterists such as Gary DeMar and Kenneth Gentry believe that Jesus came locally, through the Roman army in A.D. 70.

Such a view contradicts verse 27 which teaches that the Messiah's return will be global in nature. Randolph Yeager says of verse 27:

> Thus we have Jesus' reason for telling us not to believe the false teachers who will seek to localize Messiah's coming. It will be universally observed. No one will find it necessary to go anywhere in order to see Him, any more than it is necessary to move to a better vantage point in order to see the flash of lightning is conspicuous—something impossible to overlook. Satan, the shinning one fell from heave, with the speed of the lightning—(Lk. 10:18). Christ will come to earth with the universality of the lightning.[1]

We see that the teaching of this passage means that second coming of Christ will be something that no human being—not even the anti-Christ—will be able to fake. It will be of such a nature that only God will be able to pull it off. It will be a global and miraculous event that does not in any way parallel the Roman destruction of Jerusalem in A.D. 70. This will be an event that will not need to be reported in the media, since God will accomplish this event in such a way that everyone will know what has happened. Thus, it *must* be a future event to our own day since nothing like this has yet to occur in history.

THE MEANING OF THE PROVERB

There are two main interpretations of verse 28. One holds that it speaks of judgment of the unsaved. The other view sees a continuation of the theme of the context denoting suddeness and universality. I believe that both ideas are intended in verse 28.

Our Lord speaks of a "corpse," coupled with the expression of "eagles" or more accurately in this context, "vultures." This provides a picture of judgment. Thomas Figart notes:

> Taken literally, it means that wherever dead bodies are, there the *aetoi* (either eagles or vultures) will descend upon them. From a physical point of view, the vast carnage will result in this very thing.

> Symbolically, it can be related to the parallel passage in Luke 17:37 when the disciples asked *"Where, Lord"* in regard to the separation of the believers from the unbelievers at that time. He answered, *"Wherever the body is, there will the eagles (aetoi) be gathered together."* This means that these two similar statements refer to the judgment to come upon the unbelievers who are not prepared to meet Him.[2]

In addition to a judgment warning in conjunction with the return of Jesus to earth, the grammar appears to require an emphasis upon the global suddeness of the event. Heinrich Meyer points this out when he writes:

> Confirmation of the truth that the advent will announce its presence everywhere, and that from the point of view of the retributive punishment which the coming One will be called upon everywhere to execute. The emphasis of this figurative adage is on *hopou ean ê* and *ekeî*: "Wherever the carcase may happen to be, there will the eagles be gathered together,"—on no spot where there is a carcase will this fathering fail, so that, when the Messiah shall have come, He will reveal Himself everywhere in this aspect also (namely, as an avenger).[3]

That this proverb includes a global and suddeness aspect is supported by the preceding context, which I have noted before. emphasizes Christ's sudden and public return.

NOT A REFERENCE TO A.D. 70

Preterists, twist and turn this verse into a proverb that supports their first-century fulfillment assumption. Dr. Gentry declares:

> This seems to speak of the dreadful devastation Rome wreaks upon Israel. The furious soldiers who cruelly ravage the people will destroy national, political Israel. Josephus often mentions the rage of the Roman troops: ...The imagery is familiar enough to an agrarian people: the ugly, rotting corpse of an animal blanketed by bickering birds of prey.[4]

Fellow preterist Gary DeMar echoes Dr. Gentry's view stating:

> The Jerusalem of Jesus' day, because of its dead rituals, was a carcass, food for the scavenging birds, the Roman armies. This is an appropriate description of Jerusalem's acts of abomination. In addition, we know that tens of thousands (Josephus says over a million) were killed during the Roman siege. Even the temple area was not spared. The Idumean and Zealot revolt left thousands slaughtered in and around the temple.... There was no life in Jerusalem since the Lord had departed. As our High Priest, Jesus could no longer remain in the city because of its defilement. It had to be burned with fire for purification.
>
> Just as there is little life left once the vultures have gathered, so with the destruction of the temple and the desolation of the city, the shadow of heavenly things is no more.[5]

Yet, I have already argued from the context that this passage in general refers to a future return of Christ. If the surrounding context teaches a future return of Christ, which it does, then this passage cannot reference a past event. Meyer rightly notes:

> Others (Lightfoot, Hammond, Clericus, Wolf, Wetstein) have erroneously supposed that the carcase alludes to Jerusalem or the Jews, and that the eagles are intended to denote the Roman legions with their standards (Xen. Anab. I. 10. 12; Plut. Mar. 23). But it is the advent that is in question; while according to vv. 23–27, on *hopou ean ê* cannot be taken as referring to any one particular locality.[6]

Alan M'Neile echoes Meyer's point and declares, "It does not describe... the eagles on the Roman standards in the attack on Jerusalem; the last is not the subject dealt with either in Mat. or Lk."[7] Similarly, William Kelly summarizes the correct view of the passage when he states the following:

> Applied to Israel, all is simple. The carcase represents the apostate part of that nation; the eagles, or vultures, are the figure of the judgments that fall upon it. It is not only, then, that there will be the lightning-like display of Christ in judgment; but the agents of His wrath shall know where, and how, to deal with that which is abominable in God's sight.[8]

"AFTER THE TRIBULATION OF THOSE DAYS"

Having mentioned the second coming of Christ in verses 27–28 in reference to how He will appear (i.e., publicly, not privately), in this next section (verses 29–31), Jesus describes His return. The first thing Christ says is that His return will take place "immediately after the tribulation of those days." This means that the events described in the rest of verses 29–31 will occur *immediately* after the events of the tribulation. This seems obvious enough. However, not all seem to understand that.

Preterist Gary DeMar says that Christ's coming was a "coming in judgment upon Jerusalem in A.D. 70."[9] If the judgment events upon Jerusalem took place in verses 4–28 and occurred before verse 29, as DeMar teaches, then that would mean that he believes that verses 29–31 describe a second coming, different from the one spoken of in verse 27. This is exactly what preterists must do in order to maintain their view of Christ's prophetic discourse. DeMar admits, "Jesus' 'coming' in judgment upon Jerusalem (Matt. 24:27) and His coming 'up to the Ancient of Days' (Dan. 7:13) were two events that occurred within the time span of the first generation of Christians. There is no future fulfillment of those events."[10] Since DeMar is himself teaching multiple comings of Christ, it seems inconsistent that he could be so vocal against others, like pretribulationists, who also see several comings of our Lord (rapture and second coming).. Yet DeMar heaps great disdain on what he calls "a two-stage coming."[11]

Kelly rightly observes the following points about this bizarre preterist perspective:

> One can hardly be asked to notice the old effort to apply these verses to the Roman triumph over Jerusalem. On the fact of it, could this be said to be "immediately after the tribulation"? or was it not rather the crowning of Jewish sorrow, not the glorious reversal of their sufferings by a divine deliverance? Whatever prodigies Josephus reports were rather during the tribulation he records; whereas the signs spoken of here, literal or figurative, are to follow "the tribulation of those day" (*i.e.*, the future crisis of Jerusalem).[12]

If the preterist view is to be maintained, it would mean the disciples' question about "what will be the sign of your coming?" (verse 3) would have to have multiple answers. Yet we find no such thing in Christ's discourse. Should not the disciples' question read: "what will be the signs of your comings?" It appears that since neither preterist return is a bodily, physical return, but instead are spiritual or non-physical comings, that one can have Christ coming and going all over the place. One could have Christ coming every day in some spiritual way, if "coming" does not refer to an actual physical event. These are the kinds of interpretations that a preterist must hold in their attempts to make their system appear to work. James Morison notes of the preterist position:

> This word *immediately* has been a perfect rack of torture to such expositors as have lost their way in the interpretation of the chapter.... The whole difficulty arises from assuming that the tribulation of those days has reference to the tribulation that was to be experienced in connection with the destruction of Jerusalem. (See vers. 16–21.) There is not however the slightest necessity for making such an assumption. There is every reason indeed for rejecting it,...This great mistake is founded on an unwarrantably narrow view of the Saviour's aim in His discourse in general, and on an inappropriately microscopic way of peering toward telescopic objects.[13]

He is correct. In the end, preterism's iterpretations are untenable.

ENDNOTES

1 Randolph O. Yeager, *The Renaissance New Testament,* 18 Vols. (Bowling Green, KY.: Renaissance Press, 1978), vol. 3, 308.

2 Thomas O. Figart, *The King of The Kingdom of Heaven: A Commentary of Matthew* (Lancaster, PA: Eden Press, 1999), 447.

3 Heinrich August Wilhelm Meyer, *Critical and Exegetical Handbook to The Gospel of Matthew,* 2 vols. (Edinburgh: T. & T. Clark, 1879), vol. 2, 144.

4 Kenneth L. Gentry, Jr., *Perilous Times: A Study in Eschatological Evil* (Texarkana, AR: Covenant Media Press, 1999), 74.

5 Gary DeMar, *Last Days Madness: Obsession of the Modern Church* (Powder Springs, GA: American Vision, 1999), 127.

6 Meyer, *Matthew,* 144.

7 Alan Hugh M'Neile, *The Gospel According to St. Matthew* (London: MacMillan, 1915), 351.

8 William Kelly, *Lectures on The Gospel of Matthew* (Sunbury, PA: Believers Bookshelf [1868] 1971), 493–94.

9 DeMar, *Last Days Madness,* 71.

10 DeMar, *Last Days Madness,* 71.

11 Gary DeMar, *End Times Fiction: A Biblical Consideration of the Left Behind Theology* (Nashville: Thomas Nelson Publishers, 2001), 29.

12 Kelly, *Matthew,* 494.

13 James Morison, *A Practical Commentary on the Gospel According to St. Matthew* (London: Hodder and Stoughton, 1883), 477–78.

21

TRIBULATION AND TRANSITION

"Wherever the corpse is, there the vultures will gather. But immediately after the tribulation of those days the sun will be darkened, and the moon will not give its light, and the stars will fall from the sky, and the powers of the heavens will be shaken."

—Matthew 24:28–29

Upon stating the fact of His sudden, bodily, and glorious return, Christ parenthetically comments upon the judgment aspect of this advent. Then, verses 29–31 provide a more extended description of His future return to planet earth. The statement of His return in verse 27 concludes a discussion in which Jesus contrasts the coming of false messiahs with His genuine return. When He returns, there will be no doubt. One will not have to have a subscription from a special news source that reports information the mainstream media leaves out. No media will be needed at Christ's coming since His return will include a grand and glorious publicity feature.

CORPSES AND VULTURES

The phrase in verse 28 is also found in Luke 17:37, but not in Mark 13 or Luke 21. No doubt this is a judgment slogan of some kind. Interestingly in Revelation 19:17–19, we have a similar, though not verbatim, statement in conjunction with Christ's return:

> And I saw an angel standing in the sun; and he cried out with a loud voice, saying to all the birds which fly in midheaven, "Come, assemble for the great supper of God; in order that you may eat the flesh of kings and the flesh of commanders and the flesh of mighty men and the flesh of horses and of those who sit on them and the flesh of all men, both free men and slaves, and small and great." And I saw the beast and the kings of the earth and their armies, assembled to make war against Him who sat upon the horse, and against His army.... And the rest were killed with the sword which came from the mouth of Him who sat upon the horse, and all the birds were filled with their flesh." (Rev. 19:17–19, 21)

Revelation 19 clearly paints the picture of the birds coming to feast upon the corpuses of those who are about to be slaughtered by Christ at His return. This is a clear judgment use of this terminology. Since the contexts are similar in Matthew 24 and in Luke 17, I think that consistency of context demands a judgment interpretation. Robert Gundry explains:

> The preceding context determines that the saying be taken as a figure of judgment on the wicked when the Son of man has his day. The body stands for the wicked, the vultures for judgment, and the saying means that wherever the wicked are, the judgment will strike. They cannot escape; only the righteous will.[1]

Taken in context, verse 28 completes the section (verses 23–28) by noting that when Jesus suddenly appears at His return, it will result in not just judgment upon the false prophets and messiahs, but doom for all in opposition to His will. However, we should not be surprised to learn that preterists think differently.

THE ROMANS IN A.D. 70?

Preterists, such as Gary DeMar and Kenneth Gentry, believe that this passage was fulfilled in A.D. 70. DeMar says, "The Jerusalem of Jesus' day, because of its dead rituals, was a carcass, food for the scavenging birds, the

Roman armies."[2] Gentry agrees and contends, "This seems to speak of the dreadful devastation Rome wreaks upon Israel. The furious soldiers who cruelly ravage the people will destroy national, political Israel."[3]

This view is untenable because the context supports a still-future event that did not occur in the A.D. 70 destruction of Jerusalem—namely the bodily return of Christ. Alan M'Neile tells us that this passages "does not describe the Messiah descending from heaven upon the nation dead in sins, nor the false Messiahs and prophets making the people their prey, nor the eagles on the Roman standards in the attack on Jerusalem; the last is not the subject dealt with either in Mt. or Lk."[4] Gundry further explains::

> Some have thought that [the vultures] refers to the eagles of the Roman legions swooping down on Jerusalem during the first Jewish revolt (A.D. 66–73); but the context in Luke has nothing about the destruction of Jerusalem, and Matthew focuses attention on the Son of man's coming rather than on the destruction of the city.[5]

Matthew 24:28 is surrounded with a context of a future return of Christ, not an invisible coming through the Romans in A.D. 70. Thomas Figart aptly notes that, "This means that these two similar statements refer to the judgment to come upon the unbelievers who are not prepared to meet Him. They will be judged as swiftly and as surely as vultures pounce upon dead bodies."[6]

IMMEDIATELY AFTER THE TRIBULATION

As Christ's narrative transitions to a new emphasis, we move from events relating to the tribulation to an event that will follow the tribulation. Even though Jesus has already commented on the manner of His second coming in verse 27, He now focuses upon it in relation to the tribulation. He has been speaking previously about tribulation events (see verses 9, 21 and Mark 13:19), but now shifts to something that will take place "immediately" after the tribulation of those days. That event is the future, bodily return of Christ to earth, which is known as the second coming (verse 30). What Christ describes in a few verses (verses 29–31), John explains in greater detail in his recorded divine revelation (Rev. 19:11–21). The second-advent immediately follows the events of the tribulation.

Verse 29 begins with the word "immediately." *Eutheos* is a Greek adverb usually translated "immediately," as in the New American Standard Bible or "straightway, at once, directly."[7] Moulton and Milligan, in examples from the Greek papyri, emphasize that the use of this word means "at once."[8] Since "an adverb usually modifies the verb closest to it,"[9] immediately relates directly to the verb "to darken." Thus, the events of verse 29 will follow the tribulation immediately, at once, without any other events intervening, or without a time delay.

This would mean within the expanded chronology of the events of the tribulation found in Revelation 4–19, that Matthew 24:29–31 will follow immediately the final bowl judgment found in Revelation 16:17–21. This explains the parenthetical warning in the next-to-the-last bowl judgment which reads: "Behold, I am coming like a thief. Blessed is the one who stays awake and keeps his garments, lest he walk about naked and men see his shame" (Rev. 16:15). It won't be long from the time in which the sixth bowl judgment takes place, until Christ returns. Revelation 17–18 is an overview of the judgment upon Babylon, which surveys items that will take place throughout the tribulation and second coming. From a chronological aspect in Revelation, chapter 16 is followed in time by chapter 19.

Of further interest, is the fact that the word "immediately" is used in Luke 21:9 to say that during the events of the tribulation, "the end does not follow immediately." It is only later, in Luke 21:27–28, when "they will see the Son of Man coming in a cloud with power and great glory," that they are "straighten up and lift up your heads, because your redemption is drawing near." This passage speaks of the physical deliverance that will occur for Jewish believers at the second coming. To be sure, physical deliverance will occur at Christ's return for all believers, but the context is speaking specifically to Jewish believers who are under great peril during the tribulation.

Of the parallel passages on the Olivet discourse, none have the word "immediately." Luke 21 really does not have a parallel statement like verse 29 in Matthew. However, Mark 13 does have a parallel statement which reads as follows: "But in those days, after that tribulation, the sun will be darkened, and the moon will not give its light, and the stars will be falling from heaven, and the powers that are in the heavens will be shaken. And then they will see the Son of Man coming in clouds with great power and glory" (13:24–26). Mark drops the pressing term "immediately," for the less urgent phrase "in those days," but then provides a similar statement to Matthew's in the things that follow. This demonstrates that both speak of a similar event and that event is the future second coming of Christ.

PRETERIST PROTEST

Preterists DeMar and Gentry do not explain how "immediately" in verse 29 relates to their first-century fulfillment view. Gentry does not even deal with the term "immediately" in verse 29.[10] DeMar spends over a page discussing "immediately" and concludes that all the events of Matthew 24 had to occur in A.D. 70.[11] The reason this is important to the preterist interpretation is because preterists teach that Christ's coming in A.D. 70 was a "judgment-coming" that occurred through the Roman army as they assaulted and eventually destroyed Jerusalem and the Temple. Gentry calls it "a spiritual judgment-coming, rather than a bodily coming."[12] Gentry specifically links verse 30 with the overall judgment of the passage stating: "Christ specifically applies that verse to the first century.... Christ comes in judgment upon Jerusalem in the A.D. 67–70 events."[13] So Gentry describes Christ coming, as specifically mentioned in verse 30, with the events of A.D. 67–70, which is their understanding of "the tribulation."

Such a view creates a big contradiction with the text of Matthew 24 spoken by Christ Himself. When one reads the preterist interpretation of Matthew 24, it is discovered that they blend an event that is said by Jesus to take place immediately after the tribulation with those that were said to occur during the tribulation. If Christ's coming in Matthew 24:30 is a judgment-coming, as taught by preterists, then the judgment events would have had to have occurred during what Jesus called the tribulation part of Matthew 24 (verses 4–29). Yet, verse 30 is said by Christ to occur *immediately* after "the tribulation of those days." Randolph Yeager explains:

> The attempt to show that Jesus' prophecy had its fulfillment between A.D. 33 and A.D. 70, disregards vss. 29–31. None of these events took

> place ("immediately after") the troublous times connected with Titus' invasion and sack of Jerusalem in A.D. 70.... These drastic disturbances in the heavens will highlight the second coming of Christ.... How frantic the efforts of many commentators in dealing with this passage because they are prejudiced against a futurist view.[14]

In spite of the interpretations by preterists and others, we have seen and will continue to see, as we progress through this passage, that Christ speaks here of yet-future events. We will not have anyone rob the church of our wonderful hope in the glorious return of Jesus Christ to earth, as this passage so beautifully teaches.

ENDNOTES

1 Robert H. Gundry, *Matthew: A Commentary on His Handbook for a Mixed Church under Persecution*, second edition, (Grand Rapids: Eerdmans, 1994), 486.

2 Gary DeMar, *Last Days Madness: Obsession of the Modern Church* (Powder Springs, GA: American Vision, 1999), 127.

3 Kenneth L. Gentry, Jr., *Perilous Times: A Study in Eschatological Evil* (Texarkana, AR: Covenant Media Press, 1999), 74.

4 Alan Hugh M'Neile, *The Gospel According to St. Matthew* (London: MacMillan, 1915), 351.

5 Gundry, *Matthew*, 487.

6 Thomas O. Figart, *The King of The Kingdom of Heaven: A Verse by Verse Commentary on the Gospel of Matthew* (Lancaster, PA: Eden Press, 1999), 447.

7 G. Abbott-Smith, *A Manual Greek Lexicon of The New Testament*, 3rd. ed. (Edinburgh: T. & T. Clark, 1937), 186.

8 James Hope Moulton and George Milligan, *The Vocabulary of the Greek Testament: Illustrated from the Papyri and Other Non-Literary Sources* (Grand Rapids: Eerdmans, 1930), 261.

9 Wesley J. Perschbacher, *New Testament Greek Syntax: An Illustrated Manual* (Chicago: Moody, 1995), 23.

10 See pp. 75–79 where he deals with the passage but not with the term "immediately" in Gentry, *Perilous Times*.

11 DeMar, *Last Days Madness*, 141–42.

12 Gentry, *Perilous Times*, 71

13 Gentry, *Perilous Times*, 112.

14 Randolph O. Yeager, *The Renaissance New Testament*, 18 vols. (Bowling Green, KY: Renaissance Press, 1978), vol. 3., 312.

22

UNDERSTANDING FIGURES OF SPEECH

"But immediately after the tribulation of those days the sun will be darkened, and the moon will not give its light, and the stars will fall from the sky, and the powers of the heavens will be shaken."

—Matthew 24:29

One of the original questions that the disciples ask Jesus at the beginning of this discourse was "what will be the sign of your coming?" Jesus has been answering the question since verse 23. Having spoken of His coming in verse 27, Jesus now builds upon His previous point that He will not arrive clandestinely, but rather, His return will be a clear, public event that will take place suddenly. Just such a glorious appearing is exactly what is described in verses 29 and 30.

THE SUN, MOON, AND STARS

Matthew 24:29 is not a new revelation by our Lord. Old Testament passages such as Isaiah 13:9–10 and Joel 2:31; 3:15 also reference this "black out" and light show that will occur "immediately after the tribulation," in preparation for Christ's second coming as noted in Matthew 24:30. These Old Testament passages refer to the same future events that Christ describes in verse 29. In conjunction with the return of Jesus, Israel will be rescued from her tribulation by the Lord Himself as we will see (verse 31).

The theme of rescue associated with the Lord's return is reinforced from the contexts of these Old Testament passages, especially Joel 2 and 3, especially 2:31 and 3:1–2.

It is clear that our Lord has quoted part of His declaration about the sun and moon in Matthew 24:29, "But immediately after the tribulation of those days the sun will be darkened, and the moon will not give its light,..." from Joel 2:31. Both are speaking of the same time and events—the time immediately following the tribulation and in conjunction with Christ's return. It is interesting to take note of Joel 3:1–2, which provides a "time text" saying that the "black out" (Joel 2:31) will occur "in those days and at that time" (Joel 3:1). In conjunction with this is described a time when the Lord will "restore the fortunes of Judah and Jerusalem" (Joel 3:1). Not judgment, but deliverance, as in Matthew 24. This event is said to be a time when the Lord "will gather all the nations" (Joel 3:1) in the valley of Jehoshaphat just north of Jerusalem. Further, it will be a time in which Israel will have been regathered from among the nations (Joel 3:2). This will be the time in which the sun and moon will be darkened.

PRETERIST FOLLY

Of course, preterists believe that these events are connected to the first century. "Here we encounter remarkable cosmic disturbances that seem too catastrophic for applying to A.D. 70," says Gentry. He believes that "this portrays historical divine judgment under the dramatic imagery of a universal catastrophe."[1] How does he arrive at such a conclusion? "To understand it properly we must interpret it covenantally, which is to say biblically, rather than according to a presupposed simple literalism."[2] It goes without saying that any passage in the Bible must be interpreted biblically. So, why does Gentry feel compelled to make such a statement? He does this because he is getting ready to put forth an un-biblical interpretation. He already admitted that it does not seem that these events happened in the first century. Unable to provide a textual interpretation, he has to bring in his preconceived theology as the real basis for his understanding of the text. This is not interpreting the passage biblically, but theologically. Dr. Gentry uses his preconceived preterist notion as the true basis for his "interpretation" at this point. This is obvious to any attempting to understand the text from the perspective of the literal, grammatical, and contextual approach. Only those who are already committed to preterism, regardless of what the text says, will fall for the equation of covenantal interpretation with a proper biblical approach.

Dr. Gentry believes that verse 29 "draws upon the imagery from Old Testament judgment passages that sound as if they are world-ending events."[3] I have already noted such a relationship. This point is not a matter for debate, however, Gentry is typical of how preterists mishandle the recognized Old Testament relationship.

Gentry admits that this passage sounds like it did not occur in the first century. This is why, by his own admission, he must introduce his theology as a factor for interpreting this text. While those following the normal canons of sound hermeneutics—the historical, grammatical, contextual approach—cannot find Gentry's view taught from the passage. Dr. Gentry must employ a historical, grammatical, and theological hermeneutic to (mis)explain the passage. Because preterists erroneously believe that these events had to occur in the first century, they are forced to views that are not supported by the words, phrases, and context of the passage. If one is allowed to subjectively introduce their theology as part of the hermeneutical process, then it should not be surprising to find that the text supposedly teaches what is presupposed. That is not true exegesis, but it is a widely-practiced form of eisegesis. Dr. Robert Thomas' comment about this interpretative approach is on the mark when he says, "Gentry's use of symbolism is inconsistent and self-contradictory. A factoring of preunderstanding into the interpretive process inevitably leads to unimaginable extremes in hermeneutical abuse."[4] The same could be said for all preterist approaches to Matthew 24 and much of Scripture.

INTERPRETING FIGURES OF SPEECH

Literal interpretation recognizes that a word or phrase can be used plainly (denotative) or figuratively (connotative). In modern speech, as in the Bible, we talk plainly—"Grandmother died" (denotative), or more colorfully, "Grandmother kicked the bucket" (connotative). An important point to make is that even though we may use a figure of speech to refer to death, we are using that figure in reference to an event that literally happened. Ryrie says: "Symbols, figures of speech and types are all interpreted plainly in this method and they are in no way contrary to literal interpretation. After all, the very existence of any meaning for a figure of speech depends on the reality of the literal meaning of the terms involved. Figures often make the meaning plainer, but it is the literal, normal, or plain meaning that they convey to the reader."[5]

When I study the Old Testament figures of speech that preterists say speak of the passing of a great political power (Israel), I wonder how they know what the original figures mean? I do not see a textual basis for their understanding either in the Old Testament or in Matthew 24. There are no biblical passages that establish the preterist use of these figures. In 1857, Rev. D. D. Buck made the following hermeneutical points about interpreting Matthew 24:29 and they are still valid in our own day:

> (1.) The use of metaphoric language implies a knowledge or idea of what would be understood if such language were applied literally. No one ever uses figures without having in view the literal things from which the figures are derived.... If we say Christianity is the sun of the world, it implies that we have a previous understanding of the nature and fact of the sun.
>
> (2.) Now, whence did this ancient figurative use of the darkening of the luminaries arise? How did it happen that it was so common for the prophets to speak of ordinary, limited judgments, in language which all admit would, if used literally, apply to the general judgment? How became it so common to speak metaphorically of the darkening of the sun, moon, and stars, and the passing away of the heavens? Figures are the shadow of the literal. Where is the substance that originates the shadow? Metaphors are borrowed from literal speech. Where is the literal speech, and the revelation of the literal idea, of the blotting out of the bright heavens, and the downfall of the world?

(3.) This question is to be settled by those who seize upon every reference to these great events, and pronounce them figurative. Will they please to tell us where there is a spot in all the Bible where the literalist may plant his feet, and stand up in defense of orthodoxy, and give a philosophical explanation of the commonness of such language as appears to refer to the day of Judgment?[6]

COMPARING SCRIPTURE WITH SCRIPTURE

Luke 21:24 says, "and they will fall by the edge of the sword, and will be led captive into all the nations; and Jerusalem will be trampled under foot by the Gentiles until the times of the Gentiles be fulfilled." This text provides an outline of the history of Jerusalem from the time of the destruction of Jerusalem until Israel's redemption at the second coming (Luke 21:25–29). The time in which the sun and moon will be darkened will follow the end of "the times of the Gentiles," according to Luke 21:25. The fact that the black-out of Matthew 24:29 is to come at the end of the times of the Gentiles, "immediately after the tribulation of those days," makes it clear that it could not have happened in the first century since, according to Luke 21:24, the Roman destruction of the Holy City would commence that time which has gone on now for almost 2,000 years. This event must be future and in conjunction with a time in which the Lord will deliver His people, not judge them (as in A.D. 70).

If the preterist interpretation of this passage is left to stand then it creates tremendous contradictions between the text and the historical records of the Roman siege. Rev. Richard Shimeall explains the preterist problem as follows:

Historically, therefore, the state of the case amounts to this:

(1.) The high-priest of the Jewish nation and many of his associates had been murdered, and the whole body of the priesthood overthrown; and, if there were any religious services, they were conducted by such wretches as the robbers saw fit to appoint.

(2.) Their temple was changed into a citadel and stronghold of an army of the vilest and most abominable robbers and murderers that ever disgraced the human race.

(3.) Their "holy houses" (synagogues) throughout the land had been pillaged and destroyed by the ruthless and bloody Sicarii.

(4.) Their judiciary and temple officers had either fled for their lives to the Romans, or had been murdered by the robber-gangs of the city, while their nobles and men of-wealth perished by myriads. And finally,

(5.) Whether within the capital or throughout the borders of Judea, east, west, north, and south, the ecclesiastical and civil institutions of the nation were exterminated, and the country conquered and laid waste by the Romans, or ravaged by organized banditti.

And thus, reader, it continued to the end. These, we repeat, are the historical facts of the case. And yet, our commentators have trusted the interpretation of some of the most important parts of the Bible to the theory, the principal argument to sustain which lies in the assumption that the Jewish ecclesiastical and civil governments were destroyed "after" the destruction of Jerusalem!

What shall the writer say more? He claims to have settled the question by undeniable historic facts. If anything, let it be in the form of the following appeal to logic:

1. If by the heavenly luminaries be meant the ecclesiastical and civil States and rulers of the Jews, and the darkening of them refers to their destruction; and if this was effected by the Roman legions, it follows that it must have occurred either before or during the tribulation that resulted in their ruin.

> 2. But, inasmuch as the object of the war was to reduce the nation to obedience, or to bring it to ruin, it could not have preceded it.
>
> 3. It must therefore have occurred during the war. Recollect we are now speaking of the darkening of the sun, moon, and stars, as denoting the so-called Jewish tribulation at the hands of the Romans. We repeat, then, it must have occurred during the war. Now, it is undeniable, that that war did not cease until its object was effected. It is also undeniable, that the nation was in ruins before the war was ended. And it is a fact, also, that the predicted tribulation continued undiminished, if indeed it did not increase in severity, to the last.
>
> It is, therefore, we submit, settled—historically and logically settled—that it was during, and not after, that time of trouble, that the so-called Jewish luminaries were darkened. And, what is decisive of this point, are those notable words of Christ, "Immediately after tribulation of those days, the sun shall be darkened," etc.; which shows conclusively that our Lord was not speaking of that event in the 29th verse of this chapter.[7]

In the end, the preterist intrepretation of Matthew 24 creates more problems than it solves.

ENDNOTES

1 Kenneth Gentry in Thomas Ice and Kenneth L. Gentry, Jr., *The Great Tribulation: Past or Future?* (Grand Rapids: Kregel, 1999), 55.

2 Gentry in Ice and Gentry, *Great Tribulation*, 55.

3 Gentry in Ice and Gentry, *Great Tribulation*, 56.

4 Robert L. Thomas, "New Evangelical Hermeneutics and Eschatology," A paper presented at the 12th Annual Pre-Trib Study Group, (Irving, TX, December 8, 2003), 32.

5 Charles C. Ryrie, *Dispensationalism Today* (Chicago: Moody Press, 1965), 87.

6 D. D. Buck, *Our Lord's Great Prophecy* (Nashville: South-Western Publishing House, 1857), 229.

7 Richard Cunningham Shimeall, *Christ's Second Coming: Is It Pre-Millennial or Post-Millennial?* (New York: John F. Trow and Richard Brinkerhoff, 1866), 157–59.

23

DARK SKIES

"But immediately after the tribulation of those days the sun will be darkened, and the moon will not give its light, and the stars will fall from the sky, and the powers of the heavens will be shaken."

—Matthew 24:29

As we continue with an exposition of verse 29, it is important to note that we have already seen the impossibility that this passage could have been fulfilled about 2,000 years ago in the Roman destruction of Jerusalem. So to what does the darkening of the sun and moon and other astronomical events refer? Is Christ's description that of a real, physical and astronomical event, or is He merely using symbolic language in which He describes something else?

We observe that Christ's statement in this passage contains four descriptive phrases. First, the darkening of the sun; second, the moon not reflecting its light; third, stars falling from the sky; fourth, a shaking of heaven powers.

DARKENING OF THE SUN

We saw earlier that preterists believe that the reference to the sun in this passage is not to the literal, physical sun, but merely a symbol for something that occurred in the first century. Dr. Kenneth Gentry states that "this portrays historical divine judgment under the dramatic imagery of a universal catastrophe."[1] To what does he contend that this imagery is? "I will argue that this passage speaks of the A.D. 70 collapse of geo-political Israel.... of national catastrophe in terms of cosmic destruction."[2] In opposition to this interpretation I contend that sun in this context has to refer to the star that shines in the sky. If that is the case, then the events being described in verse 29 have not yet happened in history and must refer to a future time.

Before we go any further, let's examine how many of the 164 times that the word "sun" is used in the Bible as a symbol or figure of speech and not a reference to the physical sun. There are five possible uses of "sun" as a symbol in the Bible (Gen. 37:9; Psalm 84:11; Jer. 15:9; Mal. 4:2; Rev. 12:1). In Genesis 37:9 and Revelation 12:1 the sun is a symbol for Jacob, the father of Israel. Psalm 84:11 says, "the LORD God is a sun and shield," comparing an attribute of God to the sun. Jeremiah refers to the death of a mother with seven sons by an invading army as, "Her sun has set while it was yet day" (15:9). Malachi describes the coming Messiah as One Who is "the sun of righteousness," Who "will rise with healing in its wings" (4:2). About 97% of the time "sun" refers to the star and physical sphere that shines faithfully in the sky. In five instances of symbolic use, none refer to "a universal catastrophe," as suggested by Dr. Gentry. Preterists must transform Matthew 24:29, Isaiah 13:10 and Joel 2 and 3 into non-physical symbols since clearly such catastrophic events did not occur in God's creation during the A.D. 70 event. There are no textual factors in Matthew 24 that support understanding the sun, moon, and stars as mere symbols of some other natural event. Instead, context supports the role of the sun, moon, and stars as physical phenomena accompanying our Lord's return.

It makes sense that the heavens and earth are physically affected by humanity's sin at the end of history, just as nature underwent physical change in the fall of Adam and Eve at the beginning of history. With the literal view, Genesis and Revelation recount the beginning and ending of history. Revelation notes the magnitude of the shaking of the heavens and the earth in judgment. Noah's flood had physical effects, and so too will the judgment of the tribulation prior to Christ's return. Nineteenth-century Old Testament Franz Delitzsch aptly observes: "Even nature clothes itself in the colour of wrath, which is the very opposite to light."[3]

Peterists understand a number of similar, yet smaller in scale, incidents of biblical history to be literal. Did the sun literally not shine over the land of Egypt while at the same time shine in the land of Goshen during the ninth plague (Exodus 10:21–29)? Of course it did! Did the sun literally stand still for half a day in Joshua 10? You bet it did! Did the Lord cause the sun to go backward 10 degrees in the days of King Hezekiah (2 Kings 20)? It most surely did! Similarly, during the crucifixion of our Lord, did darkness really fall over the whole land of Israel about the sixth hour until the ninth hour (Luke 23:44–45)? Sure it did! It was a pattern of the final darkness that will accompany the final judgment at the end of the world. "When He died, the sun refused to shine (Lk. 23:45). When He comes again it will not shine (Mt. 24:29)."[4] Why shouldn't grandiose, supernatural phenomenon accompany the glorious return of our Lord?

Only a naturalist mentality would say that a literal occurrence of Matthew 24:29 is impossible. After all, God said in Genesis 1:14 that one of His purposes for the sun, moon, and stars is to serve as "signs" in the heavens. It would be a great mistake to think that these references to the sun, moon, and stars are to be taken merely as symbols with no physical referent. Why should not the One who created the heaven and earth have the heavens reflect His global judgment upon a sinful world? Our Lord Jesus Christ demonstrates His actual rule over all His creation upon His return to planet earth, including over the sun, moon, and stars. Delitzsch says, "when god is angry, the principle of anger is set in motion even in the natural world, and primarily in the stars that were created 'for signs' (compare Gen. i. 14 with Jer. x. 2)."[5] There may be objections in the minds of people to such heavenly displays, but no such problem exists in Scripture.

ISAIAH 13:10 AND MATTHEW 24:29

Since, as the saying goes, "necessity is the mother of invention," preterists must create new meanings to words and phrases that cannot be sustained by any of the contexts of the biblical passages. Dr. Gentry states: "Isaiah 13 speaks of remarkably similar events accompanying Babylon's collapse in the Old Testament era."[6] He is correct that Matthew 24:29 refers to Isaiah 13:10, something recognized by all commentators. He is also correct that Isaiah's prophecy speaks of Babylon's collapse. However, he is wrong about *when* this prophesied event will occur in history. He believes it occurred during Old Testament times, while I, and most futurists, believe it will unfold within the context of future tribulation events.

Twice, in the immediate context, Isaiah warns that "the day of the LORD is near" (13:6) and that "the day of the LORD is coming" (13:9). The timing of the events in verse 10 relate to when the day of the LORD occurs in history. I believe Scripture indicates that the day of the LORD will occur in conjunction with the 70th-week of Daniel, also known as the seven-year tribulation.[7] One's overall understanding of the day of the LORD will impact their understanding of the timing of the fulfillment of this and many other passages. Jesus refers to Isaiah 13:10 in Matthew 24:29 (also in Mark 13:24) and thus places it in very close proximity to the tribulation ("immediately after"). However, preterists place the events of Isaiah 13:2–16, "in the Old Testament era," hundreds of years before the first coming of Christ. This creates a major conflict between when preterists such as Dr. Gentry's believe that Isaiah 13:2–16 was fulfilled and when our Lord said it would be fulfilled. A futurist interpretation does not have such an interpretive conflict.

There are further problems with the preterist's understanding of Isaiah 13. Isaiah 13:10–11 says, "For the stars of heaven and their constellations will not flash forth their light; the sun will be dark when it rises, and the moon will not shed its light. Thus I will punish the world for its evil, and the wicked for their iniquity; I will also put an end to the arrogance of the proud, and abase the haughtiness of the ruthless." The phrase "the sun will be dark when it rises," in verse 10 requires a literal, instead of a symbolic understanding in this context. If this text is supposed to be symbolic about the fall of a nation, then why would the prophet speak of the sun rising, although darkened. That makes no sense. This is the language of real solar movement and events.

The global events described in verse 10 make sense because verse 11 says that the Lord is punishing "the world for its evil." The Hebrew word for "world" is *tebel* and "conveys the cosmic or global sense…i.e., the whole earth or world considered as a single entity."[8] "Instead of *'eretz* we have here *tebel*," notes Delitzsch, "which is always used like a proper name (never with the article), to denote the earth in its entire circumference."[9] This passage (verses 2–16) is clearly global in scope, which would rule preterism's local, symbolic, and past interpretation. It thereby requires a future fulfillment. "At this point this oracle of judgment on a great coming world-power begins to expand to cover the whole world," surmises G. W. Grogan while commenting on verses 9–13. "Matthew 24 shows Jesus, in similar fashion, relating a local judgment that was to fall on Jerusalem to the great events that would usher in his second advent and the end of the age."[10]

Isaiah 13:10 is a clear denotative statement supporting a non-symbolic intent. "Therefore I shall make the heavens tremble, and the earth will be shaken from its place at the fury of the LORD of hosts in the day of His burning anger." "I shall make the heavens tremble" looks back to our Lord's acts described in verse 10, which are in turn referred to by Jesus in Matthew 24:29. Grogan explains:

> Verse 13 seems to go even beyond v. 10 in depicting the effects of divine judgment on the natural universe. There is to be a general convulsion of the whole created order (cf. 34:4). In this way the instability of the order of things since the Fall will be disclosed (as it is seen in so many of the signs of Christ's coming in Mark 13), thus revealing the need for the eternally stable order of the kingdom of God that Christ's coming will establish.[11]

CONCLUSION

As we have examined the first of four statements in Matthew 24:29 concerning the Lord's return, we see that the overwhelming support for a futurist interpretation. Under scrutiny, the preterist interpretation is unsustainable. Not only does Matthew 24 not mean what they say it means, neither does Isaiah 13 to which they appeal. Preterists must fabricate from Isaiah 13 an alleged Old Testament genre which is not supported by the biblical text. Yet, if both Matthew 24 and Isaiah 13 are taken the way the biblical authors intended, then futurism, and not preterism, is the teaching of the text.

ENDNOTES

1 Kenneth Gentry in Thomas Ice and Kenneth L. Gentry, Jr., *The Great Tribulation: Past or Future?* (Grand Rapids: Kregel, 1999), 55.

2 Kenneth L. Gentry, Jr., *Perilous Times: A Study in Eschatological Evil* (Texarkana, AR: Covenant Media Press, 1999), 77.

3 F. Delitzsch, "Isaiah," vol. VII in C. F. Keil and F. Delitzsch, *Commentary on the Old Testament in Ten Volumes* (Grand Rapids: Eerdmans, 1975), 299–300.

4 Randolph O. Yeager, *The Renaissance New Testament* (Bowling Green: Renaissance Press, 1978), Vol. 3, 312.

5 Delitzsch, "Isaiah," 300.

6 Gentry, *Perilous Times*, 77.

7 For an excellent explanation and defense of this view see J. Randall Price, "Old Testament Tribulation Terms," in Thomas Ice and Timothy Demy, editors, *When the Trumpet Sounds* (Eugene, OR: Harvest House, 1995), 57–83. *Trumpet* is out of print, but *The Return* is still in print and contains it. See Thomas Ice and Timothy Demy, editors, *The Return: Understanding Christ's Second Coming and The End Times* (Grand Rapids: Kregel, 1999), 27–53.

8 Willem A. VanGemeren, Gen. Ed., *New International Dictionary of Old Testament Theology & Exegesis*, 5 vols. (Grand Rapids: Zondervan 1997), vol. 4, 272–73.

9 Delitzsch, "Isaiah," 300–01.

10 G. W. Grogan, "Isaiah", *The Expositor's Bible Commentary*, Vol. 6 (Grand Rapids: Zondervan Publishing House, 1986), 101.

11 Grogan, "Isaiah," 102.

24

ASTRONOMICAL ABBERATIONS

"But immediately after the tribulation of those days the sun will be darkened, and the moon will not give its light, and the stars will fall from the sky, and the powers of the heavens will be shaken."

—Matthew 24:29

Previously, we noted that this passage contains four descriptive phrases. First, the darkening of the sun; second, the moon not reflecting its light; third, stars falling from the sky; fourth, a shaking of heavenly powers. Previously we dealt with the darkening of the sun and saw that both Jesus and Isaiah (Isa. 13:10) intended their readers to understand that these were physical events, not symbolism denoting a non-physical event.

HEBREW POETRY

All too often opponents of literal interpretation will equate a biblical use of poetic structure with non-literal interpretation. Doing so is poor hermeneutics and results in faulty interpretations.

I recall that during my college days, I took a class in the Minor Prophets. When we got to the book of Jonah my liberal professor said because the style of chapter two was poetic it meant that the events depicted there should not be taken literally. Jonah 2 records the episode of Jonah and the great fish. Such an interpretive perspective is clearly wrong when compared with Scripture itself. There are many historical events, both past and future, that are recorded in the Bible using some kind of Hebrew poetic form. Many historical events are contained in the Psalms. Yet, every Psalm is written using Hebrew poetry. Even within American history, some of our greatest literature uses poetic expression to communicate historical events. One need only think of literature such as *The Midnight Ride of Paul Revere* by Henry Wadsworth Longfellow, or *O Captain! My Captain!* by Walt Whitman.

Hebrew poetic genre often can be more expressive or colorful than prose narrative, but this does not mean that it cannot be historical. Did not the Song of Deborah (Ex. 19) mention historical events that had just taken place in the Exodus, even though it is in a poetic form? Just because Isaiah 13 and many prophetic passages on the Day of the Lord are in a poetic form, it does not mean that they do not speak of actual historical events.

NO MOONLIGHT

Christ says in His discourse, that in conjunction with the sun not shinning, "the moon will not give its light." This makes physical sense in that if the sun has been darkened, the moon will not shine, since the moon does not generate its own light, as does the sun, but simply reflects the light of the sun. Because the sun has been darkened, then this would mean in a physical cause and effect that the moon would also be darkened. This argues for a literal intent by Jesus in Matthew 24:29. Robert Govett is on the mark when he says, "no proof is needed on the part of those who take them literally: reason must first be shown why we are to take them symbolically, before we need give any proof of the contrary."[1] Another commentator suggests that the description should be taken literally because, "Elsewhere in chapter 24 the dramatic events—wars, famines, earthquakes—are intended literally."[2]

The basic approach and arguments that were used to demonstrate that Christ's previous reference to the sun is of a physical nature are also applied to His use of moon in this context. Because sun and moon are linked together, as are all four of these descriptive phrases, if the sun is literal then so must be the moon. Leon Morris observes:

> There is to be no source of light here on earth in that day. It accords with what will happen to sun, moon, and stars that *the powers of the heavens will be shaken*.... Whatever functions they may be exercising at the time will be affected by the great fact that the Son of man is coming back to this earth to bring an end to the current system and to inaugurate the reign of God over all the earth.[3]

STAR POWER

The third of four descriptions that will occur "immediately after the tribulation of those days" will be "the stars will fall from the sky." These events are all in preparation for the second coming that is described in verse 30. It will be a heavenly blackout that will provide a perfect background for the brilliant arrival of Jesus Christ back to earth to set up His thousand-year rule.

Preterists do not think that this passage describes the backdrop for Christ's bodily return to Jerusalem. "When the tribulation of 'those days' is completed, the end of the temple and city is near," claims Gary DeMar. "As the time for Jerusalem's judgment draws ever closer, certain other signs would appear. These later signs are descriptive of the fall of the nations and kingdoms."[4] Concerning the stars in this passage, DeMar believes that they "represent people and nations. The people of Israel were represented as stars (Gen. 22:17; 26:4; Deut. 1:10)."[5] Once again, does Christ intend a literal or figurative event? Even if it is a figure of speech, which I do not think it is, it would not necessarily follow that DeMar's understanding would be correct. Theoretically, stars could be used figuratively and still relate to the second advent.

STARS FALLING TO THE EARTH

Why should this descriptive phrase also be taken literally, as have the sun and moon? The text says, "the stars will fall from the sky." It does not say in this passage that stars will fall to the earth. Yet, that is how DeMar attempts to finesse the passage by trying to connect it with Revelation 6:13, which says, "and the stars of the sky fell to the earth." "How can *stars* fall to the Earth and the Earth survive,"[6] asks DeMar?

First, *aster*, the Greek word for star, can refer to physical stars in the sky (Mat. 2:2, 7, 9–10) or it can be used figuratively as a symbol, referring to people and angels (Jude 13, Rev. 8:10–11; 9:1). Second, stars literally do fall from heaven upon the earth. They are called "falling stars," "shooting stars," or comets or asteroids,or "meteors," and upon reaching the earth, are known as meteorites. The Greek word for star can be used in this way.[7] "The word 'star' (Greek *aster*) refers to any luminous body in the sky other than sun and moon."[8] Such stars that fall to the earth often disintegrate and burn up as they enter the earth's atmosphere. Robert Gundry has said, "The falling of the stars refers to a shower of meteorites."[9]

A number of commentators see the falling stars as meteorites. Greek scholar, Kenneth Wuest translates Revelation 6:13 as follows: "the *meteors* of the heaven fell to the earth."[10] Grant Osborne says, "The background is a huge meteor shower."[11] In reference to the meaning of star, Robert Thomas says, "Its meaning is broad enough to include smaller objects that hurtle through space from time to time.... a very large meteor shower that invades the terrestrial atmosphere."[12] Kendell Easley declares, "we speak of 'falling stars' or 'shooting star' emanating from a meteor shower."[13] "The most likely identification of these particular falling stars is that of a great swarm of asteroids that pummel the earth," says Henry Morris.[14]

Further, the description of the falling stars to the earth in Revelation 6:13 is not a complete emptying of the heavens of all of their stellar components. It is a partial event as supported by the part of verse 13 that reads, "as a fig tree casts its unripe figs when shaken by a great wind." Robert Govett explains as follows:

> Not all of them are cast down; as the comparison appears to prove. For their fall is like that of the untimely figs of a fig-tree, much shaken by a gale. The fruit intended is the winter-fig, that comes out too late in the summer to ripen, and loses its hold of the tree during the inclement skies of the end of the year; so as to be easily shaken off by any wind, which agitates to any considerable extent the branches of the tree.[15]

Falling stars are what cause the people of the earth to hide in caves in Revelation 6:12–17.

The sixth seal judgment, which is being described this passage, is not a parallel passage to Matthew 24:29, even though there are some similar phrases in both passages. The context is totally different. The sixth seal judgment describes a partial judgment, which does not include the second coming. Matthew 24:29 describes a complete blackout of the sun, moon, and stars, followed by the second coming. Even though DeMar tries to equate these passages,[16] there are too many differences to justify such an understanding. Revelation 6:13 is the only passage which teaches that stars will fall upon the earth. The other passages referencing literal stars, which includes Matthew 24:29 and Mark 13:24, simply say that the stars will fall from the sky, not to the earth. Thus, it is in this way that the sixth seal judgment will be fulfilled literally.

REVELATION 12

DeMar also indicates (erroneously) that Revelation 12:4 is a passage that futurists believe refers to literal stars. It says of the great red dragon (Satan), "And his tail swept away a third of the stars of heaven." "Again, 'a third of the meteorites of heaven' would have a devastating effect on our planet. Earth would cease to exist," DeMar declares. "Scientists have speculated that a single meteorite threw up enough debris upon impact with Earth that it 'ended the reign of the dinosaurs.'"[17]

It is interesting that DeMar uses an evolutionary hypothesis to defend his naturalistic interpretation. Nevertheless, futurists and literalists do not believe that physical stars are in view in verse 4. I have already noted above that the word star can be used to refer to the physical stars in the sky or as a symbol referring to a personality. DeMar fails to tell his readers what is said a few verses later: "And the great dragon was thrown down, the serpent of old who is called the devil and Satan, who deceives the whole world; he was thrown down to the earth, and his angels were thrown down with him" (Rev. 12:9). Revelation 12:4 uses "stars" as a symbol for angels (as in Job 38:7), in this case fallen angels, because verse 9 repeats what is said in verse 4 using the non-symbolic term "angels." Robert Thomas notes:

> The stars must refer to angels who fell with Satan in history past. The similarity of this verse to Dan. 8:10, where "the host of heaven" is an apparent reference to angels, shows this. Already in Revelation a star has pictured an angel (9:1). That factor along with the reference to Satan's angels in 12:8–9 adds credence to this explanation.[18]

Preterists must obfuscate and misrepresent the views of others in order to make their own appear to have some merit.

ENDNOTES

1 Robert Govett, *The Prophecy on Olivet* (Miami Springs, FL: Conley & Schoettle Publishing Co., [1881] 1985), 64.

2 W. D. Davies and Dale C. Allison, Jr., *A Critical and Exegetical Commentary on The Gospel According to Saint Matthew*, 3 vols. (Edinburgh: T. & T. Clark, 1997), vol. 3, 358, fn. 200.

3 Leon Morris, *The Gospel According to Matthew* (Grand Rapids: Eerdmans, 1992), 609–10.

4 Gary DeMar, *Last Days Madness: Obsession of the Modern Church* (Powder Springs, GA: American Vision, 1999), 142.

5 DeMar, *Last Days Madness*, 143.

6 DeMar, *Last Days Madness*, 142.

7 Henry George Liddell and Robert Scott, *A Greek-English Lexicon* (Oxford England: Oxford University Press, 1968), s.v. "aster", 261.

8 Henry M. Morris, *The Revelation Record* (Grand Rapids: Baker, 1983), 122.

9 Robert H. Gundry, *Matthew: A Commentary on His Handbook for a Mixed Church under Persecution*, second edition, (Grand Rapids: Eerdmans, 1994), 487.

10 Kenneth S. Wuest, *The New Testament: An Expanded Translation* (Grand Rapids: Eerdmans, 1961), 597.

11 Grant R. Osborne, *Revelation* (Grand Rapids: Baker, 2002), 292.

12 Robert L. Thomas, *Revelation 1–7: An Exegetical Commentary* (Chicago: Moody, 1992), 454.

13 Kendell H. Easley, *Revelation* (Nashville: Holman Reference, 1998), 111.

14 Morris, *Revelation Record*, 122.

15 Robert Govett, *Govett on Revelation*, 2 vols. (Hayesville, NC: Schoettle Publishing, [1861] 1981), vol. I, 216.

16 DeMar, *Last Days Madness*, 142–43.

17 DeMar, *Last Days Madness*, 143.

18 Robert Thomas, *Revelation 8–22: An Exegetical Commentary* (Chicago: Moody, 1995), 124.

25

SHAKING OF THE HEAVENS

"But immediately after the tribulation of those days the sun will be darkened, and the moon will not give its light, and the stars will fall from the sky, and the powers of the heavens will be shaken."

—Matthew 24:29

The final phrase of verse 29 reads, "and the powers of the heavens will be shaken." Is this phrase to be taken literally, like the three previous phrases, or should one apply speculative exegesis to say that it means something other than what it appears to say? Does the phrase "powers of the heavens" refer to angelic entities or to the physical universe?

POWERS OF THE HEAVENS

The same basic phrase is used in all three accounts of the Olivet Discourse (Matt. 244:29; Mark 13:25; Luke 21:26). The phrase "powers of the heavens" most likely has the idea of "the sun, moon, and stars, spoken of in summary fashion," as they have been specifically mentioned earlier in the verse. Leon Morris says, "The word for heaven is singular in the reference to the stars, but plural where the powers are spoken of."[1] Stanley Toussaint notes: "Thus the Lord describes the astronomical bodies being shaken as the earth is in an earthquake."[2]

The specific phrase "powers of the heavens" is never used of angelic beings in the Bible nor does the context support such an understanding.[3] Since the first three phrases relate to the entities that fill the sky, this final expression is a summary of the collective. "Jesus is sayịng that, whatever the powers of the heavens may be, they are subject to God, and that at this time, that of the return of the Son of man to this earth, their power will be disturbed."[4] These "powers of the heavens" also appear to include God's decree of stability by which these celestial objects currently function with regularity. John MacArthur explains:

> All the forces of energy, here called **powers of the heavens**, which hold everything in space constant, will be in dysfunction. The heavenly bodies will careen helter-skelter through space, and all navigation, whether stellar, solar, magnetic, gyroscopic, will be futile because all stable reference points and uniform natural forces will have ceased to exist or else become unreliable.[5]

A HEAVENLY SHAKING

The verb "shaken" is used about 15 times in the Greek New Testament. The verb is sometimes used as a metaphor, as in 2 Thessalonians 2:2: "that you may not be quickly shaken from your composure." However, most of the time it refers to a physical shaking, as in Acts 16:26: "suddenly there came a great earthquake, so that the foundations of the prison house were shaken." A physical shaking of the heavens is what our Lord intends in this context.

However, preterists believe that this phrase does not reference a physical shaking, but to the A.D. 70 destruction of Jerusalem . Gentry states:

> Consequently, we may legitimately apply Matthew 24:29 to the destruction of Jerusalem in A.D. 70. Christ draws upon this imagery from Old Testament judgment passages that sound as if they are world-ending events. And in a sense it is "the end of the world" for those nations God judges. So it is with Israel in A.D. 70.[6]

Most commentators recognize that the shaking of the heavens in this passage is an allusion from Haggai 2:6 which says, "For thus says the Lord of hosts, 'Once more in a little while, I am going to shake the heavens and the earth, the sea also and the dry land.'" What does this passage mean? We have a divine New Testament commentary that we can look to in Hebrews 12 that tells us what it means:

> And His voice shook the earth then, but now He has promised, saying, "Yet once more I will shake not only the earth, but also the heaven." And this expression, "Yet once more," denotes the removing of those things which can be shaken, as of created things, in order that those things which cannot be shaken may remain. Therefore, since we receive a kingdom which cannot be shaken, let us show gratitude, by which we may offer to God an acceptable service with reverence and awe. (Heb. 12:26–28)

In this fifth warning passage, the writer of Hebrews contrasts the first shaking of the earth, a physical one, at the Exodus with a future shaking, which will include the heavens as well. He too has in mind Haggai 2:6. The future shaking will be much greater than the past shaking since it will include the heavens as well. Since the first shaking at the Exodus was physical then it follows that the second shaking will also be a physical one, just as Christ describes in His prophetic sermon of Matthew 24. "The discourse is entirely plain," notes amillennial interpreter R. C. H. Lenski, who understands this as a future physical event. "'The whole sidereal world shall collapse.... This is made plain by the last 'the powers of the heavens shall be shaken' or dislocated. All that hold the heavenly bodies in their orbits and enables sun and moon to light the earth will give way."[7] H. A. W. Meyer notes: "This convulsion in the *heavens*, previous to the Messiah's descent *therefrom*, is not as yet to be regarded as the *end of the world*, but only as a prelude to it." And again, "*The earth* is not destroyed as yet by the celestial commotion."[8]

SIGNS IN THE HEAVENS

Matthew and Mark do not record Christ's statements about the human response to these great events, but Luke does. William Kelly observes, "It is Luke only who mentions the moral signs of men's anguish spite of the deceits and pretensions of that day."[9] In what is clearly the same context that we find in Matthew and Mark, Jesus says:

> "And there will be signs in sun and moon and stars, and upon the earth dismay among nations, in perplexity at the roaring of the sea and the waves, men fainting from fear and the expectation of the things which are coming upon the world; for the powers of the heavens will be shaken" (Luke 21:25–26).

Luke is the only one to call the activity in the sky involving the sun, moon and stars a sign. Robert Stein says, "the signs associated with the Son of Man's coming are cosmic, whereas those associated with Jerusalem's fall are terrestrial, so that Luke kept these two events distinct."[10]

One of the purposes to which God gave in His creation of the sun, moon, and stars would be for "them be for signs, and for seasons, and for days and years" (Gen. 1:14b). For whom would these signs be given? They will be signs to those upon the earth. When one ponders great events down through history, in no other event would signs in the heavens be so appropriate than for the second coming of Christ from heaven to earth.

LUKE'S ACCOUNT

Clearly, Luke 21:20–24 refers to the destruction of Jerusalem by the Romans in A.D. 70. The second half of verse 24 says, "and Jerusalem will be trampled underfoot by the Gentiles until the times of the Gentiles be fulfilled." Equally clear is that the last half of verse 24 is descriptive of a period of time that commenced after the Roman vanquishing of Jerusalem in the first century. That phrase has a beginning point, which began after A.D. 70. It has a time interval described by the expression, "Jerusalem will be trampled underfoot by the Gentiles." The verse also provides an ending point when it says, "until the times of the Gentiles be fulfilled." There is no way that this event has already been fulfilled and it looks to a time when events that took place in A.D. 70 will be reversed.

Verse 24b provides a textual transition from A.D. 70 to events just before the second coming of Christ. Even a renowned preterist such as F. W. Farrar recognizes the shift from A.D. 70 in verses 20–24 to the second advent, or what he calls "the Last Coming" in verses 25–28.[11] E. H. Plumptre observes:

> From this point onwards the prophecy takes a wider range, and passes beyond the narrow limits of the destruction of Jerusalem to the final coming of the Son of Man, and the one is represented in St. Matthew as following "immediately" on the other, by St. Mark as "in those days." No other meaning could have been found in the words when they were first heard or read.[12]

At this point in Luke 21 we have an example of what Tim LaHaye and I call "The Mountain Peaks of Prophecy" in our book *Charting The End Times*.[13] Plumptre has provided an excellent explanation of this in the following statement:

> As men gazing from a distance see the glittering heights of two snow-crowned mountains apparently in close proximity, and take no account of the vast tract, it may be of very many miles, which lies between them; so it was that those whose thoughts must have been mainly moulded on this prediction, the Apostles and their immediate disciples, though they were too conscious of their ignorance of "the times and the seasons" to fix the day or year, lived and died in the expectation that it was not far off, and that they might, by prayer and acts, hasten its coming (2 Pet. iii. 12).[14]

Clearly, in Luke 21, Christ sees two different events. One in the first century (21:20–24) and the other, still future to our time (21:25–28). However, neither Matthew 24 nor Mark 13 relate in any way to the A.D. 70 event, since neither the destruction of the Temple nor Jerusalem is mentioned in them. Instead, the Matthew and Mark accounts of the Olivet Discourse clearly speak of the rescue of the Jewish people, rather than their judgment as happened in A.D. 70.

In summary, we have seen that great supernatural events will accompany Christ's return to earth. Is that so hard to imagine or believe? Scripture (both in the Old and New Testaments) speaks of Israel being regathered in her land, in unbelief (her current status today), as a national entity. She will go through a time called the tribulation that will lead to the conversion of the remnant to faith in the messiahship of Jesus. This will then precipitate the second coming of Christ for the purpose of rescuing a now-converted nation, who calls for His protection against the armies of all the nations that have gathered in Israel to destroy it. Instead, Christ destroys Israel's enemies and commences His reign in Jerusalem for a thousand years.

ENDNOTES

1 Leon Morris, *The Gospel According to Matthew* (Grand Rapids: Eerdmans, 1992), 609.

2 Stanley D. Toussaint, *Behold the King: A Study of Matthew* (Portland, OR: Multnomah, 1980), 276 .

3 Contrary to Robert Govett, *The Prophecy on Olivet* (Miami Springs, FL: Conley & Schoettle, 1881), 65.

4 Morris, *Matthew*, 609–10. For further reasons not to take this a an angelic reference see Heinrich August Wilhelm Meyer, *Critical and Exegetical Handbook to the Gospel of Matthew*, 2 vols. (Edinburgh: T. & T. Clark, 1879), Vol. 2, 148–49.

5 John MacArthur, *Matthew 24–28, The Macarthur New Testament Commentary* (Chicago: Moody, 1989), 51.

6 Kenneth L. Gentry in Thomas Ice and Kenneth L. Gentry, *The Great Tribulation: Past or Future?* (Grand Rapids: Kregel, 1999), 56–57.

7 R. C. H. Lenski, *The Interpretation of St. Matthew's Gospel* (Columbus, OH: The Wartburg Press, 1943), 947.

8 Meyer, *Matthew*, vol. 2, 149.

9 William Kelly, *An Exposition of the Gospel of Luke* (Oak Park, IL: bible Truth Publishers, 1971), 333,

10 Robert H. Stein, *Luke, The New American Commentary* (Nashville: Broadman Press, 1992), 524.

11 F. W. Farrar, *The Gospel According to St. Luke, with Maps, Notes and Introduction* (Cambridge: At The University Press, 1899), 319.

12 E. H. Plumptre, *The Gospel According to St. Luke*, 12 vols., vol. 3, *Ellicott's New Testament Commentary* (London: Cassell & Company, n. d.), 345.

13 Tim LaHaye and Thomas Ice, *Charting the End Times: A Visual Guide to Understanding Bible Prophecy* (Eugene, OR: Harvest House, 2001), 26–28.

14 Plumptre, *Luke*, 345.

26

A SIGN IN THE SKY

"and then the sign of the Son of Man will appear in the sky, and then all the tribes of the earth will mourn, and they will see the Son of Man coming on the clouds of the sky with power and great glory."

—Matthew 24:30

The second coming of Christ will be an event that has multiple aspects and phases to it. Jesus will not just appear in the sky and that is it, but there will be a multitude of specific events that will take place in the process of this advent. Christ, in Matthew 24:30 continues to note some of the sequencing that will take place at this time in the future. One of the important events that will transpire will be "the sign of the Son of Man" that will appear in the sky.

SIGN OF THE SON OF MAN

Earlier in Matthew 24:3 the disciples of Jesus ask Him, "Tell us, when will these things be, and what will be the sign of Your coming, and of the end of the age?" This passage answers the question about the sign of Christ's coming. So what is that sign?

First, it should be noted that the sign and His coming are separate events. Based upon what has preceded this verse, we know that the stage for his dramatic return begins in verse 29 with a shaking of the sun, moon and stars. This produces a blackout of the sky preparing the way for the appearance of the sign of the Son of Man, followed by the response of human mourning and fear, resulting in the second coming of Christ.

Second, this sequence of events will unfold in Jerusalem Israel. This is the location on planet earth in which these things are scripted to unfold, even though they will have a global impact.

Third, I believe that the sign of the Son of Man will be some form of the manifestation of the Shekinah (or Shechinah) Glory. Arnold Fruchtenbaum explains as follows:

> As this sign is coupled with God's glory, it is obviously the *Shechinah* Glory light that will signal the Second Coming of the Messiah. The answer to the second question, "What will be the sign of the Second Coming?" is the *Shechinah* Glory. *But immediately after the tribulation of those days,* there will be a total blackout with no light penetrating at all, followed by a sudden, glorious, tremendous light that will disperse the blackness. This *Shechinah* light will be the sign of the Second Coming of the Messiah. The light will be followed by the return of the Messiah Himself.[1]

THE SHEKINAH GLORY

What is the Shekinah Glory? Why do I think this is what Christ has in mind here? The Shekinah Glory is the visible manifestation of the presence of God, often showing up in the form of a cloud, light, fire, or combinations of these. The Hebrew word Shekinah does not appear the biblical text. The Jewish rabbis coined this extra-biblical expression called the "Shekinah Glory," in order to distinguish those biblical passages where they believe that a physical glory cloud or light was present when the Hebrew word for "glory" was used. Shekinah is a form of a Hebrew word that literally means "he caused to dwell," signifying that when God's glory appeared in this way it was a Divine visitation of the presence or dwelling of God in the glory cloud. Fruchtenbaum tells us that "the *Shechinah* Glory is the visible manifestation of the presence of God. In the Old Testament, most of these visible manifestations took the form of light, fire, or cloud, or a combination of these. A new form appears in the New Testament: the Incarnate Word."[2] In order to see the significance of the Shekinah Glory for future Bible prophecy, a survey of past appearances are necessary.

The following events are believed to be manifestations of the Shekinah Glory in biblical history:

- The Garden of Eden—the Lord's presence in the Garden and the flaming sword (Gen. 3:8, 23–24).
- The Abrahamic Covenant—the flaming torch that passed between the sacrificial pieces (Gen. 15:12–18).
- The Burning Bush—the burning that did not consume the bush (Ex. 3:1–5; 13:21–22; 14:19–20, 24; 16:6–12).
- The Exodus—the pillar of cloud by day and the pillar of fire by night (Exodus).
- Mount Sinai—the Ten Commandments written by the finger of God; thunders, lightnings, and a thick cloud (Ex. 19:16–20; 24:15–18 Deut. 5:22–27).
- The Special Meeting with Moses—the afterglow of Moses' face as a result of his meeting with the Lord (Ex. 33:17–23; 34:5–9, 29–35; 29:42–46; 40:34–38).
- The Tabernacle and the Ark of the Covenant—the glory-cloud presence often associated with these items (Exodus).
- The Book of Leviticus—the authentication of the Law and residence in the holy of holies (Lev. 9).
- The Book of Numbers—the Shekinah Glory rendered judgment for sin and disobedience (Num. 13:30—14:45; 16:1–50; 20:5–13).

- The Period of Joshua and Judges—the continued dwelling of the Shekinah Glory in the tabernacle (1 Sam. 4:21–22).

- The Solomonic Temple—the transfer of the Shekinah Glory from the tabernacle to the Temple (2 Chron. 5:2–7:3).

- The Departure in Ezekiel—Ezekiel watches the Shekinah Glory depart the Temple in preparation for judgment upon the nation (Ezek. 1:28; 3:12, 23; 8:3–4; 9:3; 10:4, 18–19; 11:22–23).

- The Second Temple—the Shekinah Glory was not present, but a promise was given that it will be greater in the future than in the past (Hag. 2:3, 9).

- The Appearance to the Shepherds—the glory of the Lord shone round about them (Luke 2:8–9).

- The Star of Bethlehem—the star or glory-cloud that guided the Magi to Jesus (Matt. 2:1–12).

- Jesus: The Glory of the Lord—the incarnation was a manifestation of the Shekinah Glory (John 1:1–14).

- The Transfiguration—the Shekinah Glory appears to the three disciples (Matt. 17:1–8; Mark 9:2–8; Luke 9:28–36, Heb. 1:1–3; 2 Peter 1:16–18; Rev. 1:12–16).

- The Book of Acts—the cloven tongues of fire on Pentecost and the blinding light shown upon Paul at his conversion (Acts 2:1–3; 9:3–8; 22:6–11; 26:13–18).

- The Revelation—Jesus Christ is dressed in the Shekinah Glory in Revelation 1 (Rev. 1:12–16).

The following is an overview of future events relating to the Shekinah Glory:

- The Tribulation—the Shekinah Glory is connected with the Bowl judgments (Rev. 15:8).
- The Second Coming of Christ—the Shekinah Glory is the sign of the Son of Man and the cloud upon which He returns (Matt. 16:27; 24:30; Mark 13:26; Luke 21:27).
- The Millennium—the Shekinah Glory will be present in its greatest manifestation in history because of Christ's physical presence on earth (Ezek. 43:1–7; 44:1–2; Isa. 4:5–6; 11:10; 35:1–2; 40:5; 58:8–9; 60:1–3; Zech. 2:4–5; 11:10)
- The Eternal State—the Shekinah Glory will provide light for the new creation where sin will be totally removed and God the Father, God the Son, and God the Holy Spirit will dwell in fullness with man (Rev. 21:1–3, 10–11, 23–24).[3]

THE SIGN

The word order of the Greek in verse 30 is as follows: "And then shall appear the sign of the Son of Man in the heaven." The Greek supports the probability that the intent of the passage is that the sign of the Son of Man will appear in the heaven or sky. To take it as a humanly visible sign in the sky, as I would, preterist Kenneth Gentry says, "requires a restructuring of the text."[4] It does not *require* a restructuring, even though many who take a futurist view do put forward translations that do not retain the original word order. When rendering a passage from Greek to English (or into any language), maintaining the original word order is not as important as providing an accurate translation. Gentry inserts a red herring at this point in his attempt to change the true intent and sense of this passage. The difference amounts to whether "in heaven" refers to an invisible sign that takes place in the throne room of God in heaven or whether it occurs as a sign in the sky that is seen by humanity. Grammarian Nigel Turner says, "Mt 24:30 is ambiguous, either *the sign which is the S.M.* [Son of Man] (appos.), or *the sign which the S.M. will give* (possess.)."[5]

I believe the context argues in favor of the futurist interpretation that the sign is visible to the human eye in heaven, which is the sky. First, the Greek word can mean either "throne room," or the visible heaven or sky that can be seen by the human eye, as understood by futurists. The majority of New Testament uses fall into this latter use.[6] The major Greek lexicon of our day classifies it as the latter and says "*then the sign of the Son of Man (who is) in heaven will appear*; acc. to the context, the sign consists in this, that he appears visibly in heavenly glory Mt. 24:30."[7]

Second, surrounding verses focus upon heavenly meteorological disturbances (cf. verse 27, 29, 30b, 31) that are visible to humanity. The appearance of a sign in the sky would certainly fit the contextual theme of a heavenly focus.

Third, "It must, in the nature of the case, be *luminous*. This is indicated by the original word for *appear*. But it must be luminous from this single consideration: it will appear, or shine, at a time of *total darkness*," declares D. D. Buck. "The sun will be previously turned to darkness, and the moon and the stars will have withdrawn their shining. All the great sources of light being thus totally obscured, whatever shall *appear* must be luminous in its nature."[8]

Fourth, the time relationships of the passage support a visible, and thus, a future understanding. Matthew 24:30 begins "and then" referring back to the astronomiical events of verse 29 which will occur "immediately after the tribulation of those days." Thus, verse 30 tells us that "the sign… will appear;" "and then" there will be human mourning in response to the sign; followed by Christ's glorious return. Amazingly, Gentry says that the sign of verse 30 means that the Jews "must flee the area if they are to preserve their lives."[9] How can this happen if the sign is the Roman conquest of Jerusalem? It will be too late. Such folly does not fit an A.D. 70 sequence of events as is noted by the nineteenth-century biblical commentator Richard Shimeall:

> Yes, reader. This is the theory of our Lord's *second* coming,...Briefly, then, as it respects the *first* branch of this theory, its inconsistency, we submit, will become apparent, from the following arguments and facts:
>
> (1.) *If* the coming of the Lord at the time here specified was merely "the coming of the Roman army to destroy Jerusalem and the unbelieving Jews," then it will follow, of necessity, that it occurred at the same time, since, in fact, it is affirmed to be the *same event.*
>
> (2.) Again. The destruction of the Jewish Church and State, and city, and people, resulted from the coming of the Romans, and must, of course, have been *after* that coming, because results must be subsequent to the causes which produce them. Accordingly, as our blessed Lord delivered the whole of this remarkable prophecy with special regard to the *chronological* order of the events,
>
> (3.) He describes the appearance of the "sign" of His coming, of the mourning of all the tribes of the earth, and of His actual coming in the clouds of heaven, as being "*after* the tribulation of those days," and subsequent, in the order of time, to the darkening of the sun, moon, and stars.
>
> Reader, which shall we believe—the comments and opinions of men, or the teachings of Christ?[10]

The events of this verse are not in the past, but in the future. The world has yet to experience them in God's prophetic plan.

ENDNOTES

1 Arnold Fruchtenbaum, *The Footsteps of the Messiah: A Study of the Sequence of Prophetic Events*, Revised Edition (Tustin, CA: Ariel Ministries, 2003), 643.

2 Fruchtenbaum, *Footsteps*, 599.

3 Adopted from Fruchtenbaum, *Footsteps*, 599–628.

4 Gentry in Thomas Ice and Kenneth L. Gentry, Jr., *The Great Tribulation: Past or Future?* (Grand Rapids: Kregel, 1999), 58.

5 Nigel Turner, *A Grammar of New Testament Greek*, Vol. III, *Syntax* (Edinburgh: T. & T. Clark, 1963), 214.

6 William F. Arndt and F. W. Gingrich, *A Greek-English Lexicon of the New Testament* (Chicago: University of Chicago Press, 1957), 598–600.

7 Arndt and Gingrich, *A Greek-English Lexicon*, 599.

8 D. D. Buck, *Our Lord's Great Prophecy* (Nashville: South-Western Publishing House, 1857), p. 292..

9 Gentry, *Great Tribulation*, 60.

10 Richard Cunningham Shimeall, *Christ's Second Coming: Is It Pre-Millennial or Post-Millennial?* (New York: John F. Trow and Richard Brinkerhoff, 1866), 159–60.

27

MOURNING TRIBES

"and then the sign of the Son of Man will appear in the sky, and then all the tribes of the earth will mourn, and they will see the Son of Man coming on the clouds of the sky with power and great glory."

—Matthew 24:30

In the previous installment we saw four reasons why the context of the passage argues in favor of the futurist interpretation that the "sign" is visible to the human eye in heaven, which is the sky. In this chapter we continue looking at verse 30 and we will see the final reason for taking this view.

Fifth, I believe that "the sign" will likely be some form of the Shekinah Glory that has been manifested throughout history. After all, it was the sign of Christ's first coming—the Shekinah Glory—that flashed upon a darkened sky announcing His birth to the shepherds. It was the Shekinah Glory star that led the wise men from the East. So it is that His sign, the sign of the Son of Man will once again be His trademark, the Shekinah Glory cloud.

A SIGNLESS SIGN?

Preterist Kenneth Gentry argues that "they will see… " Christ's "… coming on the clouds" is once again not visible sight (the eyes of faith) nor a physical coming.[1] He goes so far as to evidence "exegetical vertigo" when he says that Christ's "coming on the clouds" "actually speaks of his ascension."[2] At this point, preterists confuse coming with going. Gentry further explains that

> the sign" of verse 30 is "when the Romans lay waste the temple (vv. 6 and 15 anticipate this) and pick apart Jerusalem (v. 28). That is, when the government of Israel utterly collapses (v. 29), then it will be evident that the one who prophesies her destruction is "in heaven." The "sign" is not a visible token in the sky. Rather, the sign is that the "Son of Man" rejected by the first century Jews is in heaven. The destruction of Israel vindicates Christ.[3]

It is hard to believe that Gentry could put forth this view with a straight face, since, unlike many preterists, he understands Acts 1:11 as a second coming passage.[4] In that passage Luke states:

> And after He had said these things, He was lifted up while they were looking on, and a cloud received Him out of their sight. And as they were gazing intently into the sky while He was departing, behold, two men in white clothing stood beside them; and they also said, "Men of Galilee, why do you stand looking into the sky? This Jesus, who has been taken up from you into heaven, will come in just the same way as you have watched Him go into heaven." (Acts 1:9–11)

The language in Acts 1 is clear that Christ is ascending upward to heaven in verse 9. It is equally clear that verse 11 speaks of His return as a coming down from heaven on a cloud. Further, the Greek word for "coming" in both Matthew 24:30 and Acts 1:11 is *erchomai*. Thus, once Christ has ascended into heaven, His next act of coming could not be up, but only down—down from heaven to earth. This is clearly the picture our Lord paints, not only in the specific passage (verse 30), but throughout the overall context (verses 27–31). In the extended citation below, Stanley Toussaint observes:

> It will be conceded by all that the first part of Matthew 24:30 looks back to Zechariah 12:10. However, it is important to notice that in Zechariah the mourning of 12:10 is explained by the verses that follow. It is a repentant lamentation by Israel because it results in the purification of the nation (Zech. 13:1). The context of Zechariah

12:10 is most significant. Rather than prophesying the destruction of Jerusalem, it is predicting the opposite. "And it will come about in that day that I will set about to destroy all the nations that come against Jerusalem" (Zech. 12:9). This is the tenor of Zechariah 12:1–8. It looks ahead to God's future deliverance of Israel when Jerusalem will again be surrounded by enemies. "In that day" is prophetic of a time of deliverance of Israel, not judgment. (Note the constant repetition of "in that day" [12:3, 4, 6, 8 (2x), 9, 11; 13:1, 2, 4]). It is clear that the context of Zechariah is a mourning that results in cleansing and deliverance for Israel. Whatever the sign of the Son of Man is, it results in the national repentance of Israel. This parallels perfectly what Paul says in Romans 11:25–27. This explanation of Matthew 24:30a sets the stage for the understanding of the last half of the verse.

It is true that in the vision of Daniel 7:13 as it is translated in the NASB the Son of Man came up to the Ancient of Days to receive the dominion to rule. However, the Hebrew verb has no idea of direction; it simply means to arrive or to reach. This specific verb is only used in Daniel where it may refer to something reaching up as Nebuchadnezzar's greatness did in 4:22, or it may describe something going down as in 6:24 where the detractors of Daniel were thrown into the lion's den. It has no intrinsic sense of direction. Nor does the following preposition indicate direction in itself. The construction simply means the Son of Man approached the Ancient of Days. But even if it describes the Son of Man coming up to the Ancient of Days, it only looks at the bestowment of authority. The question is where is the authority expressed? Keil says it well when he writes:

> In this very chapter before use there is no expression or any intimation whatever that the judgment is held in heaven. No place is named. It is only said that judgment was held over the power of the fourth beast, which came to a head in the horn speaking blasphemies, and that the beast was slain and his body burned.

> If he who appears as the son of man with the clouds of heaven comes before the Ancient of days executing the judgment on the earth, it is manifest that he could only come from heaven to earth. If the reverse is to be understood, then it ought to have been so expressed, since the coming with clouds of heave in opposition to the rising up of the beast out of the sea very distinctly indicates a coming down from heaven. The clouds are the veil or the "chariot" on which God comes from heaven to execute judgment against His enemies; cf. Ps. xvii;10f., xcvii 2–4, civ. 3, Isa. xix 1, Nah. i. 3. This passage forms the foundation for the declaration of Christ regarding His future coming, which is described after Dan. vii. 13 as a coming of the Son of man with, in, on the clouds of heaven; Matt. xxiv. 20, xxvi. 64; Mark xiii. 26; Rev. 1.7, xiv. 14.

> In summary, Matthew 24:30 describes a visible appearance of the sign of the Son of Man, the repentance of Israel and the triumphant return of Christ to reign on planet earth.[5]

The information above shows why the next time Jesus comes, it will not be a "signless sign" that did not actually exist in the form of the Roman army. Rather, it will be the visible, bodily, physical return of Jesus Christ that mirrors His ascension. Matthew 24 is not concerned with the destruction of Jerusalem, but with the coming of the Lord. No one in A.D. 70 recorded a second coming of Christ, not even Josephus. The New Testament predicts the destruction of Jerusalem, which was fulfilled in A.D. 70, not a second coming in A.D. 70.

ALL THE TRIBES OF THE EARTH WILL MOURN

We have seen up to this point that God is preparing the cosmic stage to showcase the most spectacular event in all human history—the glorious return of Jesus Christ to planet earth to reign for a thousand years. First, this will occur after the events of the tribulation (24:29). Second, it will interrupt the campaign of Armageddon. Third, God will darken the sky by causing the sun, moon and stars to cease shinning. Fourth, in the midst of this blackened background, the sign of the Son of Man with burst forth in brilliant light and glory. Finally, then, and only then, will the stage be set for Jesus to return to planet earth—to the Mount of Olives in Jerusalem. It is within this scenario of events that Jesus says, "then all the tribes of the earth will mourn."

The next part of verse 30 says, "then all the tribes of the earth will mourn, and they will see the Son of Man coming on the clouds of the sky with power and great glory." Why will they mourn, because they will see the undeniable sign of the returning Christ. Gentry says, that this merely refers to the Jewish tribes of Israel in A.D. 70.[6] That is incorrect. It is a universal term used of global unbelievers. Every time this plural phrase is used in the parallel Book of Revelation it clearly refers to Gentiles. For example, Revelation 13:7 speaks of "every tribe and people and tongue and nation." Every use in the Old Testament of "all the tribes of the earth" has a universal meaning in the Septuagint. The Old Testament uses the term "all the tribes of Israel" (about 25 times) when it refers to the Jewish tribes.

Most importantly, the verse continues and states, "they will see the Son of Man coming on the clouds of the sky with power and great glory." When the text says, "they will see the Son of Man," it has to be a reference to the visible, bodily, physical return of Jesus Christ to earth! This did not happen in A.D. 70. Josephus does not record it nor is it recorded in any other sources. This cannot refer to a symbolic, naturalistic interpretation that somehow Jesus returned in conjunction with the Roman army in the first century. Jesus said, "they will see the Son of Man."

CHRIST'S RETURN STILL FUTURE

If Jesus returned in A.D. 70, as preterists contend, then, on what day did He return? Since this is a past event, we should be able to know the exact day our Lord supposedly returned and fulfilled this passage. I have never read in any preterist material where any of them who can tell the day and exact manner or event that supposedly was Christ's return in A.D. 70. In fact, this was such a non-event in terms of church history, that it was not until the seventeenth century that there is an extant record of anyone suggesting anything like a preterist view that refers Matthew 24:27 and 30 to A.D. 70.

Had Christ returned as described in that passage, surely Josephus would have observed it or written of it. But even the verbose Josephus does not record such an event. It is not recorded because it did not occur. When the second coming of Christ—as described prophetically in Matthew 24:27–31—occurs, we will all be able to note the day and the hour. The description of Christ's return in this passage is of a nature that it will be such a public event that will be observed by multitudes of people. The exact day and hour of this event will not be lost in history.

ENDNOTES

1 Gentry in Thomas Ice and Kenneth L. Gentry, Jr., *The Great Tribulation: Past or Future?* Grand Rapids: Kregel, 1999), 58.

2 Gentry, *Great Tribulation,* 57–59.

3 Gentry, *Great Tribulation,* 58.

4 Kenneth L. Gentry, Jr., *He Shall Have Dominion: A Postmillennial Eschatology* (Tyler, Texas: Institute for Christian Economics, 1992), 275.

5 Stanley D. Toussaint, "A Critique Of The Preterist View Of The Olivet Discourse," an unpublished paper presented to the Pre-Trib Study Group, Dallas, Texas, 1996, n.p. Toussaint's quotation from Keil and Delitzsch is: F. Keil and F. Delitzsch, *Commentary on the Old Testament,* 10 vols, *Commentary on the Book of Daniel,* (Grand Rapids: Eerdmans, 1975), 235–36.

6 Kenneth L. Gentry, Jr., *Perilous Times: A Study in Eschatological Evil* (Texarkana, AR: Covenant Media Press, 1999), 83.

28

GLOBAL GATEHRING

"And He will send forth His angels with a great trumpet and they will gather together His elect from the four winds, from one end of the sky to the other."

—Matthew 24:31

We have seen that the return of Jesus to earth is said to be "on the clouds of the sky" and will be accompanied "with power and great glory" (24:30). In the process of that return, apparently as our Lord descends, He will then send out His angelic company to gather in the Jewish believing remnant that He will rescue from the danger of all the world's armies who have gathered by the anti-Christ person in an attack upon Israel and Jerusalem. The passage before us now, Matthew 24:31, describes this event.

AN ANGELIC GATHERING

In Matthew 23:37 we read that Jesus weeps over Jerusalem as He pronounces the A.D. 70 judgment and declares, "How I wanted to *gather* your children together, the way a hen *gathers* her chicks under her wings, and you were unwilling." Now in chapter 24, this same Jesus is returning after at least a couple thousand years at a future time when Jerusalem is again in peril. But this second time the Jews respond positively to the messiahship of Jesus. Our Lord sends out his angels to *gather* His elect (saved Jews at the end of the tribulation) from around the world and bring them to Jerusalem, instead of scattering them as in A.D. 70 (Luke 21:24). Just such a regathering was predicted in the Old Testament:

> "So it shall be when all of these things have come upon you, the blessing and the curse which I have set before you, and you call them to mind in all nations where the LORD your God has banished you, and you return to the LORD your God and obey Him with all your heart and soul according to all that I command you today, you and your sons, then the LORD your God will restore you from captivity, and have compassion on you, and will gather you again from all the peoples where the LORD your God has scattered you. If your outcasts are at the ends of the earth, from there the LORD your God will gather you, and from there He will bring you back." (Deuteronomy 30:1–4)

> And He will lift up a standard for the nations, and will assemble the banished ones of Israel, and will gather the dispersed of Judah from the four corners of the earth. (Isaiah 11:12)

The only thing missing from the Old Testament that our Lord expands upon in His Olivet Discourse is that He will use the agency of angels to bring Jews to Israel, instead of El Al Airlines and others as they come and go today from the modern state of Israel. Deuteronomy 30:1–4 reveals an important covenantal promise made by the Lord to His people Israel. Matthew 24:31 reveals that our Lord, the same One who made the promise in Deuteronomy will fulfill His promises in history, even if it requires a miraculous solution.

Surely no one would object to the supernatural implications of angels gathering human beings and returning them to Israel. We know that Elijah was translated to heaven without dying. 2 Kings 2 records this interesting event with an emphasis upon the mode of Elijah's transportation to heaven. We read in 2 Kings 2:1 that Elijah was taken "by a whirlwind to heaven." In 2 Kings 2:11 the whirlwind is further described as "a chariot of fire and horses of fire." No doubt this was an appearance of the Shekinah Glory of God since Hebrews 1:7 says, "and of the angels He says, 'Who makes His angels winds, and His ministers a flame of fire.'" If an individual, Elijah, was taken to heaven by angels (mere human messengers could not accomplish such a task), the same type movement could happen for a group. This is exactly what we find in conjunction with an important event associated with Christ's second advent.

The Deuteronomy 30:1–4 passage also provides an answer for why our Lord used the term "elect" in Matthew 24:31 to characterize His people. It is because at this pivotal point in history, the Jews will fulfill the requirements of Deuteronomy 30:2 and will turn "to the Lord your God and obey Him with all your heart and soul according to all that I command you today." This was also our Lord's own requirement for the second coming in Matthew 23:39. The passage makes great sense with such a futuristic interpretation and is also in harmony with clear Old Testament teaching about Israel and that wonderful day when they will be converted to Messiah and receive in history their long awaited blessing. Arnold Fruchtenbaum writes:

> In the New Testament, the final regathering revealed by the Old Testament prophets is summarized in Matthew 24:31 and Mark 13:27. In this passage, Jesus stated that the angels will be involved in the final regathering and they will bring the Jews back into the land. As to locality, the emphasis is on the world-wide regathering. The two passages are a simple summary of all that the prophets had to say about the second facet of Israel's final restoration. The Matthew passage is based on Isaiah 27:12 13 and the Mark passage is based on Deuteronomy 30:4. Its purpose was to make clear that the world-wide regathering predicted by the prophets will be fulfilled only after the second coming.[1]

Isaiah 27:12–13 teaches exactly what Fruchtenbaum says and it is clear that Christ had it in mind in Matthew 24:31. Isaiah's passage reads:

> And it will come about in that day, that the Lord will start His threshing from the flowing stream of the Euphrates to the brook of Egypt; and you will be gathered up one by one, O sons of Israel. It will come about also in that day that a great trumpet will be blown;

> and those who were perishing in the land of Assyria and who were scattered in the land of Egypt will come and worship the LORD in the holy mountain at Jerusalem.

The Isaiah passage has emphasis upon a regathering of the Jewish remnant that is not in the land of Israel and restoring them back to their homeland. This is one of the reasons why Matthew 24:31 emphasizes a global regathering of saved Jews in conjunction with the return of Jesus to the Mount of Olives in Jerusalem. Fruchtenbaum notes:

> The Matthew passage is a rather simple summary of all that the prophets had to say about the second facet of Israel's final restoration. Its purpose was to make clear that the world-wide regathering predicted by the prophets will be fulfilled only after the Second Coming.[2]

THE FEAST OF TRUMPETS

As Dr. Renald Showers notes,the global gathering means that."the elect will be gathered from all over the world at Christ's coming,"[3] Dr. Showers provides three lines of proof for his view as follows:

> First, because of Israel's persistent rebellion against God, He declared that He would scatter the Jews "into all the winds" (Ezek. 5:10, 12) or "toward all winds" (Ezek. 17:21). In Zechariah 2:6 God stated that He did scatter them abroad "as four winds of the heavens."...God did scatter the Jews all over the world.
>
> Next, God also declared that in the future Israel would be gathered from the east, west, north, and south, "from the ends of the earth" (Isa. 43:5–7). We should note that in the context of this promise, God called Israel His "chosen" (vv. 10, 20).
>
> ...Just as Jesus indicated that the gathering of His elect from the four directions of the world will take place in conjunction with "a great trumpet" (literal translation of the Greek text of Mt. 24:21), so Isaiah

> 27:13 teaches that the scattered children of Israel will be gathered to their homeland in conjunction with the blowing of "a great trumpet" (literal translation of the Hebrew)....
>
> Gerhard Friedrich wrote that in that future eschatological day "a great horn shall be blown (Is. 27:13)" and the exiled will be brought back by that signal. Again he asserted that in conjunction with the blowing of the great trumpet of Isaiah 27:13, "There follows the gathering of Israel and the return of the dispersed to Zion."
>
> It is significant to note that Isaiah 27:13, which foretells this future regathering of Israel, is the only specific reference in the Old Testament to a "great" trumpet.
>
> Although Isaiah 11:11–12 does not refer to a great trumpet, it is parallel to Isaiah 27:13 because it refers to the same regathering of Israel. In its context, this passage indicates that when the Messiah (a root of Jesse, vv. 1, 10) comes to rule and transform the world as an "ensign" (a banner), He will gather together the scattered remnant of His people Israel "from the four corners of the earth."[4]

What Jesus describes in Matthew 24 and Mark 13 is the Jewish ingathering that will fulfill the prophetic aspects of the Feast of Trumpets for the nation of Israel. In fact, a prayer for this regathering of the children of Israel appears to this day in the Jewish Daily Prayer Book.[5]

THE ELECT

The term "elect" in Matthew 24:31 refers to those Jewish individuals who will become believers in the messiahship of Jesus by the time the second advent occurs. As a reference to Jewish individuals who are destined to become believers is the same way that the term is used in the previous two references in Matthew 24 (verses 22, 24). Daniel 12:1, which is set within the same context of the tribulation period reads:

> "Now at that time Michael, the great prince who stands guard over the sons of your people, will arise. And there will be a time of distress such as never occurred since there was a nation until that time; and at that time your people, everyone who is found written in the book, will be rescued."

This passage uses the phrase "everyone who is found written in the book," to refer to Jewish individuals who will come to faith in Christ during the tribulation period, which is the context of this passage. Christ, who apparently has this passage from Daniel in mind shortens the phrase "everyone who is found written in the book," to "the elect." "Elect" is an excellent term that refers to an individual, in this context a Jewish person, whom the Lord knows will come to faith in Christ. That this is not just any individual who will come to faith in Christ during the tribulation is noted by the context in which it is clear that it is a reference to Jewish individuals. This is supported in Daniel 12:1 by the modifier "your people" that appears just before "everyone who is found written in the book." Who are "your people?" In the context it can only refer to Daniel's people, the Jewish people.

We see that this passage teaches that in conjunction with Christ's return to earth, He will have His angels gather all saved Jews (the remnant) and bring them to Israel. This will be so that they will be back in their homeland in preparation to dwell there during the one thousand-year reign of Christ upon earth.

ENDNOTES

1 Arnold Fruchtenbaum, *Israelology: The Missing Link In Systematic Theology*, rev. ed. (Tustin, CA.: Ariel Ministries Press, 1992), 798–99.

2 Arnold Fruchtenbaum, *The Footsteps of the Messiah*, 2nd edition (San Antonio: Ariel Press, 2003), p. 425.

3 For more information supporting this view see Renald Showers, *Maranatha: Our Lord, Come!* (Bellmawr, NJ: The Friends of Israel, 1995), 181–84.

4 Showers, *Maranatha*, 182–83.

5 For this prayer see Showers, *Maranatha*, 183.

29

IDENTIFYING THE ELECT

"And He will send forth His angels with a great trumpet and they will gather together His elect from the four winds, from one end of the sky to the other."

—Matthew 24:31

Many non-pretribulationists contend that Matthew 24:31 teaches a posttribulational rapture. All agree that this passage teaches a return of Christ. This means that the question revolves around whether Matthew 24:31 and the parallel passage of Mark 13:27 are references to the rapture. I contend that the rapture is not in view in this passage.

POSTTRIBULATIONAL POSITION

Posttribulationists such as Irwin Baxter, believe that the rapture and the second coming "are the same event" in Matthew 24:31. "Matthew 24:29 teaches that the coming of the Son of man and the rapture are the same event," contends Baxter.[1] He arrives at this conclusion by comparing Matthew 24:29–31 to Christ's return in Revelation 19. In the discussion cited, Baxter does not refer to 1 Thessalonians 4:13–18, the undisputed rapture passage, as a baseline for defining the rapture.

Posttribulational rapture scholar, Robert Gundry, also equates the rapture with the second coming in Matthew 24:31. "Posttribulationists," contends Gundry, "equate the rapture with the gathering of the elect by angels at the sound of the trumpet (Matt. 24:31)."[2] Unlike Baxter, Dr. Gundry does interact with the rapture passage (1 Thess. 4:13–18). He says, "If we define the rapture strictly as a catching up, only one passage in the entire New Testament describes it. That passage is 1 Thessalonians 4:13–18."[3]

DEFINITION OF THE RAPTURE

Baxter does not even attempt to define the rapture but Gundry includes in his definition of the rapture "a catching up" from 1 Thessalonians 4:13–18. Dr. Gundry wants to "broaden the definition to include a gathering or reception" from Matthew 24:31.[4] Because the present debate is whether or not Matthew 24:31 is a rapture passage, it would beg the question to include Matthew 24:31 in an *a priori* definition of the rapture.

1 Thessalonians 4:17 is the only undisputed passage describing the rapture event. Only in this passage is the Greek word *harpazô* ("caught up") used, from which the English word rapture descends. Whatever else the rapture may include in 1 Thessalonians 4:17, it clearly consists of a translation of living believers.

COMPARISON OF PASSAGES

In an attempt to equate Matthew 24:31 and 1 Thessalonians 4:17 as referring to the same event, Dr. Gundry notes "parallel terminology in Paul's Thessalonian discussion of the Church's rapture, where we read of a trumpet, clouds, and a gathering of believers just as in the Olivet Discourse."[5] Indeed, there are some similarities between the rapture and the second coming. There are also some similarities between Christ's first advent 2,000 years ago and His second advent. But they are not the same events. We know they are not the same because of the differences. It is the differences that are important when comparing Matthew 24:31 and 1 Thessalonians 4:17. Enough differences exist between the two passages to conclude that they must be separate events.

Dr. Steven McAvoy notes that "the differences between Paul's Thessalonian statements and Matthew 24:30–31 far outweigh any alleged similarities."[6] Quoting John A. Sproule, he writes:

> Where does Paul mention the darkening of the sun (Matt. 24:29), the moon not giving its light (Matt. 24:29), the stars falling from the sky (Matt. 24:29), the powers of the heavens being shaken (Matt. 24:29), all the tribes of the earth mourning (Matt. 24:30), all the world seeing the coming of the Son of Man (Matt. 24:30), or God sending forth angels (Matt. 24:31)?[7]

Feinberg also notes the dissimilarities between the two accounts:

> Notice what happens when you examine both passages carefully. In Matthew the Son of Man comes on the clouds, while in 1 Thessalonians 4 the ascending believers are in them. In Matthew the angels gather the elect; in 1 Thessalonians the Lord Himself (note the emphasis) gathers the believers. Thessalonians only speaks of the *voice* of the archangel. In the Olivet Discourse nothing is said about a resurrection, while in the latter text it is the central point. In the two passages the differences in what will take place prior to the appearance of Christ is striking. Moreover, the order of ascent is absent from Matthew in spite of the fact that it is the central part of the epistle.[8]

There are more differences than similarities.[9]

In addition to the above differences, the order of events are different between the two passages. In 1 Thessalonians 4, believers are gathered in the air and taken to heaven, while in Matthew 24 they are gathered after Christ's arrival to earth. "In order for Gundry to establish his view that Matthew 24:31 refers to the rapture, he must reconcile the dissimilarities; not simply point to a few similarities."[10] Thus, the differences in the two passages support the contention that they speak of two distinct events.

WHO ARE THE ELECT?

Though not all pretribulationists agree on the identity of the "elect,", I believe the "elect" in Matthew 24:31 is a reference to the Jewish remnant who will come to faith in the messiahship of Jesus during the tribulation period. Commentators recognize that "elect" "may refer to Israel, to the Church, or to both."[11] The context is the determinative factor in any attempt to discover which nuance the author intended. I believe that the contextual usage of Matthew supports the elect as a reference to Israel because of the Jewish orientation of the passage. "Such terms as the gospel of the kingdom (24:14), the holy place (24:15), the Sabbath (24:20), and the Messiah (24:23–24) indicate that Israel as a nation is in view,"[12] observes Dr. Stanley Toussaint. Dr. Renald Showers concludes the same:

> The elect are the faithful, believing Israelite remnant in contrast with the unbelieving sinners within the nation. In Isaiah 65:7–16 God drew a contrast between these two groups and their destinies. In verse 9 He called the believing remnant "mine Elect," and in verses 17–25 He indicated that in the future Millennium His elect remnant of the nation will be blessed greatly on the earth.[13]

Because the term "elect" is used three times in Matthew 24 (verses 22, 24, 31; see also Mark 13:20, 22, 27), it is most likely that the author uses it to refer to the same entity all three times. Dr. Steven McAvoy notes, "The rule of context precludes understanding 'elect' in 24:22, 24 as referring to Israel and then nine verses later as referring to the church. Without some indication of transition from one intended meaning to another 'elect' in 24:21 must mean the same as it does in 24:22, 24."[14]

THE ANGELIC GATHERING

Perhaps the most convincing reason why Matthew 24:31 should not be interpreted as a rapture statement is found in the fact that this verse includes citations from Old Testament passages, specifically Deuteronomy 30:4. These references clearly support the notion that this angelic gathering, which was predicted in the Older Testament, references a regathering of saved Jews who need to be returned to the land of Israel in which they will live for a thousand years during Christ's millennial kingdom. Instead, of using El Al Airlines, the Lord will use angelic carriers to transport His people back to their land. What is the support for this view? Dr. Arnold Fruchtenbaum says of the use of Old Testament citations in Matthew 24:31:

> The Matthew passage is a rather simple summary of all that the prophets had to say about the second facet of Israel's final restoration. Its purpose was to make clear that the world-wide regathering predicted by the prophets will be fulfilled only after the second coming.[15]

Dr. Renald Showers has done an excellent job collecting evidence and arguing for this view.[16] After noting that "from the four winds, from one end of the sky to the other" means that "the elect will be gathered from all over the world at Christ's coming,"[17] He provides three lines of proof for his view:

> First, because of Israel's persistent rebellion against God, He declared that He would scatter the Jews "into all the winds" (Ezek. 5:10, 12) or "toward all winds" (Ezek. 17:21). In Zechariah 2:6 God stated that He did scatter them abroad "as four winds of the heavens."...God did scatter the Jews all over the world.
>
> Next, God also declared that in the future Israel would be gathered from the east, west, north, and south, "from the ends of the earth" (Isa. 43:5–7). We should note that in the context of this promise, God called Israel His "chosen" (vv. 10, 20).
>
> ...Just as Jesus indicated that the gathering of His elect from the four directions of the world will take place in conjunction with "a great trumpet" (literal translation of the Greek text of Mt. 24:21), so Isaiah 27:13 teaches that the scattered children of Israel will be gathered to their homeland in conjunction with the blowing of "a great trumpet" (literal translation of the Hebrew)....

> Gerhard Friedrich wrote that in that future eschatological day "a great horn shall be blown (Is. 27:13)" and the exiled will be brought back by that signal. Again he asserted that in conjunction with the blowing of the great trumpet of Isaiah 27:13, "There follows the gathering of Israel and the return of the dispersed to Zion."
>
> It is significant to note that Isaiah 27:13, which foretells this future regathering of Israel, is the only specific reference in the Old Testament to a "great" trumpet.
>
> Although Isaiah 11:11–12 does not refer to a great trumpet, it is parallel to Isaiah 27:13 because it refers to the same regathering of Israel. In its context, this passage indicates that when the Messiah (a root of Jesse, vv. 1, 10) comes to rule and transform the world as an "ensign" (a banner), He will gather together the scattered remnant of His people Israel "from the four corners of the earth."[18]

What Jesus describes in Matthew 24 and Mark 13 is the Jewish ingathering that will fulfill the prophetic aspects of the Feast of Trumpets for the nation of Israel. In fact, as noted in the previous chapter, a prayer for this regathering of the children of Israel appears to this day in the Jewish Daily Prayer Book.[19]

CONCLUSION

It is quite clear that because the church is not mentioned in Matthew 24, verse 31 cannot be a reference to the rapture of the church. Instead, as one studies the context and Old Testament references that our Lord alludes to, it becomes quite clear that He speaks of an end time regathering of elect Israel in order to return them to the land for the millennial kingdom. At Christ's first coming he wept over Jerusalem and expressed His desire to gather Israel to Himself "the way a hen gathers her chicks under her wings, and you were unwilling" (Matt. 23:37). At His second coming, elect Israel will look upon Him whom they have pierced (Zech. 12:10) and say, "Blessed is He who comes in the name of the LORD!" (Ps. 118:26; Matt. 23:39).

ENDNOTES

1 This information is take from the web site of Irwin Baxter under the Question and Answer section dealing with the rapture. All subsequent quotes from Baxter are from the same source.

2 Robert H. Gundry, *The Church and the Tribulation* (Grand Rapids: Zondervan, 1973), 135.

3 Robert H. Gundry, *First the Antichrist: Why Christ Won't Come Before the Antichrist Does* (Grand Rapids: Baker, 1997), 71.

4 Gundry, *First the Antichrist*, 71.

5 Gundry, *The Church and the Tribulation*, 135.

6 Steven L. McAvoy, "A Critique of Robert Gundry's Posttribulationalism," Th.D. dissertation, Dallas Theological Seminary, 1986, 136.

7 McAvoy, 137 citing John A. Sproule, "An Exegetical Defense of Pretribulationism," Th. D. dissertation, Grace Theological Seminary, 1981, 53.

8 McAvoy, 137 citing Paul D. Feinberg, "Response: Paul D. Feinberg," in *The Rapture: Pre-, Mid-, or Posttribulational?* by Richard R. Reiter, ed. (Grand Rapids: Zondervan, 1984), 225.

9 McAvoy, "Critique of Gundry," 137.

10 McAvoy, "Critique of Gundry," 138.

11 Gundry, *The Church and the Tribulation*, 135.

12 Stanley D. Toussaint, *Behold The King: A Study of Matthew* (Portland: Multnomah, 1980), 277.

13 Renald Showers, *Maranatha: Our Lord, Come!* (Bellmawr, NJ: The Friends of Israel, 1995), 182.

14 McAvoy, "Critique of Gundry," 140–41.

15 Arnold Fruchtenbaum, *The Footsteps of the Messiah* (San Antonio: Ariel Press, 1982), 299.

16 For more information supporting this view see Showers, *Maranatha*, 181–84.

17 Showers, *Maranatha*, 182.

18 Showers, *Maranatha*, 182–83.

19 For this prayer see Showers, *Maranatha*, 183.

30

PARABLE OF THE FIG TREE

"Now learn the parable from the fig tree: when its branch has already become tender, and puts forth its leaves, you know that summer is near; even so you too, when you see all these things, recognize that He is near, right at the door. Truly I say to you, this generation will not pass away until all these things take place. Heaven and earth will pass away, but My words shall not pass away."

—Matthew 24:32–35

Upon completion of His discourse about the tribulation and second coming, Jesus provided five parables that illustrate and reinforce the point of what He had just taught. Because these parables are connected to Christ's preceding discourse, they provide important parabolic focus upon the eschatology lesson Jesus has just given. All five of the parables form a group. In other words, all the parables must refer to the same event, in this case, the teaching of verses 4 through 31. This means that it would not make sense to have the first parable refer to the destruction of Jerusalem in A.D. 70 and then have the final four relate to a still future return of Christ.

THE UNITY OF THE PARABLES

Partial preterist Kenneth Gentry believes that the first of these five parables relates to verses 4 through 31, which he thinks was fulfilled in A.D. 70.

However, he then takes the last four parables to refer to a still future second advent. "Following his prophecy of the Temple's demise the Lord turns to consider his glorious Second Advent (24:36ff)," Gentry declares. "He specifically says there will be no such signs of that distant event."[1] However, fellow preterist, Gary DeMar believes that the entire Olivet Discourse (all of Matthew 24 and 25) has already been fulfilled through the A.D. 70 event. DeMar notes:

> Similarly, there is little evidence that the "coming of the Son of Man" in Matthew 24:27, 30, 39, and 42 is different from the "coming of the Son of Man" in 25:31. Compare 25:31 with 16:27, a certain reference to the destruction of Jerusalem in A.D. 70.[2]

I have argued and shown throughout this exposition why none of Matthew 24:4–31 was fulfilled in the first century. However, I agree with DeMar that the entire Olivet Discourse in Matthew 24 and 25 refers to the same time period. Even though DeMar is wrong to see all of Christ's Discourse as past, he, nevertheless, has a more stable position than that of fellow preterist Gentry who wants to break the narrative between 24:35 (past) and 24:36 (future).

All five of the parables relate to Christ's teaching in the previous section of Matthew 24:4–31 and do not introduce a new theme in His teaching. The purpose of these parables is to drive home major lessons in light of the previous teaching. It would not make literary sense for Christ to teach something, as He did in verses 4–31, and then give parables or illustration of that teaching, as He does in verses 32–51, but shift topics in the second parable to another event that He, according to Gentry, has not yet introduced. It makes no literary sense. All five parables serve as illustrations for Christ's single teaching in verses 4 –31. Why would Jesus, the master teacher, confuse His students by introducing a whole new item during His parabolic session that He had not previously touched on during His teaching session? The coming and judgment of Matthew 25: 31–46 must refer to a future event since those judged "will go away into eternal punishment, but the righteous into eternal life" (25:46).

FIVE PARABOLIC ILLUSTRATIONS

The five parables or illustrations of Jesus in Matthew 24 are: first, the fig tree illustration (24:32–35); second, the days of Noah illustration (24:36–39); third, a comparison of two men and women illustration (24:40–41); fourth, the faithful house holder illustration (24:42–44); and fifth, the wise servant illustration (24:45–51).

These parables are important lessons that relate to Israel. In fact, I would go so far as to say that all the parables in the New Testament relate directly to Israel. They often relate to Israel's rejection of Jesus as their Messiah and speak of consequences that will flow from such an act. Christ told His disciples in Matthew 13:10–17 that He would speak to "this people" (Israel) in order to blind them to the truth because of their rejection of Jesus as the Messiah. However, believers could come to understand the meaning of His parables because we are receptive of the revelation offered by Christ. Therefore, they all relate to Israel in some way and usually teach something about God's plan for the future.

The parables within the Olivet Discourse, when they speak of a coming, all relate to the second coming and not the rapture of the church. The entire Olivet Discourse was given to Israel and relates to her tribulation and Christ's return at the end of that period. Truths relating to the rapture of the church are revealed exclusively in the New Testament Epistles, which were written specifically for the purpose of explaining the intent and nature of the church age. The only exception to this is Christ's initial unveiling of the church's hope in the Upper Room Discourse (John 14:1–3) given shortly before His death.

THE FIG TREE ILLUSTRATION

The first of the parables, the lesson of the fig tree illustration, is a widely-noted passage. For example, my good friend Hal Lindsey teaches that the fig tree represents Israel, which it might, and that this means that within a generation of the founding of the modern state of Israel, Christ will return. In his famous book *The Late Great Planet Earth* (which was my first significant exposure to prophecy in 1970), Lindsay writes:

> But the most important sign in Matthew has to be the restoration of the Jews to the land in the rebirth of Israel. Even the figure of speech "fig tree" has been a historic symbol of national Israel. When the Jewish people, after nearly 2,000 years of exile, under relentless persecution, became a nation again on 14 May 1948 the "fig tree" put forth its first leaves.
>
> Jesus said that this would indicate that He was "at the door," ready to return. Then He said, "Truly I say to you, *this generation* will not pass away until all these things take place" (Matthew 24:34 NASB).
>
> What generation? Obviously, in context, the generation that would see the signs—chief among them the rebirth of Israel. A generation in the Bible is something like forty years. If this is a correct deduction, then within forty years or so of 1948, all these things could take place. Many scholars who have studied Bible prophecy all their lives believe that this is so.[3]

I agree with so much of what Lindsey teaches in the area of Bible prophecy, but on this particular passage I have to disagree with him, even though I previously held this view in the 1970s. I agree that the fig tree is sometimes used as a symbol for national Israel (see Judges 9:10–11; Jer. 8:13; Hosea 9:10; Hab. 3:17; Hag. 2:19; Matt. 21:19; Mark 11:13, 20–21; Luke 13:6–7). However, whether or not the "fig tree" is a symbol for Israel is not what a proper understanding of this passage turns upon. That is a non-issue when it comes to interpreting this passage. I also agree with Lindsey that the establishment of Israel as a nation in 1948 is prophetically significant and indicates that we are likely near the beginning of the tribulation, but I don't think that the parable of the fig tree is support for such a view.

The basic problem with Lindsey's view is that he takes the parable of Jesus and turns this illustration into a prophecy. Christ is simply illustrating that when one sees a fig tree begin to produce leaves (in the spring), then you know that the next season is approaching (summer). (In Luke's version of the same teaching, Christ says in 21:29, "Behold the fig tree and all the trees.") Christ then concludes, "even so you too, when you see all these things, recognize that He is near, right at the door." In the context, our Lord does not put an emphasis upon Israel as a symbol. He is saying that when you see the events of the seven-year tribulation take place then you know that His second advent is near.

Those who hold the view that the fig tree refers to Israel in this passage have taken Christ's illustration, which was meant to demonstrate a point about verses 24:4–31, and created a prophecy out it that does not exist. The prophecy that they create is that Christ's coming will occur 40 years after the founding of the modern state of Israel. Christ's illustration was not intended to be a prophecy about anything; it is an illustration about the preceding context. It should be clear by now that such a view is wrong, especially since we are many years beyond his 40-year prediction. Therefore, it does not matter how long a "generation" is, since the events of 4 through 31 will take place within a seven-year period. The generation that sees the events of the seven-year tribulation will not pass away (in other words, it will not take hundreds of years or a long time) until Christ's second coming (see 24:33). This first parable emphasizes the point through illustration what Christ said in 24:29–30: "But immediately after the tribulation of those days...they will see the Son of Man coming."

CONCLUSION

What is the lesson to be learned from the parable of the fig tree? It is that when a fig tree reaches a certain stage in the seasonal cycle (in this case, produces leaves) then one knows that they have reached a certain time of the year (in this case, that summer is near). A parable is a lesson of comparisons, moving from the known in order to explain the unknown. In this instance the leaves before summer would refer to the events of the tribulation as outlined by Christ in verses 4–31. Thus, when one sees these events, they are to know that Christ's return is near, "right at the door" (24:33). How is it that they know that Christ's advent is near? They will know because "this generation will not pass away until all these things take place" (24:34). In other words, that time period of events culminating in Christ's return will not exceed seven years. One day "heaven and earth will pass away, but My words shall not pass away" (24:35). Christ's words will be fulfilled; they will not simply pass away and go unfulfilled.

ENDNOTES

1 Kenneth L. Gentry, Jr., *Perilous Times: A Study in Eschatological Evil* (Texarkana, AR: Covenant Media Press, 1999), 89.

2 Gary DeMar, *Last Days Madness: Obsession of the Modern Church* (Powder Springs, GA: American Vision, 1999), 200.

3 Hal Lindsey, *The Late Great Planet Earth* (Grand Rapids: Zondervan, 1970), 53–54.

31

INTERPRETING "THIS GENERATION"

"Truly I say to you, this generation will not pass away until all these things take place."

—Matthew 24:34

Preterism teaches that most, if not all, of the Book of Revelation and the Olivet Discourse (Matt. 24–25; Mark 13; Luke 21) were fulfilled in conjunction with the destruction of Jerusalem by the Romans in A.D. 70. If this notion is granted, then almost all of Bible prophecy is not to be anticipated in the future, but is history. Their false scheme stems from a misinterpretation of Matthew 24:34 (see also Mark 13:30; Luke 21:32), by which they launch an upside-down view of eschatology, which does not look to the future but instead, gazes at the past.

PRETERIST VIEW

Preterist Gary DeMar says, "the generation that was in existence when Jesus addressed His disciples would not pass away until all the events that preceded verse 34 came to pass."[1] In contrast with fellow preterist, Kenneth Gentry, DeMar believes that this passage requires that all of Matthew 24 and 25 must have been fulfilled in some way by A.D. 70 through the Roman invasion and destruction of Jerusalem and the Temple.[2] DeMar says, "Every time 'this generation' is used in the New Testament, it means, without exception, the generation to whom Jesus was speaking."[3] But DeMar's assertion is simply not true. "This generation" in Hebrews 3:10 clearly refers to the generation of Israelites that wandered in the wilderness for 40 years during the Exodus.

Preterist, Hank Hanegraaff takes a similar position in his novel *The Last Disciple*, when the character Caleb says, "I want it remembered that we have all agreed that the truth of the prophecies of Jesus on the Mount of Olives is meaningless unless *all* the events He predicted occur, not just some."[4] The narrative in the novel supports a first-century fulfillment of Christ's prophetic discourse in a manner commonly espoused by preterists.[5] "When Jesus says 'this generation,' He doesn't mean 'that generation,'..." declared Hanegraaff in an interview. "This was the archetypal tribulation and it took place in the first century."[6]

CONTEXT MATTERS

But how do we know that almost all of the other New Testament uses of "this generation" refer to Christ's contemporaries? We learn this by going and examining how each is used in its context. For example, Mark 8:12 says, "And sighing deeply in His spirit [Jesus is speaking], He said, 'Why does this generation seek for a sign? Truly I say to you, no sign shall be given to this generation.'" Why do we conclude that "this generation," in this passage refers to Christ's contemporaries? We know this because the referent in this passage is to Christ's contemporaries, who were seeking for a sign from Jesus. Thus, it refers to Christ's contemporaries, because of the controlling factor of the immediate context.

When interpreting the Bible you cannot just say, as DeMar and many preterists do, that because something means X...Y...Z in other passages that it has to mean that in a given verse.[7] Rather, you must make your determination from the passage under discussion and how it is used in that particular context. Context is the most important factor in determining the exact meaning or referent under discussion.[8] That is how one is able to realize that most of the other uses of "this generation" refer to Christ's contemporaries.

Jesus says in Matthew 23:36, "Truly I say to you, all these things shall come upon this generation." To whom does "this generation" refer? In this context, "this generation" refers to Christ's contemporaries because of contextual support. "This generation" is governed or controlled grammatically by the phrase "all these things." All these things refer to the judgments that Christ pronounces in Matthew 22–23. We should now realize that in each instance of "this generation," the use is determined by what it modifies in its immediate context. The scope of use of every occurrence of this generation is determined in the same way.

The same is true for Hebrews 3:10, which reads, "Therefore I was angry with this generation." "This generation" is governed or controlled grammatically by the contextual reference to those who wandered in the wilderness for forty years during the Exodus.

CONTEXT AND VERSE 34

Why does "this generation" in Matthew 24:34 (see also Mark 13:30; Luke 21:32) not refer to Christ's contemporaries? Because the governing referent to "this generation" is "all these things." Because Jesus is giving an extended prophetic discourse of future events, one must first determine the nature of "all these things" prophesied in verses 4 through 31 to know what generation Christ is referencing. Because "all these things" did not occur in the first century, the generation that Christ speaks of must be future. Christ is saying that the generation that sees "all these things" occur will not cease to exist until all the events of the future tribulation are fulfilled. This is a literal interpretation and one that was not fulfilled in the first century. Christ is not ultimately speaking to His contemporaries, but to the generation to whom the signs of Matthew 24 will become evident. Dr. Darrell Bock concurs:

> What Jesus is saying is that the generation that sees the beginning of the end, also sees its end. When the signs come, they will proceed quickly; they will not drag on for many generations. It will happen within a generation.... The tradition reflected in Revelation shows that the consummation comes very quickly once it comes.... Nonetheless, in the discourse's prophetic context, the remark comes after making comments about the nearness of the end *to certain signs.*

> As such it is the issue of the signs that controls the passage's force, making this view likely. If this view is correct, Jesus says that when the signs of the beginning of the end come, then the end will come relatively quickly, within a generation.[9]

Preterists have *reversed* the interpretative process by declaring first that "this generation" *has* to refer to Christ's contemporaries, thus all these things had to be fulfilled in the first century. When one points out that various events in Matthew 24 were not fulfilled, preterists merely repeat their mantra of "this generation," saying that all these things had to be fulfilled in the first century. Yet, when one compares the use of "this generation" at the beginning of the Olivet Discourse in Matthew 23:36 (which is an undisputed reference to A.D. 70) with the prophetic use in Matthew 24:34, a contrast seems obvious. Jesus is contrasting the *deliverance* for Israel in Matthew 24:34 with the predicted *judgment* of Matthew 23:36.

As a futurist with respect to Bible prophecy, I do not think that any of the events in Matthew 24:4–31 occurred in the first century. We have seen in earlier commentary on Matthew 24:4–31 that none of these events took place in the past, thus, this is still a future time of which our Lord speaks.

PROPHETIC PERSPECTIVE

It is common for preterists to speak of what they call "audience relevance." By this, preterists believe that since the New Testament was written in the first century, it then has to relate and apply directly to the original audience. "The original audience factor cannot be overlooked; the message of Revelation must be relevant to them,"[10] proclaims Kenneth Gentry. "With the particularity of the audience emphasized in conjunction with his message of the imminent expectation of occurrence of the events," continues Gentry, "I do not see how preterism of some sort can be escaped."[11] The same logic is often applied to the Olivet Discourse. E. B Elliott notes, "Not a vestige of testimony exists to the fact of such an understanding."[12] Such a notion is pure assumption and if true would render it impossible for Scripture to provide a prophetic statement beyond the generation (40 years) that received the prediction.

I believe that Jesus uses the phrase "this generation" in Matthew 24:34 as a means of literary emphasis. As noted earlier, Jesus is contrasting the *deliverance* for Israel in Matthew 24:34 with the predicted *judgment* of Matthew 23:36, based upon the varied responses of two different generations of Israelites. This provides the basis for Christ's contrast of the two generations—the first generation unbelieving while the final one is trusting. Randall Price writes of "this generation" and its meaning:

> The future sense of "this generation" in a judgment context sets a precedence for its interpretation in contexts that are both judicial and eschatological. If the desolation experienced by "this generation" in Matthew 23:36 can be understood as a future fulfillment that came some 40 years later, it should not be a problem to understood the Tribulation judgment as a future fulfillment that will come on the generation that will experience it at the end of the age. However, the difference is not simply a span of time, but the nature of that time as eschatological. For the "this generation" of Matthew 24:34, Mark 13:30, and Luke 21:32, "all these things" (Matthew 24:34; Mark 13:30; Luke 21:28) must refer contextually to the events of the "Great Tribulation," the conclusion of "the times of the Gentiles," the coming of Christ in glory, and the regathering and redemption of Israel, all of which are not only declared to be future by Jesus at the time of speaking (Mark 13:23), but also cast in typical eschatological language (for example, "end of the age," "such as not occurred since the beginning of the world until now, *nor ever shall*," "powers of the heavens will be shaken").[13]

Instead of audience relevance, it important to know the prophetic relevance from which a prophecy is given. This means that sometimes a prophetic revelation is spoken from the timeframe of when a prophecy will take place. Such is often the case in Revelation (e.g, 21:9–10). John is often shown a vision of the future and thus he speaks from the perspective as if those future events were taking place at the time in which he is observing them and writing them down. Jesus is speaking in His Olivet Discourse in verse 34 of Matthew from the timeframe of a still future time and is saying "this generation."

We see the same kind of thing going on in Psalm 2:7, where the Father says of the Son, "Thou art my Son; *this day* have I begotten thee." This passage speaks of the Father's incarnation of the Son, which interpreters believe occurred at Christ's first coming. Yet David wrote this Psalm a thousand years earlier. An audience relevance assumption would surely lead to a gross misinterpretation of this prophetic Psalm. Looking at the Psalm as one that is speaking from a timeframe of the distant future is the only way that it makes contextual sense. The same is true of Christ's statement about "this generation" in His Olivet Discourse. He is speaking from the timeframe of the distant future.

ENDNOTES

1 Gary DeMar, *End Times Fiction: A Biblical Consideration of the Left Behind Theology* (Nashville: Thomas Nelson Publishers, 2001), 67–68.

2 Gary DeMar, *Last Days Madness: Obsession of the Modern Church* (Powder Springs, GA: American Vision, 1999), 198–201.

3 DeMar, *End Times Fiction*, 68.

4 Hank Hanegraaff and Sigmund Brouwer, *The Last Disciple* (Wheaton: Tyndale House Publishers, 2004), 93.

5 Hanegraaff and Brouwer, *Disciple*, 92–96. Matthew 24:34 is featured in a two-page layout following the acknowledgments connoting a preterist interpretation. Preterism is also clearly communicated in the "Afterword" on page 395.

6 Hank Hanegraaff on the preterist radio program "Voice of Reason," (November 21, 2004) on the Internet at www.lighthouseproductionsllc.com/broadcast.htm.

7 See D. A. Carson, *Exegetical Fallacies* (Grand Rapids: Baker, 1984), 65.

8 See Roy B. Zuck, *Basic Bible Interpretation: A Practical Guide to Discovering Biblical Truth* (Wheaton, IL: Victor Books, 1991), 106–09.

9 Darrell L. Bock, *Luke 9:51–24:53* (Grand Rapids: Baker, 1996), 1691–92.

10 Kenneth L. Gentry, Jr., *He Shall Have Dominion: A Postmillennial Eschatology* (Tyler, TX: Institute for Christian Economics, 1992), 396.

11 Gentry, *He Shall Have Dominion*, 397.

12 E. B. Elliott, *Horae Apocalypticae*, revised edition, 4 vols. (London: Seeleys, 1851), vol. iv, 535.

13 J. Randall Price, "Historical Problems with a First-Century Fulfillment of the Olivet Discourse," in LaHaye and Ice, editors, *End Times Controversy: The Second Coming Under Attack* (Eugene, OR: Harvest House, 2003), 379–80.

32

THE TEMPORAL AND THE ETERNAL

"Heaven and earth will pass away, but My words shall not pass away. But of that day and hour no one knows, not even the angels of heaven, nor the Son, but the Father alone."

—Matthew 24:35–36

Jesus said in verse 34 that "this generation will not pass away until all these things take place." Now, in verse 35, He speaks of one thing that will pass away and another thing that will not pass away. The passing away in verse 34 would not happen *until* "all these things take place." In verse 35 Christ does not mention *until* but issues a pronouncement concerning two things—"heaven and earth," and "My words."

HEAVEN AND EARTH WILL PASS AWAY

Verse 35 begins with the word pair "heavens and earth." There can be little doubt that this phrase refers back to Genesis 1:1, which says, "In the beginning God created the heavens and the earth." Allen Ross explains:

> What God created is here called "the heavens and the earth," a poetic expression (merism) signifying the whole universe. Other examples of this poetic device are "day and night" (meaning all the time) and "man and beast" (meaning all created physical beings). "Heaven and

> earth" thus indicates not only the heaven and the earth but everything in them. Genesis 2:4 also uses this expression in a restatement of the work of creation throughout the six days."[1]

The Greek word for "pass away" is *parerchomai* and has the general meaning of "come up to," "pass by," and "pass away."[2] In this context it has the connotation of "pass away." What does this mean? Ed Glasscock observes:

> Once the unveiling of this "great tribulation" (v. 21) begins, that generation will not pass away until everything is brought to completion. To add weight to what He had just said, the Lord added the proclamation that His words were more lasting than even the universe itself. The heaven and the earth will be taken away, but what He has proclaimed will last eternally.[3]

The verb "pass away" and the double negative *ou me* both occur in 24:34 and carry the same force in both references.

PRETERIST FOLLY

Amazingly, in spite of such a clear statement by our Lord, many full preterists[4] teach that heaven and earth will not pass away. For example full preterist John Anderson states, "the world will last forever, it will never be destroyed."[5] So what do they do with passages such as Matthew 24:35? Full preterist Don Preston writes:

> When he spoke of his coming on the clouds with power and great glory, Jesus was not using literal language. He was, in the established manner of Israel's prophets, using hyperbole to describe the coming judgment on Israel. And in light of the consistent figurative application of the passing of heaven and earth to the destruction of a nation, we can better understand that when Jesus said "heaven and earth will pass" Mat. 24:35, he was responding to the disciples' questions about *the destruction of Jerusalem*, Mat. 24:2. The focus was on the *world of Israel*, not on material creation.[6] (italics original)

Even if it can be established that, in general, the Old Testament prophets used language as Preston claims (which is debatable), there is no basis for using it as he says in the specific instance of Matthew 24:35. I don't think it can be demonstrated lexically that there is a single instance where "heaven and earth" is ever used in a hyperbolic, non-literal way, as claimed by Preston. Preston's conclusion is the product of assertion and not exegesis. The only motive for taking such a view is not a consequence of the study of the biblical text but is driven by his preterist assumption.

When one examines the 36 uses of "heaven and earth" in the Bible, there is not a single possible instance of it occurring as a "figurative application of the passing of heaven and earth to the destruction of a nation." With four exceptions (Deut. 4:26; 30:19; 31:28; Jer. 51:48), every use of "heaven and earth" refers to God's physical creation as in Genesis 1:1.[7] These other four instances use "heaven and earth" as angelic and human witnesses. For example, "I call heaven and earth to witness against you today,..." in Deuteronomy 30:19. This is clearly nothing like the allegorical understanding that Preston suggests.

Because the basis for saying that "heaven and earth" does not have a physical understanding in Matthew 24:35 has (no lexical basis), nor support from the context, the full preterist view should be rejected as erroneous, in fact, in serious error. The preterist interpretation not only nullifies the actual meaning of this passage, but would also distort parallel passages (Mark 13:31; Luke 21:33), but also similar passages like Matthew 5:18 and Luke 16:17. If the preterist misunderstanding of this passage were true, Luke 16:17 would read as follows: "But it is easier for *the world of Israel* to pass away than for one stroke of a letter of the Law to fail." This is such an absurd view that it is clear that the preterist mythology cannot stand in light of exegesis of the text.

CHRIST'S WORDS WILL NOT PASS AWAY

This passage states that, "heaven and earth *will* pass away" one day, but in contrast, Christ's words "shall not pass away." In order to strengthen the emphasis upon the impossibility of His words passing away, Christ uses not one, but two Greek words that mean "not," (grouped together), to say that something will not happen. "The double negative *ou me* with the subjunctive is the usual form for the emphatic negation," notes Randolph Yeager.[8] Lenski agrees and says that *ou me* is used "all-inclusively" and calls it "the strongest negation."[9]

Because Jesus speaks in such an authoritative way, He identifies Himself with Old Testament prophets such as Isaiah (40:8) and Zechariah (1:1–6). Christ's statement of the certainty of the fulfillment of His prophetic word can only mean that He has the stamp of God's approval on His ministry. Arno Gaebelein elucidates as follows:

> Yeah heaven and earth may pass away but *His Words* will not pass away. How solemn this is! Here we read still the same great and mighty Words, which were hated by thousands of God's enemies in the past; words which have been attacked and denied. And still the old enemy of the written Word is at it, and through his chosen instruments (alas! many of them in the midst of the professing church) attacks and belittles these Words. They stand! They are as eternal and divine, as infallible and true, as He, the eternal Son of God, is from whose lips they came.[10]

THE DAY AND THE HOUR

At least six passages (eight if parallel passages are included) in the New Testament specifically warn believers against date setting in relation to the second coming and the rapture. It is impossible to set the date of the time of the rapture because it is a signless, yet imminent event. How can anyone even come up with a scheme for datesetting the rapture since we are told to always be waiting for Christ's any-moment return in the air? This explains why rapture date-setters have never used rapture passages as a basis for their date-setting schemes. There is no basis in rapture passages to attempt what is forbidden. These speculators invariably go to passages related to Israel (rather than the church), or passages that confuse the second coming with the rapture.

It is enough for something to be stated only once in the Bible for it to be true, but when God says something many times the emphasis should make such assertions even clearer. Below are specific passages showing these important biblical admonitions:

- Matthew 24:36: "*But of that day and hour no one knows, not even the angels of heaven, nor the Son, but the Father alone.* Mark 13:32 is an exact parallel.

- Matthew 24:42: "*Therefore be on the alert, for you do not know which day your Lord is coming.*

- Matthew 24:44: "*For this reason you be ready too; for the Son of Man is coming at an hour when you do not think He will.*

- Matthew 25:13: "*Be on the alert then, for you do not know the day nor the hour.* Mark 13:33–37 is a parallel passage.

- Acts 1:7: *He said to them, "It is not for you to know times or epochs which the Father has fixed by His own authority;*

- 1 Thessalonians 5:1–2: *Now as to the times and the epochs, brethren, you have no need of anything to be written to you. For you yourselves know full well that the day of the Lord will come just like a thief in the night.*

These passages are absolute prohibitions against date setting. They do not teach that it was impossible to know the date in the early church, but in the last days some would come to know it. They do not say that no one knows the day or the hour, except those who are able to figure it out through some scheme. Rather, the date of Christ's coming is a matter of God's revelation and He has chosen not to reveal it even to Christ in His humanity during His first advent (Mt. 24:36).

The Bible teaches that God's Word is sufficient for everything needed to live a life pleasing unto Christ (2 Tim. 3:16–17; 2 Pet. 1:3–4). This means that if something is not revealed for us in the Bible then it is not needed to accomplish God's plan for our lives. The date of Christ's return is not stated in the Bible, therefore, in spite of what some may say, knowing it is not important for living a godly life. The Lord told Israel "The secret things belong to the Lord our God, but the things revealed belong to us and to our sons forever, that we may observe all the words of this law" (Deut. 29:29). The date of Christ's coming has not been revealed, thus it is a secret belonging only to God.

CONCLUSION

At least two things always occur when one mishandles a biblical text: First, the passage at hand is distorted and one does not learn the lesson intended by the author. Second, a wrong understanding produces a false teaching that would not surface but for the incorrect handling of a given passage.

From this passage we know: that heaven and earth will one day pass away, or as a friend of mine used to say, "its all going to burn" (2 Pet. 3:10). We also equally know that God's Word is inerrant, infallible and trustworthy. It will most certainly come to pass. This is the basis upon which prophecy is built and for that all Bible-believing Christians can be grateful.

ENDNOTES

1 Allen P. Ross, *Creation & Blessing: A Guide to the Study and Exposition of Genesis* (Grand Rapids: Baker Book House, 1988), 106.

2 Horst Balz and Gerhard Schneider, editors, *Exegetical Dictionary of the New Testament*, 3 vols. (Grand Rapids: Eerdmans, 1993), 3: 38.

3 Ed Glasscock, *Moody Gospel Commentary: Matthew* (Chicago: Moody Press, 1997), 475.

4 Full preterists teach that all Bible prophecy has been fulfilled in the past and there will be no future second advent of Christ.

5 See the following website: http://www.lighthouseproductionsllc.com/broadcast.htm

6 Don K. Preston, *Into All The World: Then Comes The End* (Ardmore, OK: Don K. Preston, 1996), 90–91.

7 Based upon searching the computer program *Accordance*, version 6.4, the following references to the physical creation as in Genesis 1:1 are as follows: Gen. 1:1; 14:19, 22; Ex. 20:11; 31:17; 2 Sam. 18:9; 2 Ki. 19:15; 2 Chron. 2:12; Ezra 5:11; Psalm 69:34; 115:15; 121:2; 124:8; 134:3; 146:6; Isa. 37:16; Jer. 23:24; 32:17; 33:25; Haggai 2:6, 21; Matt. 5:18; 11:25; 24:35; Mark 13:31; Luke 10:21; 16:17; 21:33; Acts 4:24; 13:15; 17:24; Rev. 14:7.

8 Randolph O. Yeager, *The Renaissance New Testament*, 18 vols. (Bowling Green, KY: Renaissance Press, 1978), 3:322.

9 R. C. H. Lenski, *The Interpretation of St Matthew's Gospel*, (Minneapolis: Augsburg, 1943), 953.

10 Arno C. Gaebelein, *The Gospel of Matthew: An Exposition* (Neptune, NJ: Loizeaux Brothers, [1910] 1961), 514.

33

"LIKE THE DAYS OF NOAH"

"But of that day and hour no one knows, not even the angels of heaven, nor the Son, but the Father alone. For the coming of the Son of Man will be just like the days of Noah. For as in those days which were before the flood they were eating and drinking, they were marrying and giving in marriage, until the day that Noah entered the ark, and they did not understand until the flood came and took them all away; so shall the coming of the Son of Man be."

—Matthew 24:36–39

With the prohibition clearly stated against attempts to date-set regarding His return, our Lord says that no one knows the time of His return, not the angels nor the Son, but only the Father. But, what does this mean in light of the fact that Matthew 24:4–31 speaks concerning the tribulation period that is seven 360-day years, divided at the midpoint by the abomination of desolation? In other words, alert believers in the tribulation should be able to know the exact day of the second coming. I believe that believers in the tribulation will indeed be able to know the day of Christ's return because Luke 21:28 says, "But when these things begin to take place, straighten up and lift up your heads, because your redemption is drawing near." Also, Matthew 24:34 is a time-related statement saying that the generation that sees "all these things," (i.e., the events of the seven-year tribulation) will not pass away until Christ returns. So what does Matthew 24:36 mean in light of these things?

NO ONE KNOWS

In this passage Jesus is referred to as "the Son." When the New Testament uses terms such as "the Son," or "the Son of Man," as occurs in the next verse, it stresses His humanity and the incarnation. This passage does not say, "that no man will ever know. This He did not say."[1] I agree with most commentators that this passage is saying that in His incarnation as the Son of Man it was not given to Him (or revealed to Him) the time of His return. I am sure that He knows the day and the hour upon His return to heaven. John MacArthur notes the following:

> Therefore, even on this last day before His arrest, the Son did not know the precise day and hour He would return to earth at His second coming. During Christ's incarnation, the Father alone exercised unrestricted divine omniscience.[2]

Ed Glasscock echoes this understanding: "The Lord did not attempt to display His deity but rather, in contrast, emphasized His humanity. As an obedient servant in His humanity, Jesus did not know the day or the hour of His return."[3]

In essence, Jesus is saying that He was not telling them at that time when He was returning. However, this does not mean that those at a future time would not be able to know when He was returning. Yeager says: "The thought of the context is that at the time that Jesus spoke this to His disciples, and even yet now, at the current writing, nobody knows the day and the hour."[4] It is not until after the rapture, when one is in the tribulation that God's prophetic clock will resume ticking. For believers living during that time they will be able to know at least the day when Christ will return to earth.

"THE DAYS OF NOAH"

In the second illustration following His Olivet Discourse (24:4–31) Jesus announces a parabolic comparison between His second coming and that of the days of Noah (24:37). While not specifically called one in the passage, it has the distinctives of a parabolic comparison. "The coming of the Son of Man will be *just like* the days of Noah" (emphasis added). Christ is making a comparison between His return (24:36) and the antediluvian days of Noah.

The passage says that the second coming of Christ will be *just like* the days of Noah. The word order in the original language reads as follows: "For just as the days of Noah, in this way is the coming of the Son of Man." The intensive particle "just as," *osper,* is a "marker of similarity between events and states."[5] When combined with the demonstrative adverb "in this way," *houtos,* Christ is saying that the days of Noah were exactly the same as will be the time of Christ's return.

Does this mean that there is an extensive list of items that can be compared with the days of Noah? I do not think so. There is a single point that Christ emphasizes in each of the parables that He gives. In this one it is preparedness. "The likeness is seen in the suddenness of the coming of the judgment and the unpreparedness of the world for it," declares Toussaint.[6] Similarly, Daniel Harrington observes, "The point of the comparison between the days of Noah and the coming of the Son of Man is the unexpectedness of the crisis.... So unexpected was the flood that people did not recognize it until it had already come upon them."[7]

On more than one occasion the New Testament compares the second coming to the flood in Noah's days (Luke 17:26–27; 2 Pet. 2:4–11), as well as to other judgments such as the days of Lot (Luke 17:28–30). The central point found in these passages is that unbelievers were not prepared for God's judgment. This is the same idea that Christ is teaching in this passage as well.

EATING AND DRINKING

The teaching on the lack of preparedness is then reinforced by the examples that our Lord cites. The Greek word used here for "eating," *trogo,* is not the word normally used. It means, "to bite or chew food, *eat* (audibly), of animals...chew, nibble, munch."[8] It is only used six times in the Greek New Testament; the other five uses are all found in John, usually of symbolically eating Christ's flesh. The normal New Testament Greek word for "eating," which is used in the parallel passage (Luke 17:27), is *esthio.* It occurs

158 times in the Greek New Testament and means, "to take something in through the mouth, usually solids, but also liquids, *eat*."[9] What's the point? The point appears to be "implying luxurious living."[10] The unprepared of that day will be so absorbed in pleasing themselves, or said another way, chomping on food, that they miss the fact that they are living in extraordinary times that would justify the abandoning the normal routines of life. Alfred Plummer explains as follows:

> The special point of the analogy is not that the generation that was swept away by the Flood was exceptionally wicked; none of the occupations mentioned are sinful; but that it was so absorbed in its worldly pursuits that it paid no attention to solemn warnings. Instead of saying: "It is certain to come; therefore we must make preparation and be always on the watch," they said: "No one knows when it will come; therefore there is no need to trouble oneself about it yet. Others matters are much more urgent."[11]

The events that Christ had just described (the tribulation in 24:4–31) should evoke concern about God's plan for history. Instead, the unbelievers want to continue their own pursuits of their daily routines. Robert Govett explains: "The love of the world is displayed by men's being given over to eating and drinking. Had they believed the message of wrath just about to come, they would have fasted and wept."[12] A desire for the status quo is a manifestation of unpreparedness.

MARRYING AND GIVING IN MARRIAGE

While "eating and drinking" relates to daily unpreparedness, "marrying and giving in marriage" illustrates unpreparedness concerning one's long-range perspective. Marriage is certainly an institution ordained of God that is good in-and-of itself, but the point here is that one should not be engaged in long-ranged planning while unprepared for impending judgment. Meyer observes that it is "descriptive of a mode of life without concern, and without any foreboding of an impending catastrophe."[13] Just as it would make no sense to plan a marriage in the days of Noah leading up to the Flood if one was unprepared to face God's judgment, in the same way, it makes no sense to plan for marriage in the face of the events of the tribulation that will lead up to the second coming of Christ.

In the days of Noah, Noah had been preaching concerning the coming judgment of God (2 Pet. 2:5), yet no one, other than Noah's family paid attention to his message. Instead, they went about business as usual, ignoring the warnings of God's Word. Govett captures the sense well, stating:

> Hence these pursuits are spoken of, not as evil in themselves, but as they practically give the lie to the warnings of God. These are only reasonable, so long as the present scene is to go on as it is. The accumulating property, when both life, property, and posterity are to be destroyed, is folly.[14]

These practices by the unprepared ceased "the day that Noah entered the ark," just as they will cease in the future when Christ returns.

THEY DID NOT UNDERSTAND

Perhaps the most sobering statement in this passage is that "they did not understand." They did not put two and two together, Jesus said, "*until* the flood came and took them all away." Jesus then said, "so shall the coming of the Son of Man be." Here we have a similar construction that we saw in verse 37, which is the "marker of similarity between events and states."[15]

Not only should similarities be noted, but it is also important to see contrasts as well. It is important to note that the rejecters of God's Word, who "did not understand," in verse 39 is juxtaposed with the admonition to believers in verse 33, which says, "even so you too, when you see all these things, recognize that He is near, right at the door." The Greek verb *ginosko* is used in both passages and translated "recognize" in verse 33 and "understand" in verse 39. This Greek word has the meaning in these contexts of "to grasp the significance or meaning of something, understand, comprehend."[16] The difference between the one who understands and the one who does not is based upon who accepts God's Word and who does not accept it.

Actually, verse 39 does say that they, the unbelievers, did come to understand these things. However, their understanding did not come *until* the flood came and took them all away. This is one of the many things that separates believers from unbelievers. Believers accept God's Word before an event occurs because they trust Him and His prophetic word. On the other hand, an unbeliever has to be shown these things through experience, in this case, a very bad experience. What about you? Do you trust God and His Word because He says it, or are you one who has to be shown things from experience? There is a big difference between the two.

ENDNOTES

1 Randolph O. Yeager, *The Renaissance New Testament* (Bowling Green: Renaissance Press, 1978), Vol. 3, 324.

2 John MacArthur, *The New Testament Commentary: Matthew 24–28* (Chicago: Moody Press, 1989), 72.

3 Ed Glasscock, *Matthew: Moody Gospel Commentary* (Chicago: Moody Press, 1997), 476.

4 Yeager, *Renaissance*, Vol. 2, p. 326.

5 Walter Bauer, William F. Arndt, and F. Wilbur Gingrich, *A Greek-English Lexicon of the New Testament and Other Early Christian Literature*, 3d ed., rev. Frederick W. Danker (Chicago: University of Chicago Press, 2000),1106. (abbreviated as *BDAG*)

6 Stanley D. Toussaint, *Behold The King: A Study of Matthew* (Portland: Multnomah Press, 1980), 280.

7 Daniel J. Harrington, *Sacra Pagina: The Gospel of Matthew* (Collegeville, MN: The Liturgical Press, 1991), 342.

8 *BDAG*, 1019.

9 *BDAG*, 396.

10 A. Carr, *Cambridge Greek Testament for Schools and Colleges. The Gospel According to St. Matthew* (Cambridge: At The University Press, 1896), 273.

11 Alfred Plummer, *An Exegetical Commentary on the Gospel According to S. Matthew*, 2nd edition (Minneapolis: James Family, n.d.), 340.

12 Robert Govett, *The Prophecy on Olivet* (Miami Springs, FL: Conley & Schoettle Publishing Co., [1881] 1985), 95.

13 Heinrich August Wilhelm Meyer, *Critical and Exegetical Handbook to The Gospel of Matthew*, 2 vols. (Edinburgh: T. & T. Clark, 1879), vol. 2, 155.

14 Govett, *Prophecy*, 96.

15 *BDAG*, 1106.

16 *BDAG*, 201.

34

TWO, THEN ONE

"Then there shall be two men in the field; one will be taken, and one will be left. Two women will be grinding at the mill; one will be taken, and one will be left. Therefore be on the alert, for you do not know which day your Lord is coming."

—Matthew 24:40–42

In the early 1970s, probably the most popular song within the "Jesus Movement," was one entitled: "I Wish We'd All Been Ready," by Larry Norman. I was involved in this movement and rarely did we meet when we did not sing Norman's song. This song about the rapture includes the following lines:

A man and wife asleep in bed.
She hears a noise and turns her head, he's gone.
I wish we'd all been ready.
Two men walking up a hill.
One disappears and one's left standing still.
I wish we'd all been ready.

While I tend to like songs about the rapture, (I generally like this song), I do not think Matthew 24:40–42 (compare Luke 17:34–37) is a reference to the rapture. Instead, Christ if referencing His second coming.

ONE WILL BE TAKEN

The illustration used in this parable is straightforeword in both examples. There will be a separation where one individual will be taken and the other left behind. Also, in context, it is clear one is a believer and the other is not. This describes a clear separation process. The question related to this passage is who is taken and who is left behind. Does this refer to the believer being taken and the unbeliever left behind, or just the reverse, where the unbeliever is taken away and the believer is left to enter the kingdom? Those who hold to pretribulationism have argued both ways on this issue. I believe the latter view is correct. It is the unbeliever who is taken away in judgment.

As I have been arguing throughout Matthew 24, the focus is upon the second coming while the rapture is nowhere to be found in this passage. In Matthew 24, our Lord is teaching about the events leading up to His return (tribulation events in verses 4–26), followed by a revelation of His second coming, which is then followed by parables that drive home lessons related to His previous teachings (32–51). I think it would be inconsistent to introduce parables about the rapture when He has not taught about that event in this passage.[1]

It is true that when the rapture occurs there will be a separation of believers from unbelievers when believers are snatched away from earth. It is true that somewhere there will two people together and one is taken while the other is left; however, that is not what is spoken of in Matthew 24 because of the context. These parables are making points about what Christ taught in 24:4–31.

TAKEN IN JUDGMENT OR SALVATION?

The Greek word used in verses 40 and 41 is *paralambano* and is made from the root word *lambano*, which means "to take" or "receive" and the preposition *para*, which means "along side of." Thus, the meaning of this verb is "to take into close association, take (to oneself), take with/along."[2] The only place that I find where this word is clearly used of the rapture is of Christ's initial disclosure of this mystery in John 14:3: "I will come again, and *receive* you to Myself." Since *paralambano* is not a technical term that has the same meaning in every instance it is used in the New Testament, like any word in any language, usage must be determined by how it is used in a given context.

Some have argued that "taken" here refers to the pretribulational rapture. There is a small minority of pretribulationists who interpret these two verses as a reference to the rapture.[3] For example, David L. Cooper said, "The dominant idea is that the one who is a child of God will be taken, whereas the one who has never made his peace with the Lord will be left to pass into the Great Tribulation."[4] But, as Louis Barbieri has noted: "The Lord was not describing the Rapture, for the removal of the church will not be a judgment on the church. If this were the Rapture, as some commentators affirm, the Rapture would have to be posttribulational, for this event occurs immediately before the Lord's return in glory."[5]

Some have said *paralambano* is only used of positive relations. However, such is not the case. It is used of the Roman soldiers taking Jesus away from the Garden of Gethsemane to the Praetorium and eventual crucifixion (Matt. 27:27; John 19:16). It is used of the devil taking Jesus with him to show Him all the kingdoms of this world (Matt. 4:5, 8). This verb is also used of the exercised demon returning to the newly swept house and taking with it seven other spirits (Matt. 12:45; Luke 11:26). Stanley Toussaint discusses this matter stating:

> Is this a description of the rapture of the church or of the taking of the wicked to judgment? Those who take the former position argue that "to take" (*paralambano*), the verb used her, is to be differentiated from "to take" (*airw*), the verb used in verse thirty-nine. It is asserted that *paralambano* signifies the act whereby Christ receives His own to Himself. However, *paralambano* is also used in a bad sense (cf. Matthew 4:5, 8; John 19:16). Since it is parallel in thought with those who were taken in the judgment of the flood, it is best to refer the verb to those who were taken for judgment preceding the establishment of the kingdom. The difference in verbs can be accounted for on the basis of accuracy of description. "The flood came and swept them all away" is a good translation.[6]

CONTEXTUAL CONSIDERATION

I believe that the strongest reason to take the separation depicted in this passage as a reference to ones taken away in judgment is the context. It appears verses 40–41 are illustrating that which preceded it in verses 36–39, namely those who were not prepared in the days of Noah were taken away, in judgment, by the flood. Verse 39 ends by saying, "so shall the coming of the Son of Man be." Clearly the emphasis in this verse is on unbelievers being taken away in the judgment of the flood. Therefore, verses 40–41 drive that point home by giving a couple examples of the coming separation that will occur at this time of judgment. Arno Gaebelein notes:

> Two classes were living in Noah's day. The one who were unbelieving and these were swept away by the divine judgment. The other class was Noah and his house, and he and his own were left and not destroyed by the judgment. It will be so again in the coming of the Son of Man. The unbelievers will be *taken* away in the day of judgment and wrath; the others will be *left* on the earth to receive and enjoy the blessings of the coming age and enter into the kingdom, which will then be established.[7]

PARALLEL PASSAGE

Another reason to interpret verses 40–41 as illustrating ones who are taken in judgment is the parallel passage found in Luke 17:24–37. In a previous section (17:26–30), Christ speaks of the coming of the Son of Man being just like the days of Noah and Lot. In both illustrations it was the wicked one who was taken in judgment. Luke 17:27 says, "the flood came and *destroyed* them all." Verses 28 and 29 say: "It was the same as happened in the days of Lot...and *destroyed* them all." (emphasis added) Verses 34–36 gives three illustrations of the separation of believers and unbelievers. Then the following question is asked by the disciples: "Where Lord?" This question means where are the unbelievers taken? Jesus answers: "Wheresoever the body is, there will the eagles be gathered together." Eagles in this context imply vultures who hover over and scavenger a dead corpse. Thus, anyone would be able to see where a dead body is because of the vultures hovering above (Rev. 19:17–21). Such language clearly supports the notion that the ones taken are removed to judgment.

ENDNOTES

1 Christ introduces the rapture in the "Upper Room Discourse" found in John 13–17. Jesus not only discloses the new truth of the rapture (John 14:1–3), but many other things relating to the impending church age. There is an emphasis in the Upper Room Discourse upon Christ's introduction of a number of topics that He said would be expanded upon later when the Spirit of Truth would come to the Apostles (John 14:26; 15:26; 16:7). The result of the later activity of the Holy Spirit is the New Testament Epistles where they were given greater revelation about New Testament truths like the rapture of the church.

2 Walter Bauer, William F. Arndt, and F. Wilbur Gingrich, *A Greek-English Lexicon of the New Testament and Other Early Christian Literature*, 3d ed., rev. Frederick W. Danker (Chicago: University of Chicago Press, 2000), 767.

3 I did find a published pretribulationist who says that this passage refers to both the rapture and the second coming. He called it a dual reference. See Allen Beechick, *The Pre-Tribulation Rapture* (Denver: Accent Books, 1980), 231–68.

4 David L. Cooper, *Future Events Revealed: According to Matthew 24 and 25* (Los Angeles: Published by David L. Cooper, 1935), 101. See also Arnold G. Fruchtenbaum, *The Footsteps of the Messiah: A Study of the Sequence of Prophetic Events*, Revised Edition (Tustin, CA: Ariel Ministries, [1982], 2002), 650, a disciple of Cooper.

5 Louis A. Barbieri, Jr., "Matthew," in John F. Walvoord and Roy B. Zuck, *The Bible Knowledge Commentary: New Testament* (Wheaton: Victor Books, 1983), 79.

6 Stanley D. Toussaint, *Behold The King: A Study of Matthew* (Portland: Multnomah Press, 1980), 281.

7 Arno C. Gaebelein, *The Gospel of Matthew: An Exposition* (Neptune, NJ: Loizeaux Brothers, [1910] 1961), 515–16.

35

PREPARED AND ALERT

"Therefore be on the alert, for you do not know which day your Lord is coming. But be sure of this, that if the head of the house had known at what time of the night the thief was coming, he would have been on the alert and would not have allowed his house to be broken into. For this reason you be ready too; for the Son of Man is coming at an hour when you do not think He will."

—Matthew 24:42–44

Three major themes are emphasized in the parables concluding the twenty-fourth chapter of Matthew. Watchfulness was the emphasis concerning the parable of the fig tree (24:32–34). The comparison of Christ's return to the days of Noah focuses on preparedness (24:36–41). The section we are now entering (24:42–51) provides two parables that teach lessons of faithfulness in service to our Lord. The first parable in the section is found in verses 42–44. Mark's account of the Olivet Discourse does not have this identical parable, but Luke does have it in a different context (12:39–40).

This parable speaks about an owner of a house who received a warning that a thief was coming to break into his house. Because he knows the time in which the thief was to arrive, the responsible owner prepares for this impending event by setting a watch to guard the house and protect it from a possible break-in. The point of the lesson is that if one knows the time and place of when something will occur, then the responsible thing to do would be to take conscientious action in light of the impending event.

BE ON THE ALERT

Following on the heels of the "one taken and the other left" passages, Jesus exhorts that one needs to be alert concerning His coming. Verse 42 provides a hinge between the preceding context, advocating preparedness, and the following context emphasizing alertness concerning that day. "This exhortation is the chief exhortation of a parenthetical section of parables," observes James R. Gray. "It is the result of the preceding parable (indicated by the word 'therefore'), and an incentive or bridge for the parables that illustrate the need for such watchfulness."[1]

The Greek verb *gregoreo* is translated "alert" in this passage and is used 22 times in the Greek New Testament. It has the idea of "to stay awake, be watchful"[2] in some passages. This word is used of Christ's appeal to his sleepy disciples as He prayed in the Garden of Gethsemane shortly before His crucifixion (Matt. 26:38, 40, 41; Mark 14:34, 37, 38). It is also used in this way in the next verse of this passage (Matt. 24:43). However, the majority of its uses have the nuance of "to be in constant readiness" and to "be on the alert,"[3] which is how it is used here in Matthew 24:42. "The phrase **be on the alert** translates a present imperative, indicating a call for continual expectancy," notes John MacArthur.[4]

RAPTURE OR SECOND COMING?

Some argue that since one is told to be on the alert, this passage and surrounding context do not speak concerning the second coming, but instead, of the rapture. For example, Dave Hunt contends:

> When Christ says, "As it was in the days of Noah and Lot," it is absolutely certain that He is not describing conditions that will prevail at the time of the Second Coming. Therefore, these must be the conditions which will prevail just prior to the Rapture at a different time—and, obviously, before the devastation of the tribulation period.[5]

Of course, I certainly believe in the pretribulational rapture, but I do not believe that is what Christ was referencing in this passage.

Even though one passes through the momentous events of the tribulation, Scripture teaches that unbelievers will not be alert to the coming of Christ because of their deadness to the things of God. Consider two other important passages that use the Greek word for "alert": First, look at Paul's teaching in 1 Thessalonians 5 about how believers and unbelievers relate to the coming tribulation period. Paul says that unbelievers will be seeking peace and safety at this time, but "then destruction will come upon them suddenly like birth pangs upon a woman with child; and they shall not escape" (5:3). In contrast to this, believers "are not in darkness, that the day should overtake you like a thief" (5:4). The explanation given by Paul as to why believers will not be surprised is because "you are all sons of light and sons of day" (5:5). Following the rationale that Paul has provided thus far, he says, "so then let us not sleep as others do, but let us be alert and sober" (5:6). Here is the word "alert" that is used by our Lord in Matthew 24, which is employed in a similar way by Paul to denote constant readiness or being alert in relation to "the day of the Lord," since we are children of the day. The point is that unbelievers (children of darkness) are not alert and are asleep to the things of God. They are caught off guard by virtue of the fact that they are unbelievers. Because of their unbelief they are not prepared.

A second significant use of the word "alert" is found in Revelation 16:15, which says, "('Behold, I am coming like a thief. Blessed is the one who stays awake and keeps his garments, lest he walk about naked and men see his shame.')" This is translated as a parenthetical statement at the end of the sixth bowl judgment. Using the logic of those who say that "coming like a thief" would not catch unbelievers off guard does not account for this passage. Here we have seen 18 of the 19 major judgments of the tribulation and the earth is just about destroyed along with over half of the world's population and yet there is issued a warning about being alert. Why? Because unbelievers are never alert to what God is doing. That is the point! It is not whether the world is experiencing a time of disruption, but whether one is listening to God's Word and is prepared. Believers at this time will be alert while unbelievers, as always, will not be alert.

THE JEWISH REMNANT

The meaning of this parable is clear and understandable. Believers will be watching because they know a thief is coming during this time. Thus, they are prepared and alert. Christ presents the key line of the parable in verse 44 when He says, "For this reason (as stated in the two previous verses), you be ready too." To whom does the "you" reference? I believe it refers to the Jewish remnant. Jesus has been using the generic "you" throughout the Olivet Discourse as a reference to the Jewish people (cf. verses 4, 6, 9, 15, 26). The Lord uses the same language many times throughout Scripture, for example Deuternomy 4:25–31 also uses the generic "you." Since He clearly has in mind believers in verse 44, because only believers will be alert, then this passage refers specifically to the Jewish remnant during the tribulation. "This warning will be understood and heeded by the Jewish remnant, to which it is addressed," writes Arno Gaebelein. "They are to *watch* for the Son of Man; the church is to *wait* for her Lord."[6]

Israel was not prepared and ready when Christ came the first time, but the remnant will be prepared and ready when He arrives the second time. That the Jewish remnant is in view here is further supported by the observation that all of the parables that Christ speaks relate to Israel and their response to Messiah. John MacArthur notes: "In this context, being **ready** seems to refer primarily to being saved, of being spiritually prepared to meet Christ as Lord and King rather than Judge."[7] Our Lord is letting Israel know they need to be prepared for His return, whenever it occurs. Preparation is made when one trusts Jesus as their Messiah. Stanley Toussaint concludes: "The lesson is evident. When the householder knows the general time in which the thief should come, he prepares himself accordingly. 'For this reason" the believers of the age of the tribulation should be prepared. The signs of the end will equip them to know generally or 'in which watch' the Son of Man should come."[8]

The parables in this section, prepare the way for the parable lessons in Matthew 25. Randolph Yeager has summarizes this present section observing:

> The entire passage in context from verse 36 teaches that (1) in Jesus' day, no one knew the date of the advent except the Father, (2) that Noah's days were analogous to the last days; (3) that the unsaved in Noah's day did not know when the flood would come; (4) but that the saved (Noah and his family) did know at least seven days in advance; (5) further, that since, when the Lord comes, He will divide between the saints and sinners, (6) we ought to be watching the signs of the times for hints that will tell us when He will come, inasmuch as (7) we do not now have such information.[9]

Having emphasized the need for preparedness and alertness, Jesus continues His discourse with a parable regarding faithfulness.

ENDNOTES

1 James R. Gray, *Prophecy on The Mount: A Dispensational Study of the Olivet Discourse* (Chandler, AZ: Berean Advocate Ministries, 1991), p. 101.

2 Walter Baur, William F. Arndt, and F. Wilbur Gingrich, *A Greek-English Lexicon of the New Testament and Other Early Christian Literature*, 3d ed., rev. Frederick W. Danker (Chicago: University of Chicago Press, 2000), 209.

3 *BDAG*, 209.

4 John MacArthur, Matthew 24–28, *The MacArthur New Testament Commentary* (Chicago: Moody, 1989), 75.

5 Dave Hunt, *How Close Are We? Compelling Evidence for the Soon Return of Christ* (Eugene, OR: Harvest House, 1993), 210–11.

6 Arno C. Gaebelein, *The Gospel of Matthew: An Exposition* (Neptune, NJ: Loizeaux Brothers, [1910] 1961), 516. (emphasis original)

7 MacArthur, *Matthew 24–28*, 77.

8 Stanley D. Toussaint, *Behold The King: A Study of Matthew* (Portland: Multnomah Press, 1980), 282.

9 Randolph O. Yeager, *The Renaissance New Testament*, 18 vols. (Bowling Green, KY: Renaissance Press, 1978), vol. 3., 335.

36

FAITHFULNESS IN SERVICE

"Who then is the faithful and sensible slave whom his master put in charge of his household to give them their food at the proper time? Blessed is that slave whom his master finds so doing when he comes. Truly I say to you, that he will put him in charge of all his possessions. But if that evil slave says in his heart, 'my master is not coming for a long time,' and shall begin to beat his fellow slaves and eat and drink with drunkards; the master of that slave will come on a day when he does not expect him and at an hour which he does not know, and shall cut him in pieces and assign him a place with the hypocrites; weeping shall be there and the gnashing of teeth."

—Matthew 24:45–51

Christ's final parable of Matthew 24 teaches lessons of faithfulness in service to our Lord in light of His return as presented in verses 27–31. This parable, like all of the other parables of Christ, relates to Israel, especially in light of her rejection of the messiahship of Jesus. Because all of these parables are focused upon the return of Christ, this one emphasizes proper behavior in light of the absence of Jesus between the two comings. Mark does not record this parable, but Luke does in a different context (12:41–46).

WHO IS THE SENSIBLE SERVANT?

The "faithful and sensible" (24:45) servant is related to Israel, who did not discharge her responsibilities in a faithful and sensible manner, as noted in a number of other parables spoken by Christ. Of course, this standard that Christ expected of Israel can certainly be applied to any servant of Christ, but the context for this parable is national Israel. The faithful and sensible servant was not the nation of Israel.

The Greek word that is translated "sensible" (*phronimos*) is from the root word for "wise." It is used in reference "to understanding associated with insight and wisdom, sensible, thoughtful, prudent, wise."[1] Of the fourteen times that this adjective is used in the Greek New Testament, half of them are found in Matthew (four times in Matthew 25:2, 4, 8, 9). Two of the remaining seven instances are found in Luke in parallel passages to Matthew (Luke 12:42; 16:8). Paul uses this word five times in Romans and Corinthians (Rom. 11:25; 12:16; 1 Cor. 4:10; 10:15; 2 Cor. 11:19). All of the Pauline nuances connote a false human wisdom. However, in this passage, Christ uses the word positively of a servant who is skillful in managing his master's household.

Within this parable, the household is Israel. The faithful and sensible servant references the leadership of Israel. To give them food at the proper time is a responsibility cited concerning the leadership of Israel. The emphasis in this verse is placed upon doing something "at the proper time." What was the responsibility with which Israel's leadership was entrusted? They were entrusted with knowing that the time of the Messiah had arrived. Randolph Yeager notes: "the inferential conjunction used here in direct question. On the basis of verses 42–44 with their admonition to watch the time signals on God's prophetic clock, who will be judged faithful and wise, as a servant of the Lord."[2] Yet, the leadership of Israel led the people astray by not knowing much about what their own Scriptures taught about the expected Messiah. Hence, the comparison to the evil steward who says, "my master is not coming for a long time."

MY MASTER DELAYS HIS COMING

The emphasis in this parable is upon the fact that Christ has forewarned His servants concerning these matters. He had sent the prophets and others to warn the nation that their Messiah was coming, yet, most did not pay attention to these matters because they did not fit into their personal agendas. They were not good stewards and it had consequences, bad consequences for the nation of Israel. This is why there will be consequences when the Master returns and evaluates the faithfulness of His servants who witness the signs. Rewards of higher authority and rule are given to the faithful servant (24:46–47), while severe judgment is pronounced upon the derelict servant (24:51). "The reward of faithfulness is to be trusted with higher responsibilities; cf. xxv.21, 23 Lk. xvi.10a," notes A. H. M'Neile. "Since the parable deals with the Parousia, the words apply to higher activities in the age to come."[3] That age to come is the millennial kingdom.

A focus of this parable is upon the wrong attitude of the faithless servant who says, "My master is not coming for a long time" (24:48). Dr. J. Dwight Pentecost observes:

> Christ was revealing that if people are unfaithful to the stewardship entrusted to them, and if they ignore the signs that will be given of the return of the Lord, they will be kept from the kingdom to be established at His coming. In these parables the servants represent the people of the nation of Israel who will be god's stewards during the Tribulation. At Christ's return the nation will be judged, the faithful will be received into the kingdom, and the unfaithful will be excluded from the kingdom. Here again the faithfulness is that which springs from faith in Christ, while the unfaithfulness is produced because of lack of faith in Christ. Thus in view of the signs given to Israel, the people are exhorted to be watchful, prepared, and faithful.[4]

This parable looks back to the unfaithfulness of Israel (perhaps focusing upon her leadership) but also looks ahead to the coming again of Jesus Christ. The unfaithful steward "employs his authority for tyranny over those who will not support him in his evil ways, and for self-indulgence with those who will."[5] How will the nation respond to a second opportunity during the tribulation to demonstrate faithfulness and wisdom? This is an emphasis found in this parable: "Blessed is that slave whom his master finds so doing when he comes" (24:46).

FUTURE ORIENTATION

This parable provides an instance in which what one thinks about the future will impact their behavior in the present. The servant who has a proper future orientation thinks that his master could return at any time. This is an important reason why he acts responsibly in the present. On the other hand, the servant who says, "my master is not coming for a long time," acts irresponsibly. Therefore, it is very important what one thinks about the future since it impacts present behavior. Jesus is wanting Israel to think about the future and its impact upon them.

There are also consequences to how a servant dispenses his responsibilities. This likely relates to the role that Israel will have in the kingdom, or for those individuals within Israel who are unfaithful stewards, the role they will not have in the kingdom. Clearly many will be outside of the kingdom since the passage says of the unfaithful stewards: "shall cut him in pieces and assign him a place with the hypocrites; weeping shall be there and the gnashing of teeth" (24:51).

JUDGMENT UPON HYPOCRITES

The Greek verb (*dichotomeo*) is translated "shall cut him in pieces." The Greek lexicon says, "cut in two of the dismemberment of a condemned person."[6] Its only two New Testament uses are in Matthew 24:51 and the parallel passage in Luke 12:46. The lexicon admits that it could be a figurative expression denoting to "cut him off," but no exact linguistic support has been found for this rendering.[7] Yeager admits that it literally means, "to cut into two, a reference to a most severe form of Hebrew punishment." However, he notes that "the text, both in Mt. 24:51 and Lk. 12:46, represents the victim as remaining alive. Hence we suppose that the term is used in the same sense in which the western cowboy 'cuts out of the herd' a cow. A severing for the purpose of separation from others."[8] M'Neile, however, notes the following: "A punishment literally inflicted in ancient times; cf. I Chr. xx. 3,... In Exod. xxix. 17, the verb is used of dividing a sacrificial victim into pieces."[9] This word could be associated with covenantal unfaithfulness, which would be the case of those within Israel who did not properly dispense their stewardship.

Here is an instance where both the denotative (plain or literal) and connotative (figurative) uses make sense in this context. However, I favor the literal use since it is used that way in the Old Testament and in secular literature, while the figurative use is nowhere attested in other literature. Also, when this phrase is coupled with the companion phrase, "weeping shall be there and the gnashing of teeth," which it is, then it appears to support a literal, final judgment.

The phrase "weeping shall be there and the gnashing of teeth" speaks of the response of the hypocrite while experiencing judgment. That person will weep and gnash their teeth together in bitter anger for having been an unwise steward. Stanley Toussaint notes: "Invariably throughout Matthew this phrase refers to the retribution of those who are judged before the millennial kingdom is established (Matthew 8:12; 13:42, 50; 22:13; 25:30)."[10] As we will see, this theme of faithful stewardship in relation to Israel will be continued in Matthew 25.

ENDNOTES

1 Walter Bauer, William F. Arndt, and F. Wilbur Gingrich, *A Greek-English Lexicon of the New Testament and Other Early Christian Literature*, 3d ed., rev. Frederick W. Danker (Chicago: University of Chicago Press, 2000), 1067. (hereafter *BDAG*)

2 Randolph O. Yeager, *The Renaissance New Testament*, 18 vols. (Bowling Green, KY: Renaissance Press, 1978), vol. 3., 340.

3 Alan Hugh M'Neile, *The Gospel According to St. Matthew* (London: MacMillan, 1915), 358.

4 J. Dwight Pentecost, *The Parables of Jesus* (Grand Rapids: Zondervan, 1982), 151.

5 M'Neile, *Matthew*, 359.

6 *BDAG*, 254.

7 *BDAG*, 254.

8 Yeager, *Renaissance New Testament*, vol. 3, 346.

9 M'Neile, *Matthew*, 359.

10 Stanley D. Toussaint, *Behold The King: A Study of Matthew* (Portland: Multnomah Press, 1980), 282.

37

PARABLE OF THE TEN VIRGINS

"Then the kingdom of heaven will be comparable to ten virgins, who took their lamps, and went out to meet the bridegroom. And five of them were foolish, and five were prudent. For when the foolish took their lamps, they took no oil with them, but the prudent took oil in flasks along with their lamps. Now while the bridegroom was delaying, they all got drowsy and began to sleep. But at midnight there was a shout, 'Behold, the bridegroom! Come out to meet him.' Then all those virgins rose, and trimmed their lamps. And the foolish said to the prudent, 'Give us some of your oil, for our lamps are going out.' But the prudent answered, saying, 'No, there will not be enough for us and you too; go instead to the dealers and buy some for yourselves.' And while they were going away to make the purchase, the bridegroom came, and those who were ready went in with him to the wedding feast; and the door was shut. And later the other virgins also came, saying, 'Lord, lord, open up for us.' But he answered and said, 'Truly I say to you, I do not know you.' Be on the alert then, for you do not know the day nor the hour."

—Matthew 25:1–13

Alas, we wave goodbye to chapter 24 and say hello to chapter 25. "Instead of faithful and unfaithful servants, now we have wise and foolish bridesmaids."[1] There are a number of items that need to be addressed as we move into Matthew 25 which impact how we should understand Christ's intent in this passage. If we are wrong on these issues it will guarantee that we will misinterpret the passage (unless we are illogical in the process).

One of the first issues that should be recognized is that the parables and teachings in Matthew 25 are a continuation of the flow of the previous chapter. Jesus has not totally changed topics and started speaking about something completely new when we enter this chapter. This means that these parables are related to Israel, (not the church), her first-century rejection of His messiahship, and the coming spoken of here relates to the second coming and judgment that will take place upon Christ's arrival. Stanley Toussaint explains as follows:

> This parable as well as the next one deals with the Jews in the tribulation period. This is seen from various facts. The context favors this view (Matthew 24:3, 8, 14, 15, 30, 31, 33, 42, 44, 47, 51). The subject being discussed is the end time, the final years before the kingdom is established. At the time the church will be absent from the earth. Therefore this section deals with a Jewish period of time.[2]

Chapter 25 highlights that because the Jewish people missed Messiah's first coming because of unbelief and were judged temporally in A.D. 70, they need to be prepared for His return so that they will escape judgment and enter into blessing (the millennial kingdom). Matthew 24:50–51 asks the question, "on what ground would the nation be judged?" The parable of the ten virgins answers that question by saying: "on the basis of preparedness." Although not explicitly stated, one is prepared by recognizing Jesus as the Messiah at His second coming.

"He taught that following His return (Matt. 24:30) and the regathering of the nation Israel to their land (v. 31), the nation would be brought under judgment (25:1–30)," says Dr. J. Dwight Pentecost. "Christ used two parables to teach that the regathered nation will be judged to determine who is saved and who is unsaved. The purpose of this judgment will be to exclude the unsaved from, and to receive the saved into, the kingdom that He will establish following His Second Advent."[3] Jesus accomplishes His goal as He continues presenting parabolic lessons and teachings about judgment upon His return. Matthew 25 can be divided into the following three sections: First, the parable of the ten virgins (25:1–13), second, the parables of the talents (25:14–30), and third, the judgment of the Gentiles (25:31–46). All three relate to the issue of preparedness for Christ's coming kingdom.

THE PARABLE OF THE TEN VIRGINS

We see a continuation of Christ's parabolic lessons in chapter 25 that were begun in 24:32. There are no chapter or verse breaks in the original manuscripts of Matthew's gospel. Matthew 24:50–51 raises the question: "On what basis will Israel be judged?" The answer in 25:1–13 is preparedness. The parable of the ten virgins provides a picture of living Israel brought back to the land at the end of days for a judgment to see who is prepared and who is unprepared the second time for the coming of Messiah since the nation was not prepared at Christ's first coming. The focus is on Israel in the last days (i.e., the tribulation period just described in Matthew 24:4–28). The prepared Israelites enter the millennial kingdom while the unprepared are excluded. To be excluded refers to unsaved Israel.

The ten virgins represent the nation of Israel as a whole. The use of the term "virgin" depicts a woman of marriable age waiting for her groom to come for the wedding. This assumes they are already betrothed. The nation is divided into two groups of five each. The first group, the wise, is depicted as prepared and genuinely waiting since they have obtained extra oil in case a delay occurs in the coming of the bridegroom. The five prepared virgins picture a responsible believing and prepared Israel truly waiting for her groom, the Messiah. The second group, the foolish, did not prepare and they represent unbelieving Israel. They were not ready for the coming of Messiah. The ratios of two groups of five each is not related to the percentage of Jewish believers or unbelievers. Dr. Pentecost tells us the following:

> Although a strong testimony will be given to the nation of Israel during the Tribulation (Matt. 24:14), some people will be unprepared when the King comes to institute His millennial kingdom. The prepared will be received into the kingdom to enjoy its bounty but the unprepared will be excluded. Thus this parable teaches that there will

be a judgment of living Israelites to determine who is and is not prepared. This is an expression of Christ's previous statement that "you also must be ready" (Matt. 24:44).[4]

THE JEWISH WEDDING MOTIF

Generally speaking, there were three stages to the Jewish marriage process in first-century Israel. First, was the marriage contract known as the betrothal. These could be arranged as early as a child's infancy. To abrogate such an engagement required a certificate of divorce, as alluded to by Joseph in relation to Mary's virgin conception of our Lord Jesus by the Holy Spirit. Second, was the marriage ceremony at the bride's house known as the procession. This is the aspect that is described in Matthew 25:1–13. The betrothed virgin was to prepare for the any-moment coming of her groom, whether day or night. "The betrothal contract, or *ketubah*, would already have been executed, and so it remains for the virgins to meet the groom when he takes the bride to the wedding celebration that begins their life together."[5] The depiction in this parable shows the bride was to have a lamp with oil and ready to go to meet the groom whenever he might come, especially if he came during the night, which is what happens in this parable. Third, there would be a wedding feast later at the groom's house. This would be the marriage supper of the Lamb as depicted in Revelation 19:9, which occurs at the beginning of the millenium.

THE BRIDEGROOM'S DELAY

The focus of the parable is upon the long delay of the bridegroom. His return takes longer than the foolish virgins thought, thus they were not prepared. "The context similarly shows that the overriding theme is preparedness for the coming of the Son of Man," notes D. A. Carson. "Even when this involves certain form of behavior (24:45–51; 25:14–30), that behavior is called forth by the unexpectedness of the master's return."[6] The focus of the passage is on the fact that prepared virgins are described as wise, while the other virgins are called foolish. "The sole distinction between the two groups is this: the wise bring not only oil in their lamps but an extra supply in separate jars, while the foolish bring no oil (either no extra oil or no oil at all."[7] Preparedness is an individual responsibility that cannot be given to another. One must make necessary arrangements for their own needs and if not it is said to be a foolish characteristic. Both groups had the same time for preparation and both groups are asleep when the bridegroom comes.

The key point is preparedness. If one has not prepared ahead of time, then when the key moment comes, it is too late. This parable teaches the lesson that at the second coming of Christ, some within Israel will be prepared having trusted Jesus as their Messiah, while other Jewish people will not have done so, even though they are supposed to be waiting for the Messiah.

The final section of the parable, verses 10–12, depicts unbelieving Israel during the tribulation that does not come to faith in Christ in order to welcome the arrival of Jesus, the Messiah. "Though this passage does not specifically interpret the meaning of the oil, many commentators see it as representing the Holy Spirit and His work in salvation. Salvation is more than mere profession for it involves regeneration by the Holy Spirit. Those who will merely profess to be save, and do not actually possess the Spirit, will be excluded from the feast, that is, the kingdom."[8] The note about the prepared virgins going into the wedding feast "and the door was shut" (verse 10), speaks of the security of believing Israel at the second coming. Yet, unbelieving Israel has been shut out. The late arrivers bang on the door of the wedding feast crying to be let in, but it is too late as noted by the chilling words, "Truly I say to you, I do not know you." The perfect tense verb is used in this statement which denotes past action with results that continue into the present. Therefore, God never knew them in the past, resulting in the fact that He does not know them in the present.

The parable ends in verse 13 by noting a lesson to be learned from the episode. The parable does not depict those who loose their salvation in the end, rather, it notes that some who profess to be believers have never actually been a believer. A true believer is going to be responsive to their Lord and His word. "'Keep watch' does not mean 'keep awake,; as if an ability to fight off sleep were relevant to the story. Rather, in the light of the entire parable, the dominate exhortation of this discourse is repeated: Be prepared! Keep watching!"[9]

SOME RAPTURE IMPLICATIONS

Because this parable deals with the future nation of Israel (perhaps the current nation of Israel that exists today), this is not a passage that comes into play concerning the rapture. This means that the parable of the ten virgins does not support the notion of a partial rapture position, which has been argued from this, as well as other passages (Matt. 24:40–51; Mk. 13:33–37; Lk. 20:34–36; 21:36; Phil. 3:10–12; 1 Thess. 5:6; 2 Tim. 4:8; Tit. 2:13; Heb. 9:24–28; Rev. 3:3, 10; 12:1–6). This view teaches that the rapture occurs before the tribulation, but only "spiritual" Christians will be taken, while other Christians will remain through the tribulation. They also believe that multiple raptures will occur throughout the seven-year tribulation period. This view is thought to have been developed by Robert Govett in the mid-nineteenth century in England, and held mainly by British advocates such as J. A. Seiss, G. H. Lang and G. H. Pember.[10] More recently a midtribulational view has been advocated by Gleason Archer.[11]

Because this passage, by and large, is not thought to relate to the rapture by pretribulationists because it contextually refers to Israel after the rapture and in the tribulation, it is even harder to make a case for a partial rapture. "We shrink from the partial rapture idea because other passages seem plainly to suggest that every member of the body of Christ will be caught up (2 Thess. 4:16–17; 1 Cor. 15:51–58, etc.)," notes Randolph Yeager. "Partial rapture would seem to imply rupture in the Body of Christ."[12] Quite frankly, the same grace that saves each believer is the grace that will take one out at the rapture. One does not have to qualify through their own words or reach a certain level of sanctification to be taken at the rapture. Qualification for being taken in the rapture is not a reward for faithfulness, but like salvation itself is a free gift. One's name is added to "the rapture manifest" when their name is added to the roll of the saved the moment one trusts Christ as his Savior. Even if a believer does not believe in the pretribulational rapture, they will be taken anyway if they are indeed a believer. I am sure some will be taken by surprise, and perhaps some kicking and screaming, but they will be taken nevertheless!

Partial rapturists contend that this parable pictures the part of the church that is watching and waiting for the Lord's return as the five wise virgins who had oil and the carnal church who is left behind as the five foolish virgins. This they believe supports the notion of the partial rapture theory.

There are major problems with anyone's attempt to apply this parable to the church to begin with, since Israel is in view. Further, the imagery does not match with what it should be if this were actually teaching a partial rapture doctrine. The imagery used in the parable of the ten virgins does not comport with that used of the church in other New Testament passages. "The passage itself uses none of the characteristic terms relating to the church, such as *bride*, *body*, or the expression *in Christ*,"[13] notes John Walvoord. Instead we see that the ten virgins are merely bridesmaids who would be attending at a wedding and not brides themselves. Were this portraying in some way the church, then these virgins would need to be portrayed as brides who were waiting upon their bridegroom, which would be Christ. This is not what is found in the passage. Dr. Walvoord further explains in the following:

> If watchfulness is necessary for worthiness, as partial rapturists characteristically argue, then none of the ten virgins qualify for "they all became drowsy and fell asleep." The command to "watch" in verse 13 has, then, the specific meaning of being prepared with oil—being genuinely regenerated and indwelt by the Spirit rather than having unusual spirituality. The clear teaching is that "watching" is not enough. This passage will serve to refute the partial rapturists instead of sustaining their viewpoint. Only by the power and presence of the Holy Spirit can one be qualified for entrance into the wedding feast, but *all* the wise virgins enter the feast.[14]

The parable of the ten virgins is not a rapture passage. Rather, it is a passage pertaining to the second coming of the Messiah and the need for believing Israel to be prepared for that coming.

ENDNOTES

1 Craig L. Blomberg, *The New American Commentary: Matthew*, vol. 22 (Nashville, TN: Broadman & Holman Publishers, 1992), 369.

2 Stanley D. Toussaint, *Behold The King: A Study of Matthew* (Portland: Multnomah Press, 1980), 283.

3 J. Dwight Pentecost, *The Words and Works of Jesus Christ: A Study of the Life of Christ* (Grand Rapids: Zondervan, 1981), 407.

4 J. Dwight Pentecost, *The Parables of Jesus* (Grand Rapids: Zondervan, 1982), 154.

5 David L. Turner, *Matthew* (Grand Rapids, MI: Baker Academic, 2008), 595.

6 D. A. Carson, "Matthew" in *The Expositor's Bible Commentary, Matthew, Mark, Luke*, vol. 8 (Grand Rapids, MI: Zondervan, 1984), 511.

7 Carson, "Matthew," 513.

8 Louis A. Barbieri, Jr., "Matthew" in John F. Walvoord and Roy B. Zuck, editors, *The Bible Knowledge Commentary*, vol. 2 (Wheaton, IL: Victor Books, 1983), vol. 2:80.

9 Carson, "Matthew", 514.

10 Charles C. Ryrie, *Basic Theology: A Popular Systematic Guide To Understanding Biblical Truth* (Wheaton: Victor Books, 1986), 480.

11 Gleason L. Archer, Jr., Paul D. Feinberg, Douglas J. Moo, *Three Views of the Rapture, Revised ed.* Grand Rapids, MI: Zondervan, 1996.

12 Randolph O. Yeager, *The Renaissance New Testament* (Bowling Green: Renaissance Press, 1978), Vol. 3, 345.

13 John F. Walvoord, *The Rapture Question*, Revised and Enlarged Edition (Grand Rapids: Zondervan, 1979 [1957]),104.

14 Walvoord, *The Rapture Question*, 104.

38

PARABLE OF THE FIVE TALENTS

"For it is just like a man about to go on a journey, who called his own slaves, and entrusted his possessions to them. And to one he gave five talents, to another, two, and to another, one, each according to his own ability; and he went on his journey. Immediately the one who had received the five talents went and traded with them, and gained five more talents. In the same manner the one who had received the two talents gained two more. But he who received the one talent went away and dug in the ground, and hid his master's money. Now after a long time the master of those slaves came and settled accounts with them. And the one who had received the five talents came up and brought five more talents, saying, 'Master, you entrusted five talents to me; see, I have gained five more talents.' His master said to him, 'Well done, good and faithful slave; you were faithful with a few things, I will put you in charge of many things, enter into the joy of your master.' The one also who had received the two talents came up and said, 'Master, you entrusted to me two talents; see, I have gained two more talents.' His master said to him, 'Well done, good and faithful slave; you were faithful with a few things, I will put you in charge of many things; enter into the joy of your master.' And the one also who had received the one talent came up and said, 'Master, I knew you to be a hard man, reaping where you did not sow, and gathering where you scattered no seed. 'And I was afraid, and went away and hid your talent in the ground; see, you have what is yours.' But his master answered and

> *said to him, 'You wicked, lazy slave, you knew that I reap where I did not sow, and gather where I scattered no seed. 'Then you ought to have put my money in the bank, and on my arrival I would have received my money back with interest. 'Therefore take away the talent from him, and give it to the one who has the ten talents.' For to everyone who has shall more be given, and he shall have an abundance; but from the one who does not have, even what he does have shall be taken away. And cast out the worthless slave into the outer darkness; in that place there shall be weeping and gnashing of teeth."*
>
> —Matthew 25:14–30

The second section of Matthew 25 is one of the most well-known parables of Jesus. The parable of the faithful and unfaithful stewards continues lessons for the nation of Israel in light of Christ's return, which was noted in Matthew 24. This parable is often the subject of sermons today without notation of its context relating to Israel and Christ's return. When we examine parallel accounts of this parable (Mark 13:34 and Luke 19:11–27) they both are also in the context of the second coming and judgment. The account in Matthew contains the most extensive version.

THE PARABLE OF THE TALENTS

In keeping with previous parables in Christ's discourse, this one deals with the issue of faithfulness. How will a true servant of the kingdom act during the time of his master's absence? Will he be faithful to his lord or will he be a worthless servant? The servants were evaluated for how they dispensed their responsibilities during the absence of their master. Upon the return of the master, those servants that were faithful in the execution of their duties were rewarded with greater responsibility and wealth during the future reign of the king. "So here the heirs of the kingdom will receive greater blessing, while the ones who do not inherit it will be shut off from even an opportunity for entrance," notes Stanley Toussaint. "Those who do receive rewards will be rewarded according to their faithfulness and not the measure of their work."[1]

This parable relates to Israel's accountability before God for their stewardship that will occur in conjunction with Christ second coming. Dr. Toussaint notes:

> The last three parables give practical instructions in the light of the King's coming to judge and to reign. The principle which underlies each is the same one which was given in the Sermon on the Mount (Matthew 7:16–21). The fruit of faithfulness and preparedness would indicate the character of those living in the days before His coming. In each parable, character is manifested by works. This thought forms the key to the following passage which deals with the judgment of the nations. (Matthew 25:31–46).[2]

The parables of the ten virgins (25:1–13) and the talents (25:14–30) deal with Israel's faithfulness in light of her responsibility, while the remainder of Matthew 25 (31–46) deals with Messiah's judgments of the nations, which will relate to how Gentiles treat the Jewish remnant during the tribulation. In both instances, Israel and the nations, there will be a mixed response. Some will be prepared and faithful, while others will not.

In the instance of the unfaithful slave, he attempts to excuse his slothful behavior based on his perception of the master's personality and the servant's fear. "Master, I knew you to be a hard man, and gathering where you scattered no seed. And I was afraid, and went away and hid your talent in the ground; see, you have what is yours" (25:24–25). Once again, the problem is not with the master but with the slave since the master demonstrated in his treatment of the other slaves was fair and not unjust. The master takes away the talent from the unfaithful slave and gives it to the faithful (25:28).

The final verse of this passage (25:30) speaks of the worthless slave being cast into "outer darkness" and in which "in that place there shall be weeping and gnashing of teeth." The term "outer darkness" is used earlier in this passage in 24:51, as well as in 8:12 and Luke 13:28 and is a clear reference to the place more popularly known as hell.

The unfaithful slave is to be seen as an unbeliever in this passage, not a carnal believer as some have suggested. The point is that unbelievers, in this case unbelieving Israel, will experience eternity in the Lake of Fire as a result of rejection of Jesus as Messiah and refusal to recognize and serve Him. John MacArthur notes: "The slave was not simply unfaithful but faithless.... Outer darkness is a common New Testament description of hell."[3]

The phrase "weeping shall be there and the gnashing of teeth" speaks of the response of the hypocrite while experiencing judgment. That person will weep and gnash their teeth together in bitter anger for having been an unwise steward, which denotes the unrelieved agony of judgment in the lake of fire. The focus in this passage that refers to hell is of endless torture and the pain the unbeliever experiences for all eternity. Dr. Toussaint notes: "Invariably throughout Matthew this phrase refers to the retribution of those who are judged before the millennial kingdom is established (Matthew 8:12; 13:42, 50; 22:13; 25:30)."[4]

PARALLEL PASSAGES

All three synoptic gospels deal with this parable (Mark 13:34–37; Luke 19:11–27). The passage in Mark does not present it as a parable but as an admonition. "Take heed, keep on the alert; for you do not know when the appointed time is" (13:34). The focus in the passage is on alertness in connection to the Lord's second coming since Mark's version is at the end of his section on the Olivet Discourse. The section ends as follows: "And what I say to you I say to all, 'Be on the alert!'" (13:37). Alert to what? Alert to the return of Christ. Alertness is required because no one knows the day or hour of His return (13:32).

As we look at Luke's parallel passage in chapter 19 we see that it is similar to the one in Matthew. We know from Luke's statement in 1:3 that his account is "in consecutive order." Interestingly, Luke places our Lord's parable following His encounter with Zaccheus. It was the prevailing opinion of Judaism in Christ's day that when Messiah entered Jerusalem then the Kingdom would have come. Just such a notion is supported by verse 11 which says, "... He went on to tell a parable, because He was near Jerusalem, and they supposed that the kingdom of God was going to appear immediately." This is the context for the parable which begins with the words: "A certain nobleman went to a distant country to receive a kingdom for himself, and then return" (19:12).

In Luke's rendition of the parable each servant was given the same amount of money to invest and Jesus says that the nobleman told them, "Do business with this until I come back" (19:13). This parable is about Israel's treatment of Jesus at His first coming. "But the citizens hated him, and sent a delegation after him, saying, 'We do not want this man to reign over us'" (19:14). Verse 15 speaks of Christ's return at the second coming "after receiving the kingdom" in spite of Israel's response at His first coming. Upon His return Christ calls His rejectors to account for their stewardship in His absence. Similar to Matthew's account, He praises and rewards the faithful servants (19:15–19). In contrast to the faithful, the "worthless slave" (19:22) hide his money in a handkerchief because he "was afraid of you, because you are an exacting man; you take up what you did not lay down, and reap what you did not sow" (19:21).

Unbelievers stress God's judgment because they have rejected His grace. Jesus said that since this was the worthless slave's view of his master, he should have put the money in the bank and at least earned interest (19:23). Likely the reason the worthless slave did not invest the money is because he doubted the master's return. That slave thought by not depositing in a bank, if his master did not return, he could keep the money for himself. As in the Matthew account, the master took the worthless slave's money and gave it to the most productive slave who had invested the money (19:24).

The lesson to be learned from this parable is stated by Jesus in verse 26: "I tell you, that to everyone who has shall more be given, but from the one who does not have even what he does have will be taken away." Jesus then concludes concerning those who did not want Him to reign over them as noted in verse 14, "bring them here and slay them in my presence" (19:27). This is no doubt a reference, in context, to Jewish individuals who rejected Him at His first coming. We know from other biblical passages that this is also the destiny of anyone, Jew or Gentile, who does not trust in Christ as their Saviour at any point in history.

Since the parable in Luke 19 followed the encounter of Jesus with Zaccheus, "And while they were listening to these things, He went on to tell them a parable" (19:11), it is important to see the Zaccheus story and the parable that followed as relating to one another. Jesus is providing a contrast of responses to Him. Zaccheus was a wealthy Jewish tax collector, an outcast within Israel's society, who recognized Jesus as the Messiah and is so affected from his encounter with Jesus that he repented. The Jewish leaders who saw this "began to grumble, saying, 'He has gone to be the guest of a man who is a sinner'" (19:7). The "sinner" Zaccheus said to the Lord, "'Behold, Lord, half of my possessions I will give to the poor, and if I have defrauded anyone of anything, I will give back four times as much'" (19:8). It is important to note that Zaccheus did what the rich young ruler refused to do in Luke 18:22, who was viewed by the Jewish community as a good Jew. Also, by his willingness to give back four times what he had unjustly taken from people, Zaccheus was following the dictate of the Mosaic Law (Exodus 22:1; Leviticus 6:5).

DISPENSATIONAL TRUTH PICTURED

In this parable Jesus portrays Himself as the master of a house who is set to embark on a journey and He gives various responsibilities to His servants. The parable contains all of the basic elements dispensationalists[5] teach are related to the testing of the various ages within God's plan for history.[6]

A leading spokesman for dispensationalism, Dr. Charles Ryrie, notes that *The Oxford English Dictionary* defines a theological dispensation as "a stage in a progressive revelation, expressly adapted to the needs of a particular nation or period of time...also, the age or period during which a system has prevailed."[7] The English word "dispensation" translates the Greek noun *oikonomía*, often rendered "administration" in modern translations. The verb *oikonoméô* refers to a manager of a household.[8] "In the New Testament," notes Ryrie, "*dispensation* means to manage or administer the affairs of a household, as, for example, in the Lord's story of the unfaithful steward in Luke 16:1–13."[9]

The Greek word *oikonomía* is a compound of *oíkos* meaning "house" and *nómos* meaning "law." Taken together "the central idea in the word *dispensation* is that of managing or administering the affairs of a household."[10] Ryrie continues:

> The various forms of the word *dispensation* appears in the New Testament twenty times. The verb *oikonoméô* is used once in Luke 16:2, where it is translated "to be a steward." The noun *oikonómos* appears ten times (Luke 12:42; 16:1, 3, 8; Rom. 16:23; 1 Cor. 4:1, 2; Gal. 4:2; Titus 1:7; 1 Pet. 4:10), and is usually translated "steward" or "manager" (but "treasurer" in Rom. 16:23). The noun *oikonomía* is used nine times (Luke 16:2, 3, 4; 1 Cor. 9:17; Eph. 1:10; 3:2, 9; Col. 1:25; 1 Tim. 1:4). In these instances it is translated variously ("stewardship," "dispensation," "administration," "job," "commission").[11]

Dr. Ryrie formulates the following description and definition of dispensationalism:

> Dispensationalism views the world as a household run by God. In this household-world God is dispensing or administering its affairs according to His own will and in various stages of revelation in the process of time. These various stages mark off the distinguishably different economies in the outworking of His total purpose, and these different economies constitute the dispensations. The understanding of God's differing economies is essential to a proper interpretation of His revelation within those various economies.[12]

There are several characteristics of a dispensation as viewed by dispensationalists: Among them, Ryrie notes the following:

- two parties are always involved
- specific responsibilities
- accountability as well as responsibility
- a change may be made at any time unfaithfulness is found in the existing administration
- God is the one to whom men are responsible
- faithfulness is required of the subordinate party

- a stewardship may end at any time
- dispensations are connected with the mysteries of God
- dispensations and ages are connected ideas
- there are at least three dispensation (likely seven).[13]

When we compare the dispensations with the specific characteristics of this parable we note the following: Each dispensation begins with a responsibility given to the steward. In this parable the stewards are the slaves (25:14) and their responsibility is faithful stewardship (25:19). While this parable pictures some who were faithful, each dispensation within God's plan ends in failure, as depicted by the unfaithful slaves (25:18, 26). Thus, each age ends in judgment, as God holds his stewards responsible for their actions, which is see in the unfaithful slave who is cast "into outer darkness" (25:30).

The scenario in this parable provides a paradigm for how God manages human history based upon His revelation (the Bible). In spite of Satan and the unbelieving world, God knows what He is doing throughout history. He is in control and even though we currently live in a time when God is allowing all of humanity and every person to go his or her own way and do their own thing, judgment day is coming when He will hold every person accountable for their stewardship toward God.

ENDNOTES

1 Stanley D. Toussaint, *Behold The King: A Study of Matthew* (Portland: Multnomah Press, 1980), 287.

2 Toussaint, *Behold The King*, 288.

3 John MacArthur, *The MacArthur New Testament Commentary: Matthew* (Chicago: Moody Press, 1989), 108.

4 Toussaint, *Behold The King*, 282.

5 For an explanation of what we mean by dispensationalism see the chapter "What is Dispensationalism?" in Mark Hitchcock and Thomas Ice, *The Truth Behind Left Behind: A Biblical View of the End Times* (Sisters, OR: Multnomah Publishers, 2004), 178–90.

6 See our chart on "The Dispensations" in Tim LaHaye and Thomas Ice, *Charting The End Times: A Visual Guide to Understanding Bible Prophecy* (Eugene, OR: Harvest House Publishers, 2001), 81–83.

7 Charles C. Ryrie, *What Is Dispensationalism?* (Pamphlet published by Dallas Theological Seminary, [1980], 1986), 1.

8 Walter Bauer, *A Greek-English Lexicon of the New Testament and Other Early Christian Literature*, a translation and adaptation by William F. Arndt & F. Wilbur Gingrich (Chicago: The University of Chicago Press, 1957), 562.

9 Ryrie, *What Is Dispensationalism?*, 1. [emphasis original]

10 Charles C. Ryrie, *Dispensationalism* (Chicago: Moody Press, [1966], 1995), 25. [emphasis original]

11 Ryrie, *Dispensationalism*, 25. [emphasis original]

12 Ryrie, *Dispensationalism*, 29.

13 Ryrie, *Dispensationalism*, 26–27.

39

JUDGMENT OF THE SHEEP AND GOATS

"But when the Son of Man comes in His glory, and all the angels with Him, then He will sit on His glorious throne. And all the nations will be gathered before Him; and He will separate them from one another, as the shepherd separates the sheep from the goats; and He will put the sheep on His right, and the goats on the left. Then the King will say to those on His right, 'Come, you who are blessed of My Father, inherit the kingdom prepared for you from the foundation of the world. For I was hungry, and you gave Me something to eat; I was thirsty, and you gave Me drink; I was a stranger, and you invited Me in; naked, and you clothed Me; I was sick, and you visited Me; I was in prison, and you came to Me.' Then the righteous will answer Him, saying, 'Lord, when did we see You hungry, and feed You, or thirsty, and give You drink? And when did we see You a stranger, and invite You in, or naked, and clothe You? And when did we see You sick, or in prison, and come to You?' And the King will answer and say to them, 'Truly I say to you, to the extent that you did it to one of these brothers of Mine, even the least of them, you did it to Me.' Then He will also say to those on His left, 'Depart from Me, accursed ones, into the eternal fire which has been prepared for the devil and his angels; for I was hungry, and you gave Me nothing to eat; I was thirsty, and you gave Me nothing to drink; I was a stranger, and you did not invite Me in; naked, and you did not clothe Me; sick, and in prison, and you did not visit Me.' Then they themselves also will answer, saying, 'Lord, when did we see You

> *hungry, or thirsty, or a stranger, or naked, or sick, or in prison, and did not take care of You?' Then He will answer them, saying, 'Truly I say to you, to the extent that you did not do it to one of the least of these, you did not do it to Me.' And these will go away into eternal punishment, but the righteous into eternal life."*
>
> —Matthew 25:31–46

The third and final section of Matthew 25 is a key New Testament passage that speaks of the sheep and goats judgment after the second coming. This final section of the Olivet Discourse (found only in Matthew) is a difficult passage for some preterists and all posttribulationists to interpret. However, the futurist (dispensationalist) has no problem understanding it because it is interpreted to mean exactly what it says.

CHRIST'S GLORIOUS COMING AND JUDGMENT

This passage is difficult for many preterists because they believe this second coming judgment passage was fulfilled in A.D. 70. Gary DeMar says, "there is little evidence that the 'coming of the Son of Man' in Matthew 24:27, 30, 39, and 42 is different from the 'coming of the Son of Man' in 25:31. Compare 25:31 with 16:27, a certain reference to the destruction of Jerusalem in A.D. 70."[1] DeMar fails to explain the details of the passage that speak of a return in glory with "all the angels with Him." In addition, when did our Lord judge the nations in A.D. 70, as depicted in this passage? This is clearly a future event and such a major event that it is hard to imagine how it can be confused with the A.D. 70 destruction of Jerusalem. Arno C. Gaebelein tells us:

> It is evident that these words must be connected with chapter xxiv:30, 31. The scene takes place after His visible and glorious appearing as Son of Man and after His elect (the remnant of His earthly people; that is, the "all Israel") have been gathered. Leaving out the central portion of the discourse, the three parables, relating to the Christian profession, we have in chapter xxiv:3–41 and chapter xxv:31–46

chronological events relating to the end of the Jewish age and the judgment which follows immediately after the Lord has come.[2]

JUDGMENT OF THE SHEEP AND GOATS

Only in Matthew does Jesus mention the judgment of the nations (*i.e.*, Gentiles) that will take place when "He will sit on His glorious throne" (25:31) immediately after His second coming to establish His kingdom (25:31–46). The Gentiles at Christ's return are pictured here as the comingling of saved and unsaved. Christ's purpose at this judgment is to separate the saved (sheep) from the unsaved (goats) since each group has a different eternal destiny. When Christ returns at the second coming He will implement what He earned at His first coming. Instead of sitting at the right-hand of God the Father in heaven making intercession for believers, Christ will return to earth to impose His righteous rule on all humanity.

Not only will Christ return to earth, He will bring with Him "all the angels." The passage says, "Then the King will say to those on His right, 'Come, you who are blessed of My Father, inherit the kingdom prepared for you from the foundation of the world'" (25:34). What a radical change in the affairs in the world with the God–Man sitting on the throne and ruling over the entire world from Jerusalem for a thousand years before the Great White Throne Judgment takes place in preparation for an endless eternity. The fact that our Lord calls this time of His rule "the kingdom" is clearly a reference to the millennium or the thousand-year reign mention in Revelation 20. At the end of the millennium is the Great White Throne judgment which ends earth's history. However, it is clear that the sheep/goats judgment occurs before the kingdom or millennium starts. This is made clear since 25:46 reads, "And these [the goats] will go away into eternal punishment, but the righteous into eternal life." Both "eternal punishment" and "eternal life" are implemented after the millennial rule of Christ as described in Revelation 20.

The dividing process is seen in the judgment of the Gentiles using the analogy of separating sheep and goats. In this context, the sheep Gentiles are those who have been good to the Jews during the seven-year tribulation, defending them at the risk of their lives, visiting them in prison and feeding them during those desperate times (25:33–40). Those who persecuted the Jews or rejected them during the tribulation will be put on the left side and are known as goats, signifying their rebellion toward God (25:41–46). For this rebellion the goats, all whom are unbelievers, "will go away into eternal punishment" (25:46).

The reason believers in the tribulation will receive these special rewards is because of the risk of their own lives they have taken as believers. During the tribulation Satan will attempt to destroy all Jews in order to prevent the second coming and the end of his activity. The Jewish people will need to recognize Jesus as their long awaited Messiah in order for Him to return to earth. Jesus said concerning Jerusalem in Matthew 23:39: "For I say to you, from now on you shall not see Me until you say, 'Blessed is He who comes in the name of the Lord!'" This is the condition for the return of Christ. This will occur as prophesied in Zechariah 12:10: "And I will pour out on the house of David and on the inhabitants of Jerusalem, the Spirit of grace and supplication, so that they will look on Me whom they have pierced; and they will mourn for Him, as one. Mourns for an only son, and they will weep bitterly over Him, like the bitter weeping over a first-born." This will be the time when "all Israel will be saved" (Romans 11:26).

The fact that the sheep are those who have been good to the Jews during the tribulation period is an indication they are born-again believers in Jesus whose "brethren" they protected and aided (25:40). These individuals from among the Gentiles will befriend the Jews because they are "righteous" (25:37), meaning they have been made "righteous" by faith in the blood of the Lamb and His subsequent resurrection. The Greek word for righteous is also used of the doctrine of justification by faith (i.e., Christ's righteousness is imputed to a believer). They are good to the Jews for the same reason. Dr. John Walvoord says, "works are presented here, not as the ground of salvation, but as the evidence of it, in the sense of James 2:26, where it is declared, 'Faith without works is dead'; that is, it is not real faith unless it produces works."[3] The Abrahamic covenant is still in effect and will continue into the millennium. It should be remembered since Jesus said in verse 46, that these "sheep," or believers during the tribulation, go "into eternal life."

There are three different groups at this judgment of the nations to determine who goes into the millennium. The unsaved followers of Antichrist left at the end of the tribulation He calls "goats." The believers who survive the martyrdom of the tribulation He calls "sheep," who demonstrate their gift of "righteousness" through the blood of the Lamb. The third category is the "brethren" whom the sheep befriend. Those whom Jesus calls "my brethren," are the Jews who go into the millennium in belief. Thus, we see that only believers will enter the millennium—Gentile believers and Jewish believers from the whole house of Israel.

POSTTRIBULATIONAL PROBLEM

Posttribulationists believe the rapture and the second coming are either the same event or occur with virtually no interval between them. This passage presents a problem for posttribulationists as noted by Dr. Ron Rhodes:

> Within premillennial eschatology, Matthew 25:31–46 is properly interpreted as referring to the judgment of the nations. The nations are comprised of the sheep and the goats, representing the saved and the lost among the Gentiles. According to Matthew 25:32, they are intermingled and require separation by a special judgment. This judgment follows the second coming of Christ, since it occurs "when the Son of Man comes in His glory, and all the angels with Him" (Matthew 25:31). However, this judgment seems somewhat infeasible (as well as unnecessary) if, as posttribulationists hold, the rapture takes place at the Second Advent. At a posttribulational rapture, a separation of the saved from the unsaved would take place at that point. Accordingly, most posttribulationists either ignore this passage entirely, or relate it to the final judgment after the millennium.[4]

Dr. Charles Ryrie notes that many posttribulationists attempt to see it as parallel to the Great White Throne judgment in Revelation 20:11–15.

A comparison of the judgment in Matthew with the one in Revelation would seem to make this view unlikely.

- *Different Time:* The judgment of the nations occurs at the second coming of Christ (Matthew 25:31); the Great White Throne occurs following the millennial kingdom (Revelation 20:11–12).

- *Different Scene:* The judgment of the nations occurs on Earth (Matthew 25:31); the Great White Throne judgment occurs at the Great White Throne (Revelation 20:11).

- *Different Subjects:* At the judgment of the nations, three groups of people are mentioned: the sheep, the goats, and the brothers (Matthew 25:32, 40). The Great White Throne judgment involves the unsaved dead (Revelation 20:12).

- *Different Basis:* The basis of judgment at the judgment of the nations is how Christ's "brothers" were treated (Matthew 25:40); the basis of judgment at the Great White Throne is their works (Revelation 20:12).

- *Different Result:* The result of the judgment of the nations is twofold: the righteous enter into the kingdom; the unrighteous are cast into the lake of fire. The result of the Great White Throne judgment is that the wicked dead are cast into the lake of fire (the righteous are not mentioned).

- *Resurrection:* No resurrection is mentioned in connection with the judgment of the nations. A resurrection does take place in connection with the Great White Throne judgment (Revelation 20:13).[5]

Believers who come to faith in Christ during the tribulation are not translated at Christ's second advent but carry on ordinary occupations such as farming and building houses, and they will bear children (Isa. 65:20–25). This would be impossible if all saints were translated at the second coming to Earth as posttribulationists teach. Because pretribulationists have at least a seven-year interval between the removal of the church at the rapture and the return of Christ to earth, this is not a problem because millions of people will be saved during that interval. Tribulation saints who survive and are alive at the second coming will be available to populate the millennium in their natural bodies in order to fulfill Scripture. Revelation 7:9 says of believers saved during the tribulation the following: "After these things I looked, and behold, a great multitude, which no one could count, from every nation and all tribes and peoples and tongues, standing before the throne and before the Lamb, clothed in white robes, and palm branches were in their hands." This passage is likely a summary observation of believers referencing the entire tribulation period even though it appears in Revelation 7.

It would be impossible for the judgment of the Gentiles to occur after the second coming if the rapture and second coming are not separated by a period of time. How would both saved and unsaved, still in their natural bodies, be separated in judgment, if all living believers are translated at the second coming? This would be impossible if the translation takes place at the second coming, but it is solved through a pretribulational gap between the two events.

Dr. Walvoord points out that if "the translation took place in connection with the second coming to the earth, there would be no need of separating the sheep from the goats at a subsequent judgment, but the separation would have taken place in the very act of the translation of the believers before Christ actually sets up His throne on earth (Matt. 25:31)."[6] If pretribulationism is true then there is no problem of how the Lord will populate the millennium with mortals. Those who will be saved during the tribulation and physically survive until Christ's return, whether Jew or Gentile, will populate the millennium in their moral bodies. This will be a great event to which Bible-believing Christians look forward.

ENDNOTES

1 Gary DeMar, *Last Days Madness: Obsession of the Modern Church* (Smyrna, GA: American Vision, 1997), 190.

2 Arno C. Gaebelein, *The Gospel of Matthew: An Exposition* (Neptune, NJ: Loizeaux Brothers, [1910] 1961), 539–40.

3 John F. Walvoord, *Matthew: Thy Kingdom Come* (Chicago: Moody Press, 1974), 202.

4 Ron Rhodes, *Posttribulationism and the Sheep/Goat-Judgment of Matthew 25—A Summary-Critique of Robert Gundry's View,* (A paper presented to the Pre-Trib Study Group, Dallas, TX, December 2003), 1.

5 Charles C. Ryrie, *Basic Theology* (Wheaton, IL: Victor Books, 1986), 518.

6 John F. Walvoord, *The Rapture Question*. Rev and enlarged ed. (Grand Rapids: Zondervan, [1957], 1979), 274.

CONCLUSION

In the previous pages we have studied the most prominent prophetic teaching of Jesus found in the New Testament. At a time when His earthly ministry and presence was coming to a conclusion, Jesus gave the disciples, and through Matthew's account, future readers such as ourselves, important knowledge about God's prophetic plan. In essence, Jesus laid out an overview of key events that will take place during the seven-year tribulation culminating in His return to earth known as the second coming (24:4–31). Christ then speaks a series of parables to show the lessons to be learned as a result of His prophetic discourse (24:32–25).

It is important to realize that none of Jesus's discourse relates to our current church age. Instead, His teaching speaks of Israel's future time known as the seven-year tribulation. Many expositors, who otherwise take a similar view as the one taken in this book, think that the first few verses speak of the end of our current church age. As a result of such understanding, it leads to thinking prophecy is being fulfilled at the end of the church age, in our own day. I think this can be demonstrated to be false when compared with the seal judgments of Revelation 6. Revelation contains the most detailed Scripture covering the tribulation period (chapter 6–19). All futurists hold that the seal judgments of chapter 6 take place within the future tribulation period. When one examines both passages and compares them we find the more extensive sequence in Revelation 6 speaks of the same events noted by our Lord in His Discourse (24:4–13). The clearer passage, Revelation 6, provides the framework for understanding the less extensive passage of Matthew 24.

As the futurist interpretation of prophecy began to rise in America after the Civil War, there was a great transition from the historicist system to futurism, which gave rise to a dominant premillennialism among conservative interpreters. However, in the transition, some elements of a historicist approach remained in the minds of otherwise futurists.

Futurists believe the entire Olivet Discourse in Matthew 24–25 speaks of events future to our own church age and is consistent with the overall futurist approach which attempts to follow a consistently literal hermeneutic.

Another important implication flowing out of a consistently literal interpretive approach to Christ's Discourse is that there is no reference to the rapture, whether pre, mid, three quarters, or post. Within the flow of events during Christ's last week before His crucifixion, Jesus finished Israel's future prophetic destiny via the Olivet Discourse. A day or so later, our Lord outlines His agenda for the previously unrevealed current church age in the Upper Room Discourse (John 13–16 and later chapter 17), the night before He was crucified. All three synoptic gospels (Matthew, Mark, and Luke) contain some or all of the Olivet Discourse. Only John's gospel contains the Upper Room Discourse. In the Upper Room Discourse, once Judas leaves the room in chapter 13, everything Jesus talks about is brand-new, church age truth called "mysteries" in the New Testament Epistles. Some of those items include the following: introduction of the rapture (14:1–3); believers will do greater works (14:5–14); New Testament ministry of the Holy Spirit (14:15–31); believers are to abide in Christ—the Christian life (15:1–17); the world will hate followers of Christ (15:18–16:6); the Holy Spirit will aid in evangelism (16:7–15); the course of the church age (16:16–24); prayer will be in the name of Jesus (16:25–33); a unique unity of love, obedience, and commitment to His will (chapter 17).

The New Testament Epistles are the development and expansion of these items. Three times in Christ's Discourse He promises the revealing and teaching ministry of the Holy Spirit (John 14:26; 15:26; 16:7). For example, "But the Helper, the Holy Spirit, whom the Father will send in My name, He will teach you all things, and bring to your remembrance all that I said to you" (14:26). This was fulfilled through the Divine provision of the New Testament canon. The Olivet Discourse, in all three iterations, are a result of Christ's promise in John 14:26.

Because the Olivet Discourse is Jesus's primary lessons concerning future events, except for the more extensive book of Revelation, it is important to correctly understand it, just as it is for all of Scripture. It appears the stage is being set for the beginning of these prophesies to unfold. Israel is back in their God-given land and largely in control of Jerusalem after almost 2,000 years. Israel's end-time enemies are also players on today's stage. No doubt that globalism is gaining increasing favor among the nations and await the rise of their leader—the Antichrist—after the rapture of church. Christ's Bride, the church is waiting for the any-moment shout of the rapture to call us home. We say with John in Revelation: Come quickly Lord Jesus! Maranatha!

BIBLIOGRAPHY

Much has been written on the Olivet Discourse. The titles below are those cited in the book with the addition of some further titles pertaining to the topic as well as to the broader subject of Bible prophecy.

Archer, Gleason L. Jr., Paul D. Feinberg, Douglas J. Moo, *Three Views of the Rapture,* rev. ed. Grand Rapids: Zondervan, 1996.

Balz, Horst and Gerhard Schneider, ed. *Exegetical Dictionary of the New Testament,* 3 vols. Grand Rapids: Eerdmans, 1991.

Bauer, Walter, William F. Arndt, and F. Wilbur Gingrich, *A Greek-English Lexicon of the New Testament and Other Early Christian Literature,* 3d ed., rev. Frederick W. Danker. Chicago: University of Chicago Press, 2000.

Beechick, Allen. *The Pre-Tribulation Rapture.* Denver: Accent Books, 1980.

Blomberg, Craig L. *Matthew,* vol. 22 of *The New American Commentary.* Nashville, TN: Broadman Press, 1992.

Bock, Darrell L. *Luke 9:51—24:53.* Grand Rapids: Baker, 1996.

Buck, D. D. *Our Lord's Great Prophecy.* Nashville: South-Western Publishing House, 1857.

Carr, A. *Cambridge Greek Testament for Schools and Colleges. The Gospel According to St. Matthew.* Cambridge: At The University Press, 1896.

Carson, D. A. *Exegetical Fallacies.* Grand Rapids: Baker, 1984.

________. "Matthew," *The Expositor's Bible Commentary,* vol. 8. Grand Rapids: Zondervan Publishing House, 1984.

Chilton, David. *Paradise Restored: An Eschatology of Dominion.* Tyler, TX: Reconstruction Press, 1985.

Cooper, David L. *Future Events Revealed: According to Matthew 24 and 25.* Los Angeles: David L. Cooper, 1935.

________. *Messiah: His Final Call to Israel.* Los Angeles, CA: Biblical Research Society, 1962.

Cooper, Robert. "The New Liberal Imperialism," in the *Observer Worldview Extra.* London: April 7, 2002.

Davies W. D. and Dale C. Allison, Jr., *A Critical and Exegetical Commentary on The Gospel According to Saint Matthew,* 3 vols. Edinburgh: T. & T. Clark, 1997.

Delitzsch, F. "Isaiah," vol. VII in C. F. Keil and F. Delitzsch, *Commentary on the Old Testament in Ten Volumes.* Grand Rapids: Eerdmans, 1975.

DeMar, Gary. *End Times Fiction: A Biblical Consideration of the Left Behind Theology.* Nashville: Thomas Nelson, 2001.

________. *Last Days Madness: Obsession of the Modern Church.* Powder Springs, GA: American Vision, 1999.

Farrar, F. W. *The Gospel According to St. Luke, with Maps, Notes and Introduction.* Cambridge: At The University Press, 1899.

Easley, Kendell H. *Revelation.* Nashville: Holman Reference, 1998.

Edersheim, Alfred. *The Life and Times of Jesus the Messiah,* 2 vols. [1883]. Grand Rapids, MI: Eerdmans, 1974

Elliott, E. B. *Horae Apocalypticae,* rev. ed., 4 vols. London: Seeleys,1851.

Evans, Craig A. *Mark 8:27—16:20. Word Biblical Commentary,* 34B. Nashville: Thomas Nelson, 2001.

Figart, Thomas O. *The King of The Kingdom of Heaven: A Verse by Verse Commentary on the Gospel of Matthew.* Lancaster, PA: Eden Press, 1999.

Fruchtenbaum, Arnold. *The Footsteps of the Messiah: A Study of the Sequence of Prophetic Events,* rev. ed. Tustin, CA: Ariel Ministries, 2003.

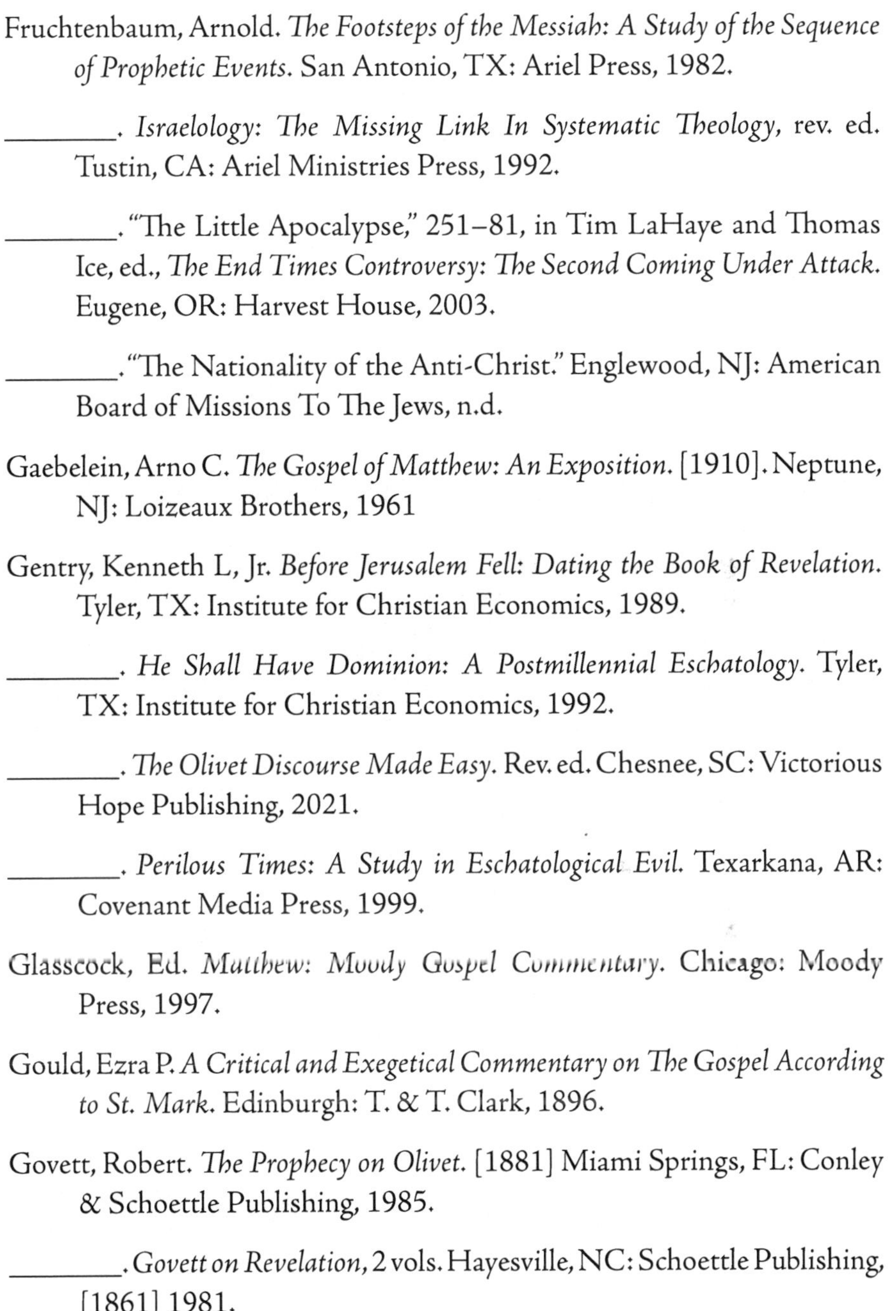

Fruchtenbaum, Arnold. *The Footsteps of the Messiah: A Study of the Sequence of Prophetic Events*. San Antonio, TX: Ariel Press, 1982.

________. *Israelology: The Missing Link In Systematic Theology*, rev. ed. Tustin, CA: Ariel Ministries Press, 1992.

________. "The Little Apocalypse," 251–81, in Tim LaHaye and Thomas Ice, ed., *The End Times Controversy: The Second Coming Under Attack*. Eugene, OR: Harvest House, 2003.

________. "The Nationality of the Anti-Christ." Englewood, NJ: American Board of Missions To The Jews, n.d.

Gaebelein, Arno C. *The Gospel of Matthew: An Exposition*. [1910]. Neptune, NJ: Loizeaux Brothers, 1961

Gentry, Kenneth L, Jr. *Before Jerusalem Fell: Dating the Book of Revelation*. Tyler, TX: Institute for Christian Economics, 1989.

________. *He Shall Have Dominion: A Postmillennial Eschatology*. Tyler, TX: Institute for Christian Economics, 1992.

________. *The Olivet Discourse Made Easy*. Rev. ed. Chesnee, SC: Victorious Hope Publishing, 2021.

________. *Perilous Times: A Study in Eschatological Evil*. Texarkana, AR: Covenant Media Press, 1999.

Glasscock, Ed. *Matthew: Moody Gospel Commentary*. Chicago: Moody Press, 1997.

Gould, Ezra P. *A Critical and Exegetical Commentary on The Gospel According to St. Mark*. Edinburgh: T. & T. Clark, 1896.

Govett, Robert. *The Prophecy on Olivet*. [1881] Miami Springs, FL: Conley & Schoettle Publishing, 1985.

________. *Govett on Revelation*, 2 vols. Hayesville, NC: Schoettle Publishing, [1861] 1981.

Gray, James R. *Prophecy on The Mount: A Dispensational Study of the Olivet Discourse*. Chandler, AZ: Berean Advocate Ministries, 1991.

Grogan, G. W. "Isaiah," *The Expositor's Bible Commentary*, vol. 6. Grand Rapids: Zondervan Publishing House, 1986.

Gumerlock, Francis X. *The Day and the Hour: Christianity's Perennial Fascination with Predicting the End of the World*. Powder Springs, GA: American Vision, 2000.

Gundry, Robert H. *The Church and the Tribulation*. Grand Rapids: Zondervan, 1973.

________. *First the Antichrist: Why Christ Won't Come Before the Antichrist Does*. Grand Rapids: Baker, 1997.

________. *Matthew: A Commentary on His Handbook for a Mixed Church under Persecution*. 2nd ed. Grand Rapids: Eerdmans, 1994.

Hagner, Donald A. *Matthew 14–28.Word Biblical Commentary*. vol. 33B. Dallas: Word Books, 1995.

Hanegraaff, Hank and Sigmund Brouwer. *The Last Disciple*. Wheaton: Tyndale House Publishers, 2004.

Harrington, Daniel J. *Sacra Pagina: The Gospel of Matthew*. Collegeville, MN: The Liturgical Press, 1991.

Hendricksen, William. *The Gospel of Matthew*. Grand Rapids: Baker Book House, 1973.

Hindson, Ed, Mark Hitchcock, and Tim LaHaye, ed. *The Harvest Handbook of Bible Prophecy*. Eugene, OR: Harvest House Publishers, 2020.

Hitchcock, Mark. *The End: A Complete Overview of Bible Prophecy and the End of Days*. Carol Stream, IL: Tyndale Momentum, 20212.

Hitchcock, Mark and Thomas Ice. *The Truth Behind Left Behind: A Biblical View of the End Times*. Sisters, OR: Multnomah Publishers, 2004.

Hooker, Morna D. *The Gospel According to Saint Mark*. Peabody, MA: Hendrickson Publishers, 1991.

Hunt, Dave .*How Close Are We? Compelling Evidence for the Soon Return of Christ*. Eugene, OR: Harvest House, 1993.

Ice, Thomas and Timothy Demy. *Prophecy Watch: What to Expect in the Days to Come*. Eugene, OR: Harvest House, 1998.

________. *The Truth About The Signs of The Times*. Eugene, OR: Harvest House, 1997.

Ice, Thomas and Kenneth L. Gentry, Jr., *The Great Tribulation Past or Future?* Grand Rapids: Kregel, 1999.

Keil, C. F. and F. Delitzsch. *Commentary on the Old Testament*, 10 vols, *Commentary on the Book of Daniel*. Grand Rapids: Eerdmans, 1975.

Kelly, William. *An Exposition of the Gospel of Luke*. Oak Park, IL: Bible Truth Publishers, 1971.

________. *Lectures on The Gospel of Matthew*. [1868] Sunbury, PA: Believers Bookshelf, 1971.

Keener, Craig S. *A Commentary on The Gospel of Matthew*. Grand Rapids: Eerdmans, 1999.

LaHaye, Tim and Thomas Ice. *Charting the End Times: A Visual Guide to Understanding Bible Prophecy*. Eugene, OR: Harvest House, 2001.

LaHaye, Tim and Thomas Ice, ed. *The End Times Controversy: The Second Coming Under Attack*. Eugene, OR: Harvest House, 2003.

Lenski, R. C. H. *The Interpretation of St. Matthew's Gospel*. Minneapolis: Augsburg Publishing House, 1943.

Lindsey, Hal with C. C. Carlson. *The Late Great Planet Earth*. Grand Rapids: Zondervan, 1970.

MacArthur, John. *The New Testament Commentary: Matthew 24—28*. Chicago: Moody Press, 1989.

McAvoy, Steven L. "A Critique of Robert Gundry's Posttribulationalism," Unpublished Th. D. dissertation, Dallas Theological Seminary, 1986.

McLean, John. "Chronology and Sequential Structure of John's Revelation," 313–52 in Thomas Ice & Timothy Demy, *When the Trumpet Sounds. Today's Foremost Authorities Speak Out on End-Time Controversies.* Eugene, OR: Harvest House, 1995.

Meyer, Heinrich August Wilhelm. *Critical and Exegetical Handbook to The Gospel of Matthew*, 2 vols. Edinburgh: T. & T. Clark, 1879.

M'Neile, Alan Hugh. *The Gospel According to St. Matthew.* London: MacMillan, 1915.

Morison, James. *A Practical Commentary on the Gospel According to St. Mark.* Boston: Bartlett & Co., 1882.

Morris, Henry M. *The Revelation Record.* Grand Rapids: Baker, 1983.

Morris, Leon. *The Gospel According to Matthew.* Grand Rapids: Eerdmans, 1992.

Mounce, Robert H. *New International Biblical Commentary: Matthew.* Peabody, MA: Hendrickson Publishing, 1991.

Osborne, Grant R. *Revelation.* Grand Rapids: Baker, 2002.

Patai, Raphael. *The Messiah Texts: Jewish Legends of Three Thousand Years.* Detroit: Wayne State University Press, 1979.

Pentecost, J. Dwight. *The Parables of Jesus.* Grand Rapids: Zondervan, 1982.

________. *The Words and Works of Jesus Christ: A Study of the Life of Christ.* Grand Rapids: Zondervan, 1981.

Perschbacher, Wesley J. *New Testament Greek Syntax: An Illustrated Manual.* Chicago: Moody, 1995.

Plummer, Alfred. *An Exegetical Commentary on the Gospel According to S. Matthew*, 2nd ed. Minneapolis: James Family, n.d.

Plumptre, E. H. *The Gospel According to St. Luke*. 12 vols. vol. 3, *Ellicott's New Testament Commentary*. London: Cassell & Company, n. d.

Preston, Don K. *Into All The World: Then Comes The End*. Ardmore, OK: Don K. Preston, 1996.

Price, Randall. *Jerusalem in Prophecy: God's Stage for the Final Drama*. Eugene, OR: Harvest House, 1998.

Price J. Randall. "Historical Problems with a First-Century Fulfillment of the Olivet Discourse," 377–398 in Tim LaHaye and Thomas Ice, editors, *The End Times Controversy: The Second Coming Under Attack*. Eugene, OR: Harvest House, 2003.

________. "Historical Problems with Preterism's Interpretation of Events in A.D. 70," 355–376 in Tim LaHaye and Thomas Ice, editors, *The End Times Controversy: The Second Coming Under Attack*. Eugene, OR: Harvest House, 2003.

________. "Old Testament Tribulation Terms," 57–83 in Thomas Ice & Timothy Demy, *When the Trumpet Sounds: Today's Foremost Authorities Speak Out on End-Time Controversies*. Eugene, OR: Harvest House, 1995.

Reiter, Richard R. ed. *The Rapture: Pre-, Mid-, or Posttribulational?* Grand Rapids: Zondervan, 1984.

Rhodes, Ron. *Posttribulationism and the Sheep/Goat-Judgment of Matthew 25—A Summary-Critique of Robert Gundry's View*. A paper presented to the Pre-Trib Study Group, Dallas, TX, December 2003.

Robertson, A. T. *Word Pictures in the New Testament*, VI vols. Nashville: Broadman Press, 1930.

Rosenthal, Marvin. *The Pre-Wrath Rapture of the Church*. Nashville: Thomas Nelson Publishers, 1990.

Ross, Allen P. *Creation & Blessing: A Guide to the Study and Exposition of Genesis*. Grand Rapids: Baker Book House, 1988.

Ryle, J. C. *Expository Thoughts on the Gospels: Luke,* 2 vols. Cambridge, UK: James Clarke & Co., n. d. [1858].

Ryrie, Charles C. *Basic Theology: A Popular Systematic Guide To Understanding Biblical Truth* Wheaton: Victor Books, 1986.

________. *Dispensationalism.* Chicago: Moody Press, [1966], 1995.

________. *What Is Dispensationalism?* Pamphlet published by Dallas Theological Seminary, [1980], 1986.

Sadler, M. F. *The Gospel According to St. Luke: with Notes Critical and Practical*[1886] London: George Bell and Sons, 1911.

________. Sadler, M. F. *The Gospel According to St. Mark: with Notes Critical and Practical.* [1884] London: George Bell and Sons, 1898.

Shimeall, Richard Cunningham. *Christ's Second Coming: Is It Pre-Millennial or Post-Millennial?* New York: John F. Trow and Richard Brinkerhoff, 1866.

Showers, Renald. *Maranatha: Our Lord, Come! A Definitive Study of the Rapture of the Church.* Bellmawr, NJ: The Friends of Israel Gospel Ministry, Inc., 1995.

Sproule, John A. "An Exegetical Defense of Pretribulationism," Unpublished Th. D. dissertation, Grace Theological Seminary, 1981.

Stein, Robert H. *Luke, The New American Commentary.* Nashville: Broadman Press, 1992.

Tacitus *Annals.*

Thomas, Robert L. "New Evangelical Hermeneutics and Eschatology," Unpublished paper presented at the 12th Annual Pre-Trib Study Group, Irving, TX, December 2003.

________. *Revelation 1–7: An Exegetical Commentary.* Chicago: Moody, 1992.

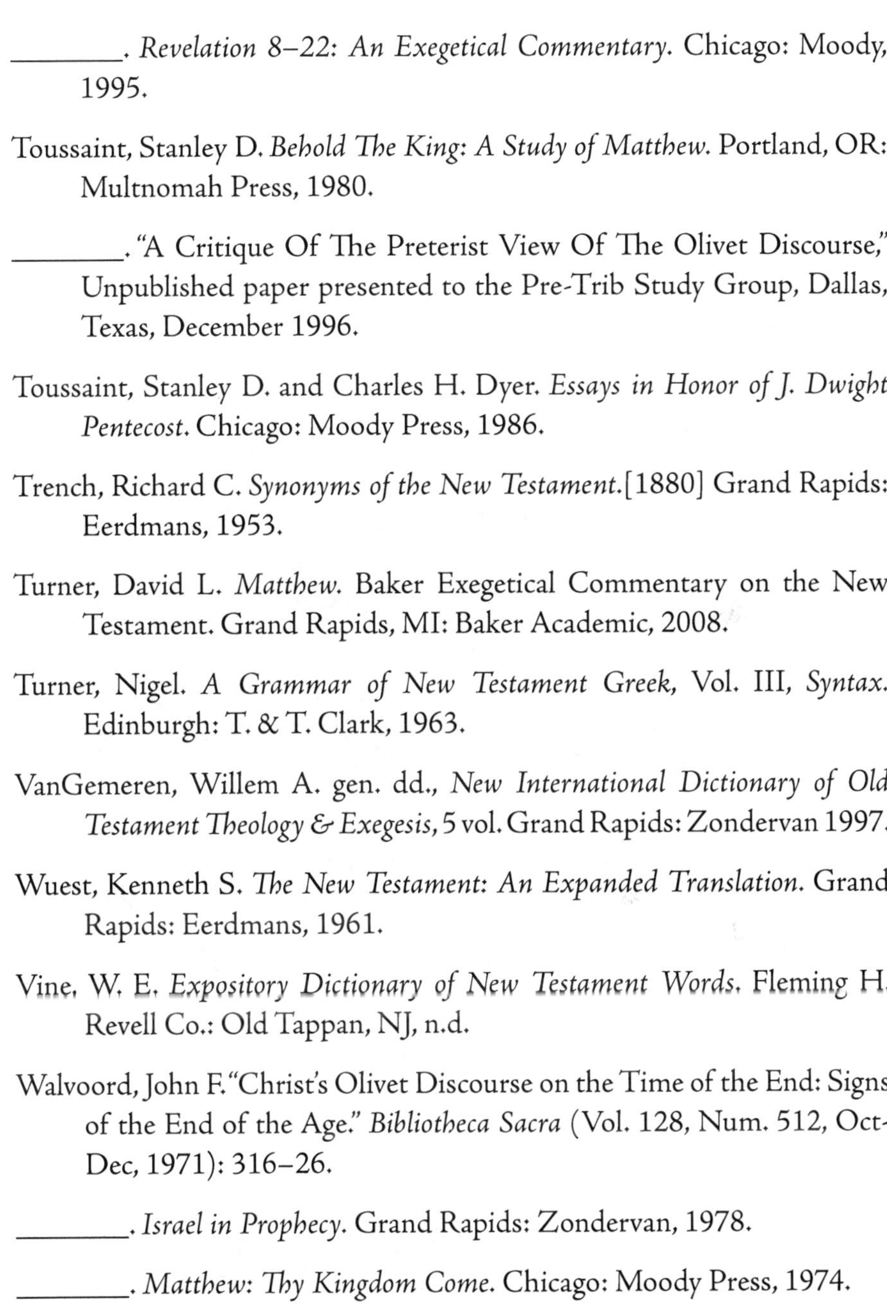

________. *Revelation 8–22: An Exegetical Commentary*. Chicago: Moody, 1995.

Toussaint, Stanley D. *Behold The King: A Study of Matthew*. Portland, OR: Multnomah Press, 1980.

________. "A Critique Of The Preterist View Of The Olivet Discourse," Unpublished paper presented to the Pre-Trib Study Group, Dallas, Texas, December 1996.

Toussaint, Stanley D. and Charles H. Dyer. *Essays in Honor of J. Dwight Pentecost*. Chicago: Moody Press, 1986.

Trench, Richard C. *Synonyms of the New Testament*.[1880] Grand Rapids: Eerdmans, 1953.

Turner, David L. *Matthew*. Baker Exegetical Commentary on the New Testament. Grand Rapids, MI: Baker Academic, 2008.

Turner, Nigel. *A Grammar of New Testament Greek*, Vol. III, *Syntax*. Edinburgh: T. & T. Clark, 1963.

VanGemeren, Willem A. gen. dd., *New International Dictionary of Old Testament Theology & Exegesis*, 5 vol. Grand Rapids: Zondervan 1997.

Wuest, Kenneth S. *The New Testament: An Expanded Translation*. Grand Rapids: Eerdmans, 1961.

Vine, W. E. *Expository Dictionary of New Testament Words*. Fleming H. Revell Co.: Old Tappan, NJ, n.d.

Walvoord, John F. "Christ's Olivet Discourse on the Time of the End: Signs of the End of the Age." *Bibliotheca Sacra* (Vol. 128, Num. 512, Oct-Dec, 1971): 316–26.

________. *Israel in Prophecy*. Grand Rapids: Zondervan, 1978.

________. *Matthew: Thy Kingdom Come*. Chicago: Moody Press, 1974.

________. *The Nations in Prophecy*. Grand Rapids: Zondervan, 1967.

________. *The Rapture Question*, Revised and Enlarged Edition. Grand Rapids: Zondervan, 1979.

Walvoord, John F. and Roy B. Zuck. *The Bible Knowledge Commentary: New Testament*. Wheaton: Victor Books, 1983.

Ware, Bruce A. "Is the Church in View in Matthew 24—25?" *Bibliotheca Sacra* (April–June 1981; Vol. 138, No. 550): 158–72.

Williams, A. Lukyn "St. Matthew" in H. D. M. Spence and Joseph S. Exell, ed., *The Pulpit Commentary*, 23 vols. Grand Rapids: Eerdmans, 1974, vol. 15.

Wohlberg, Steve *The Antichrist Chronicles: What Prophecy Teachers Aren't Telling You!* Fort Worth: Texas Media Center, 2001.

________. *The Left Behind Deception: Revealing Dangerous Errors About The Rapture And The Antichrist*. Coldwater, MI: Remnant Publications, 2001.

Yeager, Randolph O. *The Renaissance New Testament*, 18 vols. *Matthew*, vol 3. Bowling Green, KY: Renaissance Press, 1978.

Zuck, Roy B. *Basic Bible Interpretation: A Practical Guide to Discovering Biblical Truth*. Wheaton, IL: Victor Books, 1991.

ABOUT THE AUTHOR

THOMAS ICE serves as Executive Director of the *Pre-Trib Research Center*, which he founded in 1994 with Dr. Tim LaHaye to research, teach, and defend the pretribulational rapture and related Bible prophecy doctrines. Ice has authored and co-authored over 30 books, written hundreds of articles, and is a frequent conference speaker. Among his most popular books are *Charting the Bible Chronologically: A Visual Guide to God's Unfolding Plan* (co-author with Ed Hindson), and *Charting the End Times: A Visual Guide to Bible Prophecy* (co-author with Tim LaHaye) and *The Case for Zionism: Why Christians Should Support Israel*. He has served as a pastor for 17 years. Dr. Ice has a B.A. from Howard Payne University, a Th.M. from Dallas Theological Seminary and a Ph.D. from Tyndale Theological Seminary, and did postdoctoral work at the University of Wales.